MEDIAEVAL
BOOK ILLUMINATION
IN EUROPE

EDITH ROTHE

MEDIAEVAL
BOOK
ILLUMINATION
IN EUROPE

THE COLLECTIONS OF THE
GERMAN DEMOCRATIC REPUBLIC

*with 96 colour plates
and 64 monochrome plates*

W. W. NORTON & COMPANY · INC · NEW YORK

In memory of Albert Boeckler

Translated from the German
Buchmalerei aus zwölf Jahrhunderten
by Mary Whittall

Published 1966 by Union Verlag (VOB) Berlin
This edition © 1968 Thames and Hudson, London

Printed in Germany (East)

CONTENTS

THE GOTHIC AGE (1250–1500)

THE HIGH AND LATE RENAISSANCE (1500–1600)

My first reaction to the proposal to publish a study of Western illuminated manuscripts in the German Democratic Republic was rather sceptical; I had witnessed the senseless destruction of so many manuscripts during the Second World War. Nevertheless, I spent eighteen months sifting through the stock of thirty-three libraries and collections of archives, and I was astonished by what I found. My selection of material has been guided by the desirability of introducing the most valuable and the least known to the public. Of the 160 manuscripts I chose, 26 have never been published before, and a further 84 miniatures are here reproduced for the first time. I paid particular attention to ecclesiastical libraries. Only one illustration from each manuscript could be reproduced, in order to cover as much ground as possible.

I was surprised to find such a wide range of material, covering twelve centuries, from 400 to 1600, and representing most of the countries of Europe and a large number of schools. This made it possible for me to turn my commentary into a short history of Western manuscript illumination. There are no examples from Salzburg, from Spain in the early centuries or from England in the later period. Naturally the Thuringia-Meissen school is the most fully represented, since the surviving mediaeval libraries of that part of Germany, although no longer in their original locations, have not travelled far. The librarians of the thirty-three libraries and archives have been of immeasurable help to me in my work, which owes much to their suggestions. I am particularly grateful to the Abbesses of the Cistercian convents of Sankt Marienstern and Sankt Marienthal. The hospitality of convents and monasteries was a byword in the Middle Ages and is no less generous today. It would take too long to name all those who have been concerned in this publication, but I thank them all most sincerely. I am particularly appreciative of Herr Klaus G. Beyer's work in making the magnificent photographic reproductions. I must also thank the designer, Professor Horst Erich Wolter, and also Dr Jütte and Herr Rebner, whose skill and experience has made possible the production of this book. Finally I must mention the Deutsches Buch- und Schrift-Museum in Leipzig, whose new reading-rooms are an ideal place in which to work.

Leipzig, August 1965   EDITH ROTHE

THE ART of illuminating manuscripts was not invented in the Middle Ages. The earliest known form of illustrated book is the Egyptian Book of the Dead, which originated in the second millenium B.C. These books were placed in tombs and contained coloured pen and ink drawings relating to the after-life. They were made in temples and palaces for the priests and the Pharaohs. Their object was to ensure eternal life for the dead man's soul and to enhance his fame. 'The priests proclaimed the divinity of the kings in order to gain power over them. The kings built temples for the gods and the priests for their own greater glory' (Arnold Hauser). The books were written on papyrus, made out of paper reed, a kind of sedge.

The only surviving examples of Graeco-Roman illumination date from the Christian era. The Edict of Milan of 313 established Christianity as an official religion of the Roman empire, and indeed gave it pre-eminence over other religions. This gave the Church the freedom to make liturgical books; previously its artistic expression had been restricted to funerary ornaments and minor art forms. The fourth century also saw a major innovation in the material and form of books, with the replacement of the papyrus roll by the parchment codex. The texts, written by scribes, were decorated by an artist, the miniator, who followed classical models. This early Christian art form was carried on in monasteries. The Rule of St Benedict of Norcia (480–542) exhorts monks not to neglect learning and scholarship. Manuscripts were essential to study, and therefore writing and illumination were activities pleasing in God's sight. The writing rooms of Benedictine monasteries led Western Europe in the illumination of manuscripts throughout the Middle Ages. The fact that it remained an ecclesiastical art determined its development. The realism of Greek and Roman art was abandoned in favour of symbolism and imagery. Proportion and perspective were of less importance than the principles that the most important figure in a picture should be given prominence by being made larger than minor figures, and that figures should be shown full face. Naturalism still found a place in the illustration of passages of the text.

Following the eventual split of the Roman empire into Eastern and Western halves in 395, illumination in Western Europe followed a different path from Byzantine illumination. This book is concerned with the former. The oldest surviving examples of Christian illumination are the Itala fragments in the Deutsche Staatsbibliothek, which

9

are Italian and date from about 400 *(pl. 1)*. Their pictures show a kinship with classical murals and vase paintings, and, with the Vatican Vergil, constitute the earliest extant examples of an art which was to flower gloriously in the following centuries.

During the invasions of the Goths and Vandals which brought about the final collapse of the Western empire in 476, monasteries were hard put to it to protect themselves against pillage and destruction. In spite of her difficulties, however, the Church maintained her spiritual authority, and sacred art did not die out. Italy suffered most at the hands of the barbarians; other Christian countries such as Gaul and Ireland were able to carry on Rome's mission without interruption. They lacked, it is true, the Graeco-Roman and early Christian traditions of Italy, but the Irish monks in particular produced something quite new in the way of illumination. They attempted 'to create an ornamental equality of text and decoration' (Albert Boeckler). Instead of pictures illustrating the text, they evolved a new kind of ornamentation centred, in the first instance, on the embellishment of initial letters. This art was brought to perfection in Ireland and Britain *(pl. 4)*, while continental monasteries, particularly in the Merovingian kingdom, remained untouched by its influence.

The coronation of Charlemagne (768–814) in Rome in the year 800 placed Christendom under the protection of its most powerful secular ruler. The structure of the Carolingian empire, like that of the German empire which succeeded it, was based on subsistence agriculture and the rising power of a landowning aristocracy. Charlemagne made his capital at Aix-la-Chapelle (Aachen) the spiritual and intellectual centre of Christendom. His dream was to revive classical art and learning in a Christian framework. The influx of scholars and artists, influences and ideas and their adoption and development led to what is known as the Carolingian Renaissance. The greatest scholars of the age were summoned to Aix; a literary academy and an artists' studio were attached to the palace. This was the first golden age of Western manuscript illumination. The artists took their models where they found them. The two-dimensional, abstract ornamentation of the Dark Ages gave way once again to the human figure. A calligraphic innovation also took place with the introduction of the Carolingian minuscule, with its clear and regular letter forms *(pl. 8)*. The monastery schools set great store by the teaching of calligraphy, and it was there too that the miniators learnt the art of using body-colours. The monks were also concerned with the appearance and accuracy of texts, with orthography and punctuation. They produced manuscripts of an artistic quality hardly ever surpassed in later ages *(pl. 5)*. The miniatures began to cover a wider range of subject matter: as well as scenes from the Gospels they depicted Old Testament stories, the ceremonies at which a work of art was presented to the patron, scenes of everyday life, and subjects drawn from astronomy and classical literature. Most of the scriptoria lay within the boundaries of the Frankish kingdom, between the Seine and the Rhine. Differences of style allow us to distinguish between a number of Carolingian 'schools', of which one of the most productive, apart from the Aachen palace atelier, was the school of Tours *(pl. 12)*.

While the Frankish empire was multi-racial, the empire of the Ottonians, which lasted from 919 to 1024, was the first German state, comprising as it did the duchies and bishoprics inhabited by the descendants of the Germanic tribes. The spiritual and temporal rulers were members of a hereditary nobility which had evolved from a ministerial nobility at the court, and their feudal relationship to the emperor was based on mutual oaths of loyalty. The Church supported this new social structure by declaring it to be divinely ordained. The monastery, not the court, was the centre of cultural life.

Religion, thought and art concurred in emphasizing the transience of this life, relating everything in it to the life to come. Men expected the Second Coming in the year 1000; there was a growing, apocalyptic sense of rejection of this world and of longing for the next, which found one form of expression in manuscript illumination. In Ottonian manuscripts the figure is two-dimensional; 'it is an attitude that has become a form' (Hans Jantzen). Ornamentation aspired to be the representation of the text, and the script to become ornamentation; a whole-page initial became a picture in itself *(pl. 20)*. Colouring became bright, thick and completely anti-naturalistic; Ottonian illumination has been called, with some justice, an expressionist art. A new significance was won by gold backgrounds, with their transcendental glow, and by the light, which never cast a shadow; 'the world of images shines with its own light' (Wolfgang Schöne). In the Carolingian period gold had been used on the figures in the foreground, in the Ottonian it became the background. Gold backgrounds signify the celestial world, while other tints are used for terrestrial scenes.

The Ottonian dynasty came from the ruling house of Saxony, a duchy which lay in the north-east of the Holy Roman Empire of the German Nation. Bounded by the Elbe and the Saale in the east, it extended to Holstein in the north and almost to the Rhine in the west, and included the Harz mountains and Westphalia in the south. Not surprisingly it enjoyed particular favour with the Ottonian emperors, who built new castles (Quedlinburg) and cathedrals (Magdeburg) within the duchy; they also commissioned magnificent manuscripts from famous scriptoria such as that of the Benedictine monastery at Reichenau on Lake Constance. Otto III's gospel book and Henry II's Book of Pericopes are among the very finest examples of manuscript illumination; both are now in the Staatsbibliothek in Munich. Prince-bishops, too, commissioned manuscripts, for example the Codex Egberti in Treves, and this patronage led to the second golden age of illumination around the year 1000. The predominating style of this period contains not only Carolingian but also marked Byzantine elements which must be attributed, at least in part, to the influence of Otto II's empress, Theophano, a princess of Byzantium. Once again the range of subject matter was extended; series of pictures narrating New Testament stories, particularly the parables, were the most popular.

The pictures of patrons receiving a work from an artist took on a new significance; the figures of emperors, dukes, bishops and abbots were no longer portraits, they were the ideal embodiments of their office. The most important schools of illumination in Germany were Reichenau, Sankt Gallen, Fulda, Cologne and the monasteries of Bavaria and Saxony; while outside Germany, during the Ottonian period, England, France, Italy and Spain all had their own schools.

Manuscript illumination under the Hohenstaufen emperors (1138–1254) reveals traces of foreign influences. On the one hand this was the age of the crusades, which lasted intermittently from 1096 to 1270 and brought Western Europe into direct contact with Byzantium and the Orient. Crusaders took home Byzantine manuscripts and Oriental works of art. After the sack of Constantinople by the crusaders in 1204, Byzantine scholars and monks fled to Western Europe. Meanwhile, the conquest of the lands east of the Elbe and the Saale, begun by Henry I, was completed and the region was colonized and converted to Christianity, a process in which the monastic orders played the most important role. Benedictines were followed in the twelfth century by Cistercians who founded monasteries at Schulpforta in 1132, Altzella in 1162, Dobrilugk in 1165, Doberan in 1171 and Lehnin in 1182. Their missionary work required liturgical books, which at first came from the Benedictine scriptoria until the

12

Cistercians established their own. This can be followed most clearly in the marches of Meissen and Zeitz. It was Arthur Haseloff who first drew attention to the Thuringia-Saxony school which developed here *(pl. 32)*, but which is more properly named the Thuringia-Meissen school. The older centres in the west continued to flourish, so that we may regard the late Romanesque period, around 1200, as a third golden age of illumination. The great Carolingian and Ottonian achievements were not forgotten. Their lasting influence, and that of Byzantium, helped the evolution of a new style which aimed at a greater naturalism after the transcendentalism of the early Romanesque period. Colours became deeper, richer and more worldly. Purple, crimson, pale green and beige were replaced by red, blue, green and yellow. There were stronger contrasts of light and dark, as opaque white came to be used for figures. The gold background had symbolized a rejection of the world; the new, rich colours seemed to embrace it.

Outside Germany, the late Romanesque age was a great period for illumination in France and England. Italy seems to have been less active; at all events very little Italian work of the period has survived. There was another innovation in script around the end of the twelfth century and the beginning of the thirteenth: the Gothic minuscule replaced the Carolingian script which had till then prevailed all over Europe. Each minuscule is fitted into a system of four lines. The new script originated, like Gothic architecture, in northern France, and substituted angular, fractured shapes for the earlier rounded shapes *(pl. 38)*. The degree of fracture can date a manuscript, though scripts often vary from one scribe to another, and new characteristics appear earlier in Western Europe than in the east. Subject matter was extended once more in the late Romanesque period with the appearance of secular texts such as universal chronicles—these were histories of the world which began with the Genesis account of the Creation, and mixed secular und religious themes—and books on natural history such as Abbot Theofrid's *Flora (pl. 25)*.

In the Gothic age, from the thirteenth to the fifteenth century, fundamental economic and religious changes took place. The centre of gravity shifted from the land to the towns. A new form of economy evolved, based on production for sale and exchange in which merchants and craftsmen played the most important roles. A subsistence economy was replaced by a money economy. People became more aware of their identity as individuals. The influence of the Church grew less, although she remained the patron of religious art. In the Gothic era man was no longer fully enclosed in the strict order of a Christian world; he saw himself in relation to the material world and its realities, with which he had to cope independently. There was constant movement of sections of the population: knights went on crusades, the devout made pilgrimages, pedlars sold their wares from place to place, peasants left the land and settled in the towns, craftsmen and artists travelled from one workshop to another, teachers and scholars from one university to another. In the German part of the Holy Roman Empire alone, five universities were founded in the fourteenth century and nine more in the fifteenth. This made learning free of the monasteries. The great revolution, the journey away from the Kingdom of Heaven to the natural world, from the symbolic to the tangible, began. It was, of course, still accepted that everything in the real world had its proper relationship to God; the difference was that the new Gothic attitudes of thought and belief accepted a God who worked in and through the world of things. While early mediaeval art had rejected the representation of external reality, Gothic art aimed at just that, in its naturalistic depiction of landscapes and human figures, in its choice of colours and in its treatment of light. In early mediaeval art light is simply there, ra diating out of itself; during the fourteenth and fifteenth centuries it changed, it had a specific source and threw shadows. After about 1420 shading on figures became more pronounced, and they cast shadows on floors and walls.

The Gothic style began to emerge in French architecture by the middle of the twelfth century. It reached Germany later and does not appear in illumination until the second half of the thirteenth century. The demand for manuscripts grew steadily, until the monasteries were unable to cope with it alone. Guilds of scribes and miniators were formed in the towns. The monastic miniators had been content to remain anonymous, working *ad maiorem Dei gloriam*, to the greater glory of God. The lay artists, on the other hand, sought to receive credit for their work, and from the fifteenth century onwards the names of many of them are known. Manuscripts now covered an ever greater range of subjects. The Book of Hours made its first appearance in France in the first half of the fourteenth century. This was a book giving the prayers for laymen at each hour of the day, and was commissioned by princes and noblemen. Similar in layout and richness of material were the breviaries made for bishops and abbots. Manuscripts with secular content were no longer confined to classical literature and philosophy, but also covered native and vernacular literature. The universities needed books on medicine and the natural sciences. This increase in demand necessitated quicker and cheaper production and gradually paper came to be used as well as parchment. The evolution of the Gothic minuscule continued, emphasizing the vertical strokes, often at the expense of legibility. The invention of woodcuts towards the end of the fourteenth century, and Gutenberg's invention of printing from movable type around 1440, made possible the speedy distribution of many copies of the same book. At the beginning of the Middle Ages individual books were cult objects; at the end they were bought and sold like any other commodity.

France led in manuscript illumination throughout the Gothic period. The art was centred on Paris, where it was fostered by the court and the university, both of which commissioned work and financed the training of young artists. A fine example of French illumination is the miniature in a volume of Petrarch which dedicates the work to Charles VII *(pl. 89)*. In the fifteenth century Flanders and the Low Countries achieved the same high standards in the Books of Hours which they made for the whole of Western Europe *(pl. 84)*. The Flemish school of illumination dates from about 1300, but an independent Low Countries school did not emerge until the fifteenth century. English illumination of the thirteenth century was particularly fine, but it declined to a certain extent in the late fourteenth century.

In Germany the Gothic style made its earliest and deepest impression in the regions on either bank of the Rhine. In the absence of influential bibliophiles, ecclesiastical traditions proved more enduring *(pl. 116)*. The colonization of the new territories east of the Elbe encouraged the development of illumination. In 1171 the diocese of Schwerin was founded to be the spearhead of missionary work. In 1348 Mecklenburg became an independent duchy, subject only to the emperor, and ceased to be a fief of the dukes of Saxony. The first university in northern Germany was founded at Rostock in 1419. The Church and scholarship needed liturgical and educational books. Scriptoria were established with the help of miniators from further west and used Western manuscripts as their models until such time as they evolved a style of their own *(pl. 65)*.

The Cistercians who moved into Thuringia and Meissen during the twelfth century helped on the work begun by the Benedictine monasteries. The Cistercians, who were principally a preaching and missionary order, extended the sphere of their activity eastwards, while the scriptoria of the more scholarly and contemplative Benedictines provided the necessary liturgical books. With the foundation of Cistercian colleges at the university of Prague in the middle of the fourteenth century and in Leipzig at the beginning of the fifteenth century, this order too turned its attention to learning, the next step being to set up its own scriptoria. The Benedictines gradually relinquished their leading position in this field to the Cistercians.

Meanwhile, the eastern provinces of Bohemia, Silesia and Austria began to produce independent work deserving of attention. Bohemian illumination came to its peak in the fourteenth century. There are a few examples of it from the second half of the eleventh century, probably from Prague, which show the influence of Echternach and Regensburg. In the thirteenth century Italian influences were the more marked. Emperor Charles IV (1347–78) founded a school for miniators in Prague. It developed as a courtly art whose zenith was reached under the bibliophile King Wenceslaus IV of Bohemia (1361–1419), who had some magnificent manuscripts made for him. The monastic scriptoria also continued to be active *(pl. 73)*. Austrian illumination was under the influence of Italy throughout the Gothic period, while Silesia has been shown by Ernst Kloss to have had links with the Thuringia-Meissen school *(pl. 103)*.

Illumination in Italy had deep roots in native traditions and in many respects pursued an independent course during the thirteenth and fourteenth centuries. The Gothic style came late to Italy and made a relatively weak impact. The art of a Giotto already anticipates the Renaissance. Apart from liturgical works the majority of Italian manuscripts are classical texts. Legal texts were an Italian speciality. The famous law school at the university of Bologna was the centre of legal studies, and textbooks from there made their way all over Europe *(pl. 67)*.

In Spain illumination can be traced back to the Visigoth kingdom. After the Muslim invasion (711) the native population kept their Christian faith, and new monasteries were founded where illumination flourished. There are some notable Catalan manuscripts of the tenth and eleventh centuries which reveal both Oriental and Occidental characteristics of style. The Moorish influence endured into the fifteenth century, as can be seen from a breviary that belonged to Ferdinand of Aragon (1479–1516) and his wife Isabella of Castile *(pl. 121)*; this manuscript also reveals the independence of Spanish illumination in the fifteenth century from French and Italian influences.

16

The transition from Gothic to Renaissance was not, in the view of some modern scholars, the complete upheaval Jakob Burckhardt thought it. The fundamental economic changes of the twelfth and thirteenth centuries were not without effect on philosophy; the Church's domination had already begun to give way to a more materialistic outlook. Renaissance humanism was an extension and deepening of Gothic realism. The observation of nature was not new; the scientific analysis of it was. It was by no means an irreligious age, although it was to a certain extent anti-clerical. There can hardly have been so much intensive doctrinal argument at any other period or place in the Church's history as during the Reformation in Germany. With the onset of the Renaissance in Italy in the 1420s a new style was created, which did not reach the rest of Europe until the high and late Renaissance in the sixteenth century. In the Middle Ages Christendom had attached little importance to racial individuality; but now national communities took shape, each using its own vernacular. The Renaissance manifested itself in very different forms in various countries. Not only did all artists observe nature, but all works of art became 'studies of nature'. The new awareness of the world and real life brought art close to the art of the ancient world. These contacts had never been broken in Italy, which now led the rest of Europe. The great artists, not only in Italy but in Germany too, were the leaders of progress; it has been called with truth an age of genius. Artistic anonymity disappeared altogether. The Church and princes continued to commission books, and there was a growing interest in profane literature.

After one last great period shortly after 1500, manuscript illumination entered a slow and final decline. Miniatures were replaced by woodcuts, which have an affinity with printed text matter; hand-drawn illustrations could no longer be integrated with a calligraphic text. Printed books could be produced more cheaply and quickly and in greater numbers to meet the steadily growing demand. The most important scriptoria disappeared with the secularization of many monasteries. Individual works were still commissioned from well-known artists in Italy and the Low Countries, until eventually these had all taken to painting on a larger scale. In Germany, work by the great artists, such as Dürer *(pl.145)* and Lucas Cranach the younger *(pl.157)*, is to be found in manuscripts. In some cases series of woodcuts were coloured, in others they are reproductions on a miniature scale of independent works. In one respect copper-engravings and woodcuts actually enriched illuminated manuscripts, which reproduced whole series of them. But as printing gradually took over the production of liturgical books it robbed illumination of its chief *raison d'être*. One genre in which it lingered on was in the ornate *matriculae* (matriculation books) of the new universities.

Illumination survived in the ensuing centuries in two forms only: prayerbooks and albums. Albums were widespread in academic circles: they derived from *matriculae* and books of genealogy, but where these accompanied each entry with an illustration, the albums also added a motto or proverb. In the eighteenth century and on into the mid-nineteenth century, albums were records of friendship with portraits and personal mottoes. The scrapbook which subsequently developed, with its stock quotations and verses, illustrated with irrelevant pictures cut out of something else, is the last shabby remnant of a once great art form.

In this book you will see examples of illumination over a period of twelve centuries. It remained a living art throughout this period because of the constant flow of fresh impulses. First one country then another became the spearhead. In the pre-Carolingian era Southern and Western Europe, including Ireland and England, played the chief role. The centres of Carolingian illumination lay between the Seine and the Rhine. Under the Ottonian emperors Germany took the lead, while in the later Romanesque period Western Europe again came to the fore. France gave the original impulse to the Gothic age, during which Christianity was spreading across Eastern Europe, leading to the flowering of the art in Bohemia and Silesia. Already in the Gothic period the rise of lay miniators sowed the seeds of eventual decay in what was essentially a religious art. It was kept alive for a time by a number of great artists until printing, woodcuts and engraving on copper completely replaced illuminated manuscripts. This art, animated by an extraordinary power of expression, had risen to the greatest heights no less than four times, around 800, 1000, 1200 and, a final flourish, around 1500.

THE PLATES

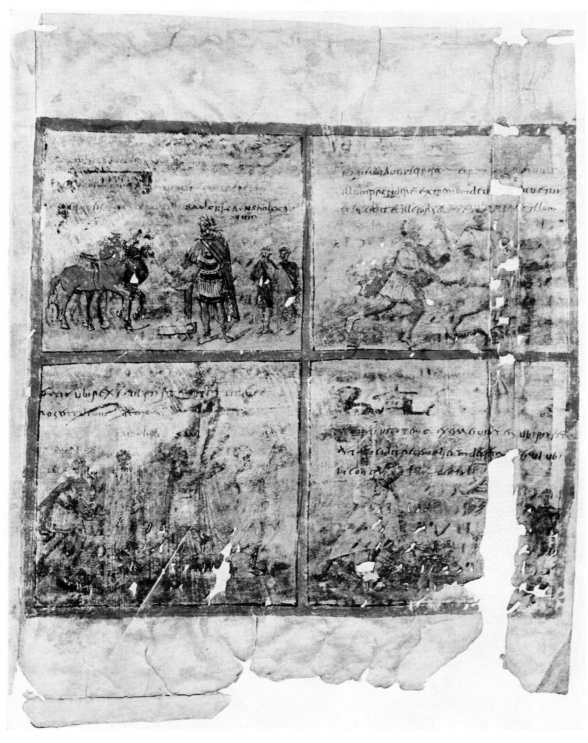

1 *Quedlinburger Itala-Fragmente · Bilder zum 1. Buch Samuelis, 15. Kapitel*
Mittelitalien, nach 400 (Text S. 183)
1 Quedlinburg Itala fragments · Illustrations to 1 Samuel 15
Central Italy, after 400 (see p. 183)

DOMINO UENERANDO MIHI PATRI
STEFANO EPISCOPO DYONISIUS

QUAM CUSTARIS SI
mus frater noster adsidua et fa
miliari conlocatione paruitate
nostram regulas ecclesiasticas de
greco transferre perpuleris Inpe
ritia credo priscae translationis of
fensus nihilominus tamen incessum
laborem tuae beatitudinis considera
tione suscepi cui xps omnipotens ds soli
tua populis pietate prospiciens Summi
sacerdotii consultu dignitate et inter
plurima tui transformamenta quibus
ecclesiam dni morum sanctitate conde
coras Et cum sacratissima iura pontifi
calibus per dignitatem digesti acconten
tibus intemerata conseruans perfec
to regimine clerum plebem quemode
reris Nullatenus nostri saeculi more
contemptus quo pronius desideramus
recta nos sequam facere Sed diuina
tus auxilio quae tu eis praecipis ante per
ficiens efficacissimo fidelibus profis
exemplo Magna est siquidem auentis
auctoritas eadem praemia iussa con
plenges quatenus in conuulsu ecclesias

uocem quidem qui euangelizas hierlm̄.;
exalta, noli timere; dic ciuitatatib; iudee.;
ecce dr̄ ur̄. ecce dn̄s dr̄ in fortitudine ueniet
& brecchiū eius dominabitur; & mer
ces eius cū eo · & opus illius corām eo. sic pas
tor gregem suū pascet. in brecchio suo
congregabit agnos · & in sinu suo leuabit.
fetatas ipse portabit · cu
uis mensus ē pugillo; aquas & celos
pelmō ponderauit; quis adpendit tb;
digitus molē terre & librauit in pondere
montes & colles in stateram; Quis ad
iubat spm̄ dn̄i. aut quis consiliarius eius ē
fuit · & ostendit illi aliquo iniit consilium.
& instruxit eum · & docuit eum semitate ius
tatie & erudiuit eū scientie & uice
prudentie ostendit illi; Ecce gentes qua
si stilla situlae & quasi momentū staterae
reputatae sunt; Ecce insule quasi puluis
exiguus & libanus insufficiet ad succendendū.

h.

3 *Bibelfragment · Christus als Knecht Gottes*
Umgebung von Chur?, Ende des 8.Jh. (Text S.184)
3 Bible fragment · Christ as the Suffering Servant
   Chur region? late eighth century (see p.184)

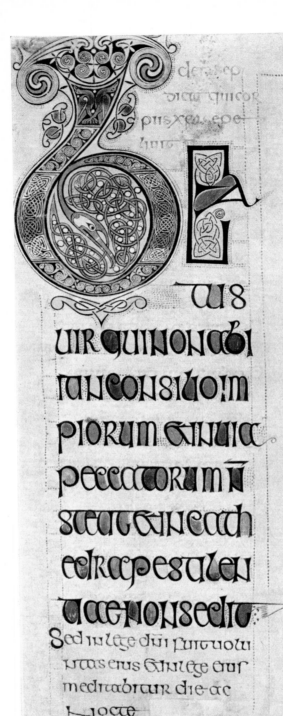

4 *Psalter der Äbtissin Salaberga · Schmuckseite mit Initiale B(eatus vir)*
Northumberland, Mitte des 8. Jh. (Text S. 184)
4 Psalter of Abbess Salaberga · Illuminated page with initial 'B(eatus vir)'
Northumberland, mid-eighth century (see p. 185)

5 Sogenannter Egino-Codex · Der hl. Ambrosius · Verona, 796–799 (Text S. 185)
5 Egino Codex · St Ambrose · Verona, 796–9 (see p. 185)

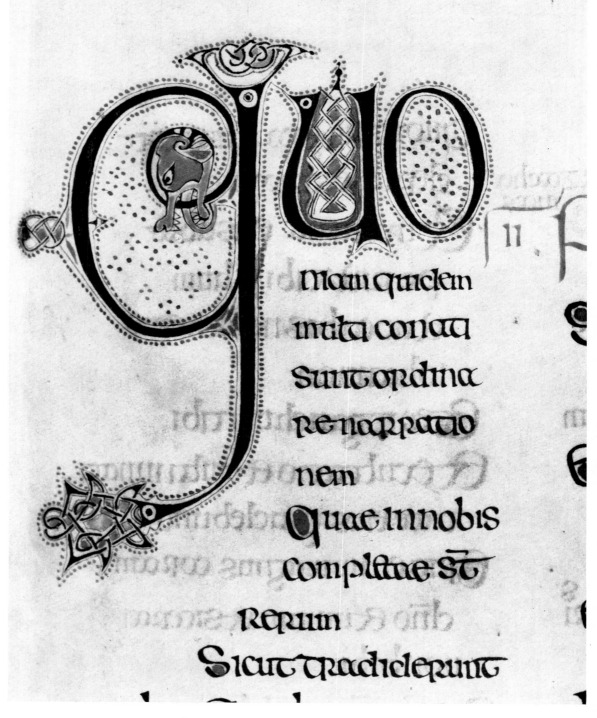

11

niam quidem
multa conata
sunt ordina
renarratio
nem
quae innobis
complitae st
rerum
sicut tradiderunt

6 *Evangeliar · Beginn des Lukasevangeliums: Quoniam quidem*
Anglo-irisch, 8. Jh. (Text S. 185)
6 Gospel book · Beginning of the argument to St Luke's Gospel: 'Quoniam quidem'
Anglo-Irish, eighth century (see p. 184)

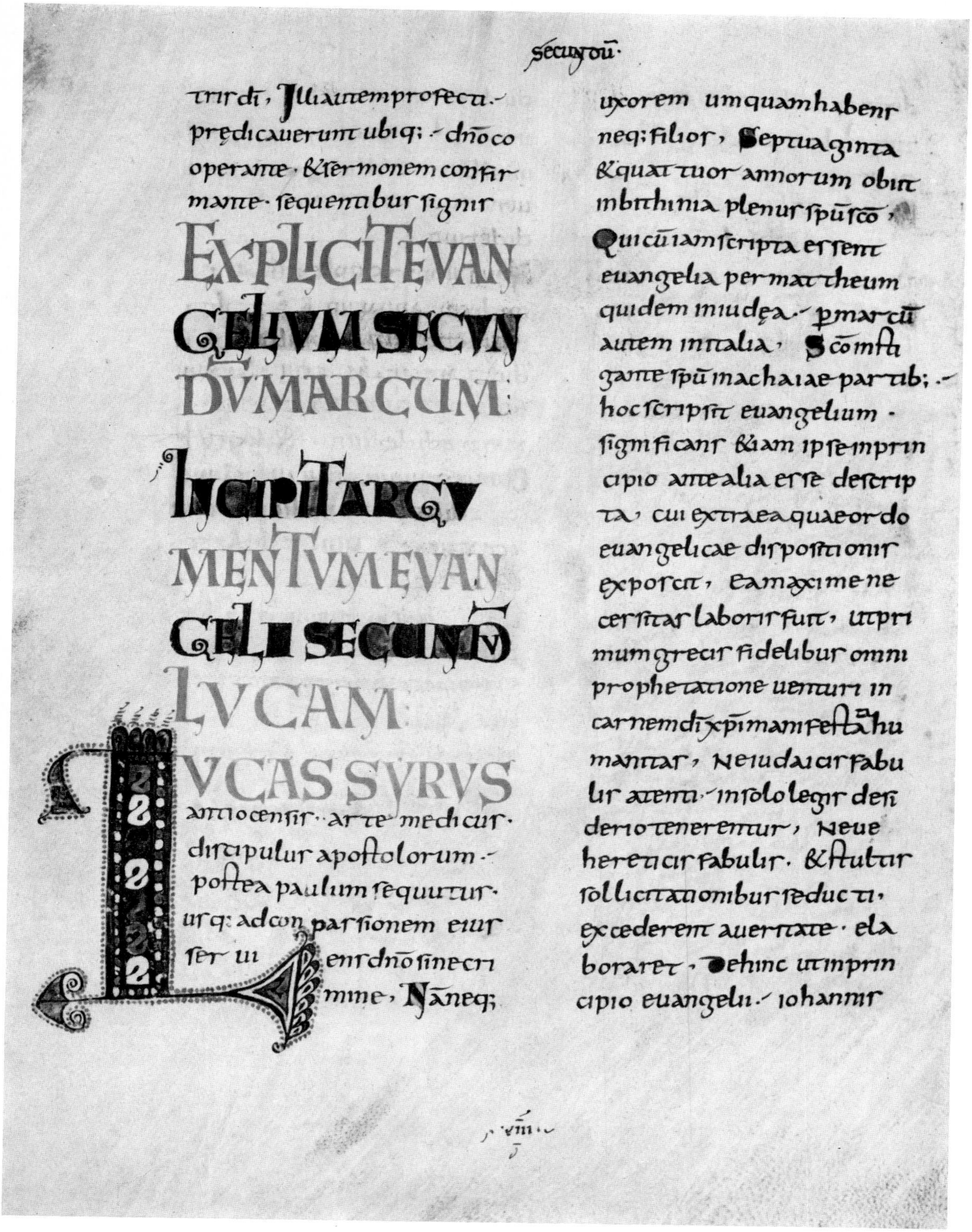

trirdī, Illi autem profecti·
predicauerūt ubiq;·dño co
operante·&sermonem confir
mante·sequentibus signis

EXPLICIT EVAN
GELIVM SECVN
DVM MARCVM·

INCIPIT ARGV
MENTVM EVAN
GELI SECVNDV
LVCAM·
LVCAS SYRVS

antiocensis·arte medicus·
discipulus apostolorum·
postea paulum sequutur·
usq; ad confessionem eius
seru ĩ ens dño sine cri
mine· Nā neq;

uxorem umquam habenr
neq; filios·Septuaginta
&quattuor annorum obiit
ĩ bithinia plenus spū sco·
Qui cū iam scripta essent
euangelia per mattheum
quidem ĩ iudea·p marcū
autem ĩ italia·sco ĩ stĩ
gante spū machaiae partib;·
hoc scripsit euangelium·
significans & iam ipse ĩ prin
cipio antealia esse descrip
ta·cui extra ea quae ordo
euangelicae dispositionis
exposcit·ea maxime ne
cessitas laboris fuit·ut pri
mum grecis fidelibus omni
prophetatione uenturi in
carnem dĩ xpī manifesta hu
manitas·Ne iudaicis fabu
lis attenti·in solo legis desi
derio tenerentur·Neue
hereticis fabulis·& stultis
sollicitationibus seducti·
excederent a ueritate·ela
boraret·Dehinc ut ĩ prin
cipio euangelii·iohannis

7 Evangeliar · Schmuckseite mit Initiale L(ucas)
Anglo-fränkisch, 1. Hälfte des 9. Jh. (Text S. 186)
7 Gospel book · Illuminated page with initial 'L(ucas)'
Anglo-Frankish, first half of ninth century (see p. 185)

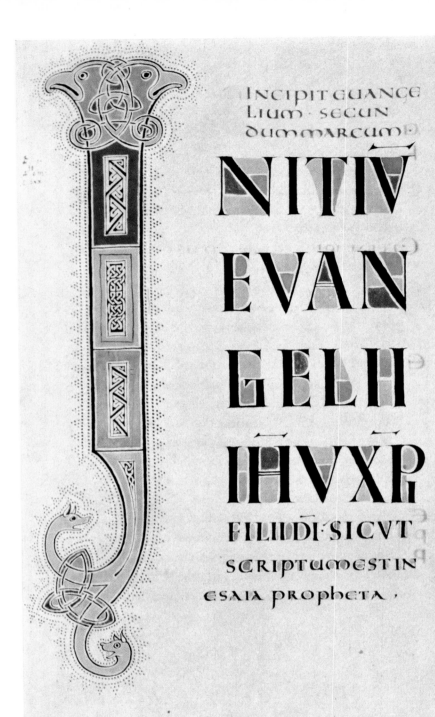

INCIPIT GUANGE
LIUM · SECUN
DUM MARCUM

NITIṼ
EVAN
GELII
IHV XRI
FILII DI · SICVT
SCRIPTUM EST IN
ESAIA PROPHETA ·

8 *Evangeliar · Beginn des Markusevangeliums mit Initiale I(nitium)*
Anglo-fränkisch, 9. Jh. (Text S. 186)
8 Gospel book · Beginning of St Mark's Gospel with initial 'I(nitium)'
Anglo-Frankish, ninth century (see p. 185)

9 *Evangelienfragment · Erste Kanonestafel*
St. Galler Zweigschule, spätes 9. Jh. (Text S. 187)
9 Gospel fragment · First canon
School of Sankt Gallen, late ninth century (see p. 186)

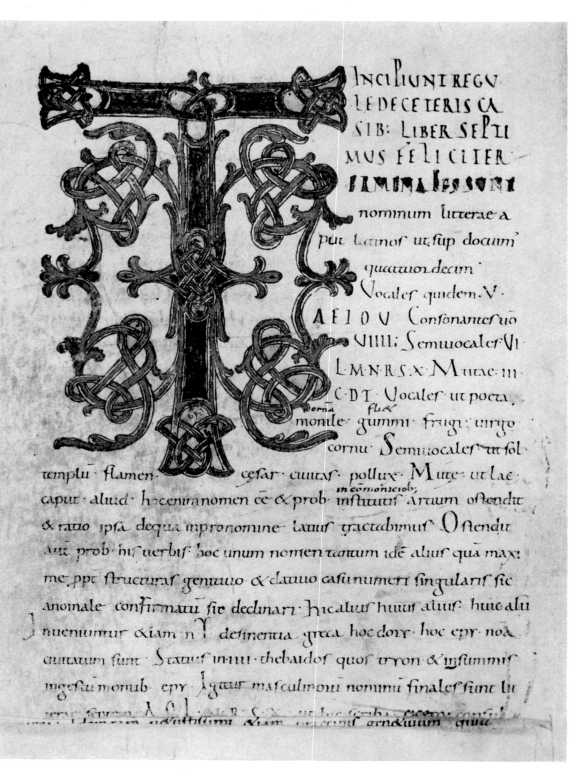

INCIPIVNT REGV
LE DE CETERIS CA
SIB: LIBER SEPTI
MVS FELICITER

TERMINALES SVNT
nominum litterae a
pud latinos ut sup docum̄
quattuor decim·
Vocales quidem. V·
A E I O V Consonantes uo
VIIII: Semiuocales VI
L M N R S X Mutae iii
C D T Vocales ut poeta·
monile gummi fragi uirgo
cornu Semiuocales ut sol
templu flamen cesar ciuitas pollux Mutae ut lac
caput aliud hec enim nomen ce & prob instituuis artium ostendit
& ratio ipsa de qua impronomine latius tractabimus Ostendit
aut prob his uerbis hoc unum nomen tantum ide aliue quā maxi
me ppt structuras genitiuo & datiuo casi numeri singularis sic
anomale confirmatū sic declinari ꝺicatur huius aliue huic alu
Inueniuntur etiam n̄ T desinentia greca hoc dorr hoc epr noā
ciuitatum sunt Statuis inuii thebaidos quos tyron & insummis
ingesu monub epr Igitur masculinoni nomini finales sunt lit
tere sunt A C L N R S X ut hic graba excep consul

10 *Priscianus: Lateinische Grammatik · Schmuckseite mit Initiale T(ermina)*
St. Gallen, nach 900 (Text S. 188)
10 Priscianus: Latin Grammar · Illuminated page with initial 'T(ermina)'
Sankt Gallen, after 900 (see p. 187)

11 *Evangeliar · Der Evangelist Markus · Karolingisch, Ende des 9. Jh. (Text S. 187)*
11 Gospel book · St Mark the Evangelist · Carolingian, late ninth century (see p. 186)

INCP̄ LIBI

DEVITA

SCIMARTI

NI EPISCOPI

ḠITUR MARTINUS

SABBARI ᴁEPANNONI

ARUM OPPIDO ORIUN

DUS FUIT SED

INTRA ITALIAM TICI

NI ALITUS EST

PARENTIBUS SECUNDŪ

SCL̄I DIGNITATĒ NON INFIMIS·

GENTILIBUS TAMEN;

12 *Sulpitius: Leben des hl. Martin · Schmuckseite mit Initiale I(gitur)*
Tours, vor 834 (Text S. 186)

12 Sulpitius: Life of St Martin · Illuminated page with initial 'I(gitur)'
Tours, before 834 (see p. 186)

PRIN

CIP₁O

13 *Evangeliar · Anfang des Johannesevangeliums mit Initiale I(n)*
Kölner Gegend, frühes 10. Jh. (Text S. 189)
13 Gospel book · Beginning of St John's Gospel with initial 'I(n)'
Cologne region, early tenth century (see p. 188)

14 *Sakramentarfragment · Kreuzigung*
Anglo-fränkisch, Anfang des 10. Jh. (Text S. 189)
14 Sacramentary fragment · Crucifixion
Anglo-Frankish, early tenth century (see p. 188)

15 *Codex Wittekindeus · Der Evangelist Matthäus · Fulda, um 975 (Text S. 188)*
15 Codex Wittekindeus · St Matthew the Evangelist · Fulda, c. 975 (see p. 188)

INCIPIT
EVANGE
LIVM·SE
CVNDV
MATTHE
VM

16 *Evangeliar · Schmuckseite: Beginn des Matthäusevangeliums*
Nordsachsen, Anfang des 10. Jh. (Text S. 190)
16 Gospel book · Beginning of St Matthew's Gospel
North Saxony, early tenth century (see p. 189)

LUCASPVI...LLUMXIMERTPONTIFICAE

17 *Evangeliar · Der Evangelist Lukas · Westsächsisch, frühes 10. Jh. (Text S. 190)*
17 Gospel book · St Luke the Evangelist · West Saxony, early tenth century (see p. 189)

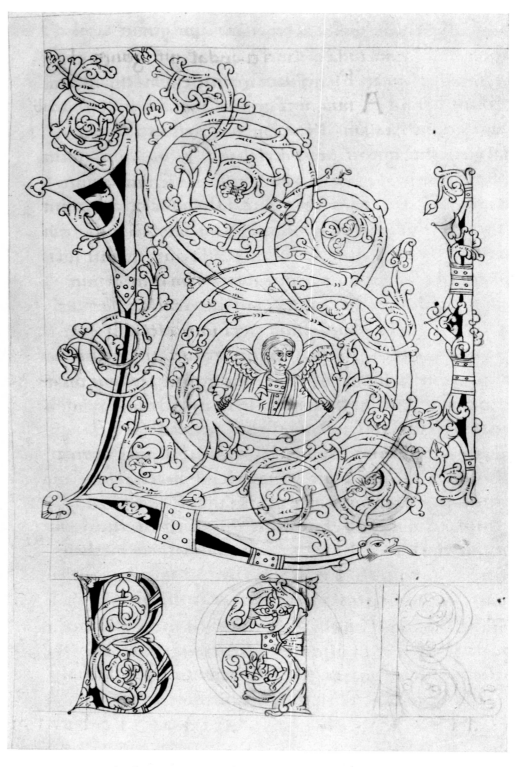

18 *Evangeliarfragment · Beginn des Matthäusevangeliums mit Initiale L(iber)*
Bayrisch, Mitte des 11.Jh. (Text S.191)
18 Gospel fragment · Beginning of St Matthew's Gospel with initial 'L(iber)'
Bavaria, mid-eleventh century (see p.190)

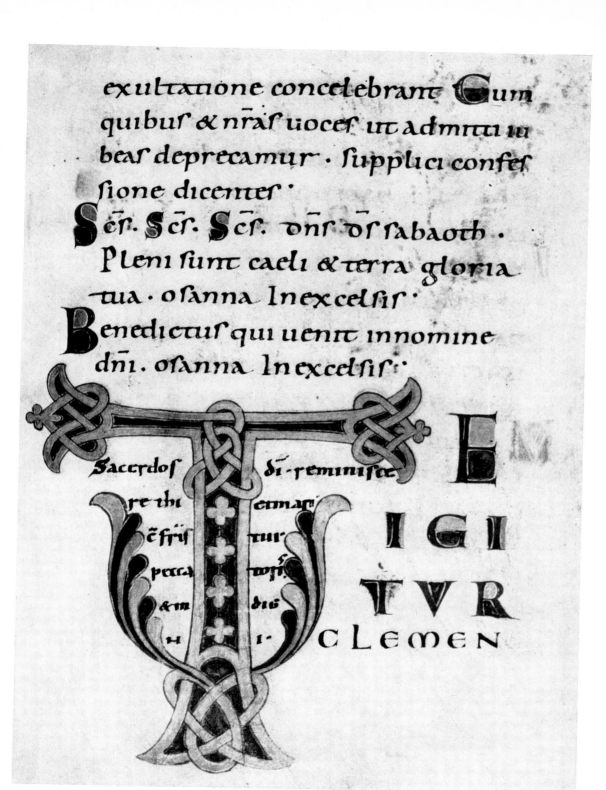

exultatione concelebrant Cum
quibus & nras uoces ut admitti iu
bear deprecamur . supplici confes
sione dicentes :
Scs. Scs. Scs. dns ds sabaoth .
Pleni sunt caeli & terra gloria
tua . osanna In excelsis :
Benedictus qui uenit innomine
dni . osanna In excelsis :

Sacerdos di reminisce
re thi etiam
e fris tur
peccat nos
& in dis
H I

E
IGI
TVR
CLEMEN

19 *Kalender und Sakramentar · Schmuckseite mit Initiale T(e igitur)*
St. Gallen?, Anfang des 11. Jh. (Text S. 188)

19 Calendar and Sacramentary · Illuminated page with initial 'T(e igitur)'
Sankt Gallen? early eleventh century (see p. 187)

20 *Evangelistar · Schmuckseite mit Initiale M(aria) · Reichenau, um 970 (Text S. 187)*
20 Evangelistary · Illuminated page with initial 'M(aria)' · Reichenau, *c.*970 (see p. 187)

21 *Sakramentar · Die Frauen am Grabe · Minden, 1. Hälfte des 11. Jh. (Text S. 190)*
21 Sacramentary · The women at the sepulchre · Minden, early eleventh century (see p. 189)

22 *Beda: Englische Kirchengeschichte · Thronender Christus · Köln, vor 1149 (Text S. 193)*
22 Bede: Ecclesiastical History · Christ in majesty · Cologne, before 1149 (see p. 191)

23 *Otto von Freising: Weltchronik · Darstellungen aus der Genesis*
Schäftlarn, zwischen 1157 und 1177 (Text S. 191)
23 Otto von Freising: Universal chronicle · Adam and Eve; Noah
Schäftlarn, 1157–77 (see p. 191)

24 *Psalter · Schmuckseite mit Initiale B(eatus vir)*
Soignies im Hennegau, 2. Hälfte des 11. Jh. (Text S. 191)
24 Psalter · Illuminated page with initial 'B(eatus vir)'
Soignies, Hainault, second half of eleventh century (see p. 190)

25 *Theofrid: Blumenbuch · Der Abt Theofrid · Echternach, um 1100 (Text S. 192)*
25 Theofrid: Flora · Abbot Theofrid · Echternach, *c.* 1100 (see p. 191)

26 *Gregor: Predigten über Hesekiel · Papst Gregor*
Thüringisch-meißnisch, spätes 12. Jh. (Text S. 196)
26 Gregory the Great: Homilies on Ezekiel · Pope Gregory
Thuringia-Meissen, late twelfth century (see p. 195)

27 *Bibel aus Hamersleben · Der Stiftsheilige Pancratius*
Halberstadt, um 1170 (Text S. 194)
27 Hamersleben Bible · St Pancras · Halberstadt, c. 1170 (see p. 192)

28 *Origines: Predigten · Schmuckseite mit Schöpfungsdarstellung*
Pegau, Ende des 12. Jh. (Text S. 196)
28 Origen: Homilies · Illuminated page with the seven days of Creation
Pegau, late twelfth century (see p. 194)

29 *Lektionar des Marcwardus · Christus in der Mandorla*
Halberstadt, 2. Viertel des 12. Jh. (Text S. 193)
29 Marcwardus' Lectionary · Christ in a mandorla
Halberstadt, *c*. 1125–50 (see p. 192)

30 *Paulusbriefe mit Anmerkungen des Petrus Lombardus · Initiale P(rincipia)*
Posa bei Zeitz?, um 1200 (Text S. 197)

30 Pauline epistles with collectanea of Petrus Lombardus · Initial 'P(rincipia)'
Posa, near Zeitz? *c.* 1200 (see p. 196)

E.C.SVNT.NOMINA
FILJORVO.JSRAHEL.QVI.IN
gressi sunt in egiptum cum iacob singu
li cum domibus suis utrouerunt.Ruben.

31 *Mildenfurter Bibel · Anfang des Exodus mit Initiale H(ec)*
Posa, um 1210 (Text S. 198)
31 Mildenfurt Bible · Beginning of Exodus with initial 'H(ec)'
Posa, *c.* 1210 (see p. 196)

32 *Augustinus: Vom Gottesstaat · Der weltliche Staat · Posa, um 1180 (Text S. 197)*

32 St Augustine: City of God · Cities of the world · Posa, *c.* 1180 (see p. 195)

33 *Bernhard von Clairvaux: Reden · Illustration zum Hohenlied*
Pegau, Ende des 12. Jh. (Text S. 196)
33 Bernard of Clairvaux: Sermons on the Song of Solomon · Christ in a mandorla;
Youth, Bride and Solomon · Pegau, late twelfth century (see p. 194)

In uigilia Natiuitatis dni. Lectio ysaie ppfe.
EC DICIT DNS.

ROPTER
syon non
tacebo. et ppr
ier ierusm non
quiescam. do
nec egrediatur
ut splendor
iustus eius? et
saluator eius ut
lampas accendatur. Et uidebunt gentes iustū
tuū. et cuncti reges inclitum tuū? et uocabitur
tibi nomen nouū. quod os dūi nominauit. Et eris
corona glie in manu dūi? et diadema regni in ma
nu dei tui. Non uocaberis ultra derelicta. et terra
tua non uocabitur amplius desolata? sed uocabe
ris uoluntas mea in ea. et terra tua inhabitabitur?
quia coplacuit dūo in te. Lc eple bi pauli apli?

AVLVS seruus ihu xpo Romanos.
xpi uocatus apls. segregatus in euuan
gelium dei quod ante pmiserat p prophas
suos in scripturis scis de filio suo. qui
factus e ei ex semine dauid secdn carnē?
qui predestinatus est filius dei in uirtu
te secdn spiritum scificationis. ex resurrec

34 *Lektionarfragment · Schmuckseite mit drei Initialen*
Magdeburger Gegend, um 1245 (Text S. 194)
34 Lectionary fragment · Illuminated page with three initials
Magdeburg region, c. 1245 (see p. 193)

xxxvi Vixit ioseph annis centū decē annis. y
ad iurauit frs suos ut eū uisitarent tol
lentt secum ossa ei in terrā suam.

Expricrvnt capitvra

In principio

creauit

deus celum

et terram.

Terra autem erat
inanis & uacua. et
tenebre erant sup
faciem abyssi. &
spiritus dei ferebat
tur sup aquas. Dix
itq; ds fiat lux. Et
facta ē lux. Et uidit
ds lucem quod es
set bona. & diuisit
ds lucem ac tene
bras. appellauitq;
lucem diem. & tene
bras noctem. Fac

Er uo
gatio
& un
Gern
facie
rū fa
cuiū
ram.
ta he
men
cien
seme
dit d
uesp
Dix
in
em &
pora
firm
Et fa
na lu
ut p
ut p
ut ea
sup
& diu
uidu
uesp
Dix

35 *Halberstädter Bibel · Initiale I(n principio) mit Gottvater*
Halberstadt, frühes 13. Jh. (Text S. 195)
35 Halberstadt Bible · Initial 'I(n principio)' with God the Father
Halberstadt, early thirteenth century (see p. 194)

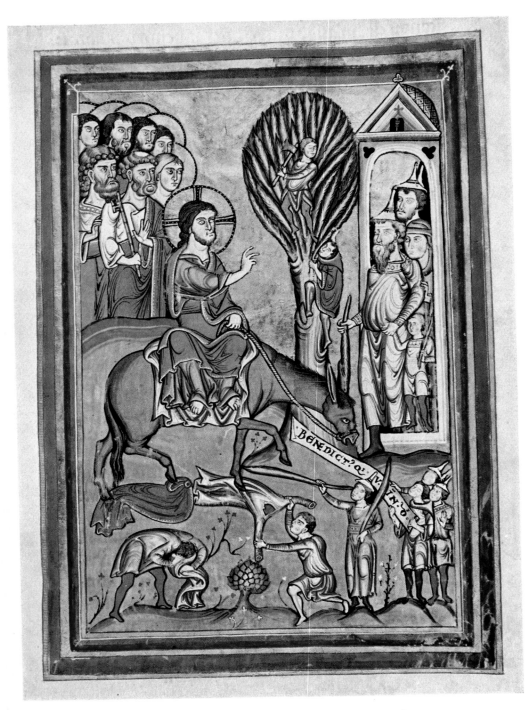

36 *Brandenburger Evangelistar · Einzug in Jerusalem*
Magdeburger Raum, Anfang des 13.Jh. (Text S.194)
36 Brandenburg Evangelistary · Entry into Jerusalem
Magdeburg region, early thirteenth century (see p. 193)

37 *Martyrologium · Das Martyrium des hl. Laurentius*
Süddeutschland, Anfang des 13. Jh. (Text S. 192)
37 Martyrology · Martyrdom of St Lawrence
Southern Germany, early thirteenth century (see p. 191)

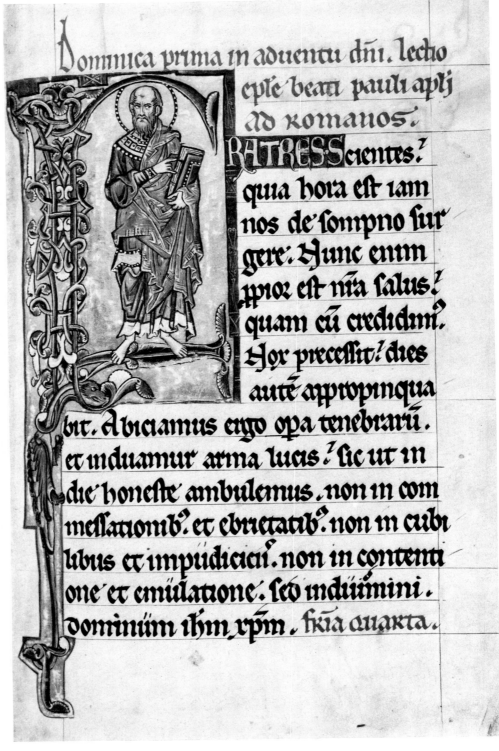

Dominica prima in aduentu dni. lectio
eple beati pauli apli
ad romanos.

FRATRES Scientes?
quia hora est iam
nos de sompno sur
gere. Hunc enim
ppior est nra salus?
quam cu credidim?
Nox precessit? dies
aute appropinqua
bit. Abiciamus ergo opa tenebraru.
et induamur arma lucis? sic ut in
die honeste ambulemus. non in com
messationib? et ebrietatib? non in cubi
libus et impudiciciis. non in contenti
one et emulatione. sed induimini.
dominum ihm rpm. feria quarta.

38 *Lektionar · Schmuckseite: Initiale F(ratres) mit Paulus*
Halberstadt, Mitte des 13. Jh. (Text S. 195)
38 Lectionary · Illuminated page with initial 'F(ratres)' showing St Paul
Halberstadt, mid-thirteenth century (see p. 193)

39 Gregor: Sittenlehre · Der Baum der Tugenden
Thüringisch-meißnisch, Mitte des 13. Jh. (Text S. 198)
39 Gregory the Great: Moralia · Tree of Virtues
Thuringia-Meissen, mid-thirteenth century (see p. 197)

40 Psalter · Initiale B(eatus vir) mit König David
Nordthüringen, 1. Hälfte des 13. Jh. (Text S. 199)
40 Psalter · Initial 'B(eatus vir)' with King David
North Thuringia, early thirteenth century (see p. 197)

41 *Fortlaufender Kalender · Auferstehung · Nordthüringen, 1. Hälfte des 13. Jh. (Text S. 199)*
41 Perpetual Calendar · Resurrection · North Thuringia, early thirteenth century (see p. 197)

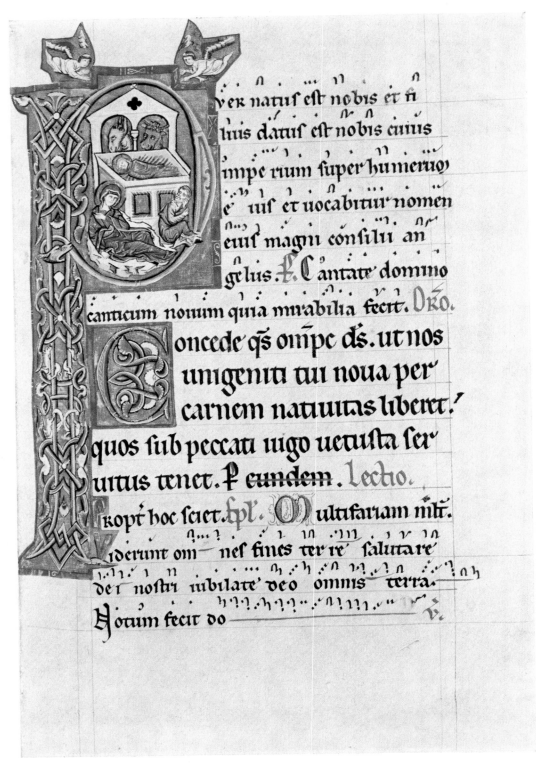

uer natus est nobis et fi
lius datus est nobis cuius
imperium super humeros
eius et uocabitur nomen
eius magni consilii an
gelus. V. Cantate domino
canticum nouum quia mirabilia fecit. ORO.
Concede qs ompc ds. ut nos
unigeniti tui noua per
carnem natiuitas liberet.
quos sub peccati iugo uetusta ser
uitus tenet. P eundem. Lectio.
ropt hoc sciet. EpL. Multifariam mlt.
iderunt om— nes fines terre salutare
dei nostri iubilate deo omnis terra.
Notum fecit do————————————

42 *Missale des Dompropstes Semeko · Initiale P(uer) mit Geburt Christi
Halberstadt, 1238–1245 (Text S.195)*
42 Provost Semeko's Missal · Initial 'P(uer)' with Nativity
Halberstadt, 1238–45 (see p.193)

43 *Psalter · Moses vor dem brennenden Busch*
Halberstadt?, 1. Hälfte des 13. Jh. (Text S. 195)
43 Psalter · Moses and the Burning Bush
Halberstadt? early thirteenth century (see p. 194)

Incipit plog regule sancti benedicti abbis.

USCULTA
o fili precepta magistri. et inclina aurem cordis tui. et admonitione pij patris libeter excipe. & efficaciter comple. ut ad eum p obedientie laborem redeas. a quo p inobedientie desidiam recesseras. Ad te ergo nunc meus sermo dirigit. quisquis abrenuncians ppriis uoluptatib. dno. xpo uero regi militaturr. obedientie fortissima atq; pclara arma assumis. inprimis ut qcqo agendum inchoas bonum. ab eo pfici instantissima oratione deposcas. ut qui nos iam infilioy

44 *Benediktinerregel · Initiale A(usculta) mit dem hl. Benedikt*
Posa, Mitte des 13. Jh. (Text S. 198)
44 Rule of St Benedict · Initial 'A(usculta)' with St Benedict
Posa, mid-thirteenth century (see p. 197)

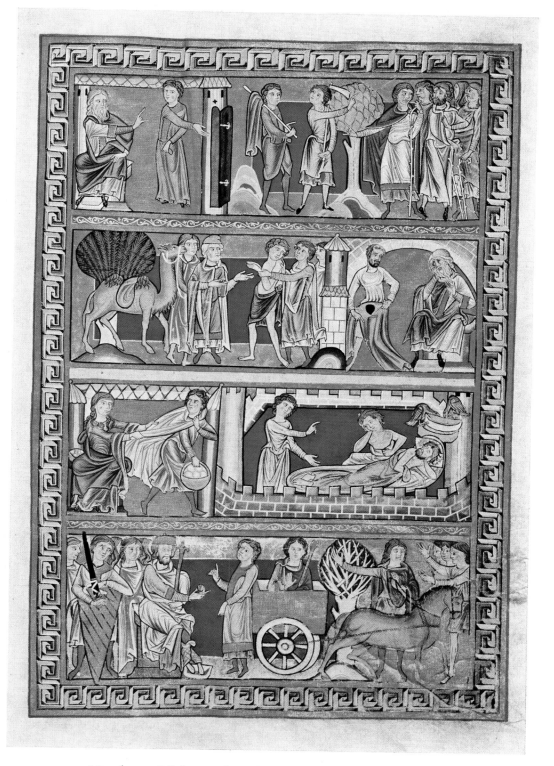

45 *Merseburger Bibel · Josephsgeschichte · Posa, um 1240 (Text S. 198)*
45 Merseburg Bible · Story of Joseph · Posa, *c.* 1240 (see p. 196)

46 *Psalter · Heimsuchung · Thüringisch-meißnisch,*
2. Hälfte des 13. Jh. (Text S. 212)
46 Psalter · Visitation · Thuringia-Meissen,
late thirteenth century (see p. 209)

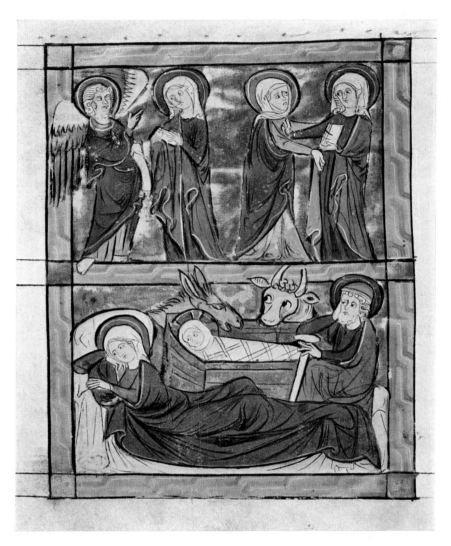

47 *Psalter · Verkündigung, Heimsuchung, Geburt*
Italienisch?, 1. Hälfte des 14.Jh. (Text S. 220)
47 Psalter · Annunciation; Visitation; Nativity
Italy? early fourteenth century (see p. 217)

48 *Missale · Schmuckseite mit Initiale P(uer), darin Geburt Christi*
Thüringisch-meißnisch, um 1300 (Text S. 212)
48 Missal · Initial 'P(uer)' with Nativity
Thuringia-Meissen, c. 1300 (see p. 209)

49 *Brevier · Auferstehung · Thüringisch-meißnisch, um 1300 (Text S. 213)*
49 Breviary · Resurrection · Thuringia-Meissen, *c.* 1300 (see p. 210)

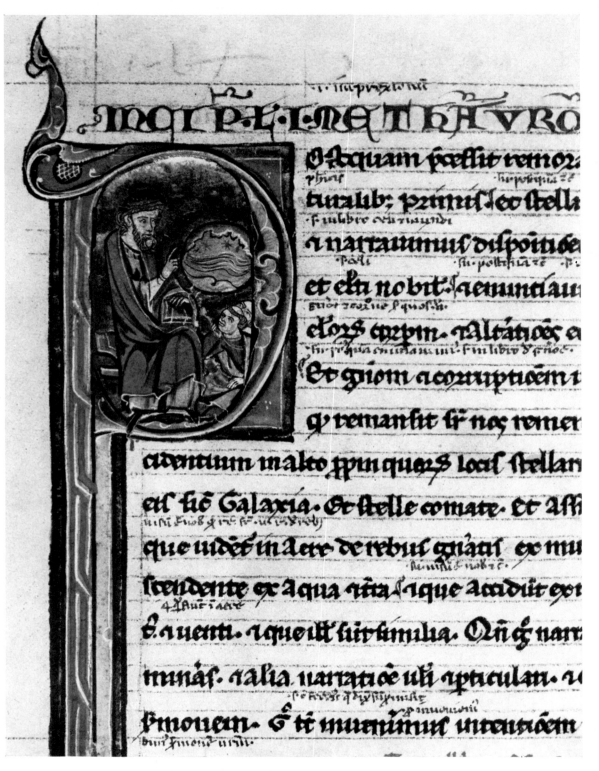

50 Aristoteles: Werke · Initiale P(ostquam) mit lehrendem Aristoteles
Norditalien, 2. Hälfte des 13. Jh. (Text S. 220)
50 Aristotle: Works · Initial 'P(ostquam)' with Aristotle teaching
Northern Italy, late thirteenth century (see p. 217)

res mei. Gratia domini nostri ihu xpi cum spi
ritu uro amen.
Incipit argumentum epistole ad hebreos.

pistola
que fer-
tur apd
hebreos.
non eiuf
dem a
postoli
creditur
pres-
stili ser
monis

et dissonantiam: sed uel barnabe iuxta
tertullianum uel luce euangeliste iuxta
quosdam. uel clementis romane postea
eccle epi quem aiunt sententias pauli p
pro ordinasse sermone. Vel certe quia pa
ulus scribebat ad hebreos: ppter inuidia
sui apud eos nominis titulum in princi
pio salutationis amputauerat. Scpserat
autem ut hebreus hebrayce: id est suo elo
quio disertissime. Ea que loquentur scrip
ta fuerant in hebreo. lucas dicitur eloque
eius uertisse in grecum: z hanc ee causa
quod a ceteris pauli eplas discrepare uide
atur. Interim apud ecclas orientis apsto
lice doctrine auctoritate habetur.

Incipit epistola ad hebreos.

olim deus loquens patribus in pphis. no
uissime diebus istis locutus est nobis in fi
lio quem constituit heredem uniusoz per
quem fecit z secula. Qui cum sit splendor
glorie et figura substantie eius portansq;
omnia ubo uirtutis sue purgationem pec
catorum faciens. sedet ad dexteram maie
statis in excelsis. tanto melior angelis effect'
quanto differentius p illis nomen heredi
tauit. Cui enim dixit aliquando angelo
rum filius meus es tu ego hodie genui te:
Et rursum. Ego ero illi in patrem: z ipse erit
michi in filium. Et cum iterum introducit
primogenitum in orbem terre dicit. et ado
rent eum omnes angli dei. Et ad anglos
quidem dicit. Qui facit anglis suos spirit
z ministros suos flammam ignis. ad fili
um autem. Thronus tuus deus in seculu
seculi. uirga equitatis uirga regni tui. di
lexisti iusticia et odisti iniquitatem: ppta
unxit te deus deus tuus oleo exultatiois
pre participibus tuis. Et tu in principio
domine terram fundasti: z opa manuum

51 *Vulgatafragment · Schmuckseite mit Initialen E(pistola) und M(ultifariam)*
Sächsische Provinzialschule, um 1260–1265 (Text S. 212)
51 Vulgate fragment · Initials 'E(pistola)' and 'M(ultifariam)'
Saxon provincial school, c. 1260–5 (see p. 209)

que qũt lathanas elt v es laïte
eglile rûïne et an freche a deu
leruir ⁊ olrur as prelais et li
aus qui paılent de celte uie eſt
uraie confeſions et les armes
de liaus rûïnent a thũtriſt et
de liauls qui inuerent en pe-
chie mortel les armes uõnté
pûïne La prenuere relurrectiõ
eſt de larme que p la deu gra
ice relieue de mort de peche
La leconde lerut de cors auut
gement Et cil qui ont pırt
en la prenuere relurrection
Ceu eſt a dıre q̃ il en celte uie
relieuent de peche p uraie cõ

feſſion et pır uraie repen
tance et par penance c̃ue
de gruıce il ont pırt en la se
conde relurrection Seu eſt
a dıre que il relieuerout au
uıgement en cors et en ar
mes a uie de gloıre et le eſt
la bien curteıs que il aue
ront car il ſeront glonfi
eſt en cors et en armes et
loueront deu ſan fin et le
eſt ceu que il dıſt que il se
ront prelles deu thũtriſt
et rammeront auec lui mıl
ans ſeu eſt p duraublemẽt

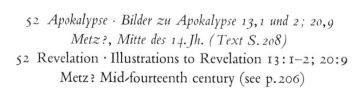

53 *Brevier · Schmuckseite mit Initialen, Randleiste mit Stamm Jesse*
Erfurt?, 14. Jh. (Text S. 213)
53 Breviary · Initials and Stem of Jesse
Erfurt? fourteenth century (see p. 210)

54 *Stitni: Gespräch des Vaters mit seinen Söhnen · Initiale gleichen Inhalts*
Böhmisch, spätes 14. Jh. (Text S. 218)
54 Thomas of Stitni: Conversation of a father with his sons · Illustration of the title
Bohemia, late fourteenth century (see p. 215)

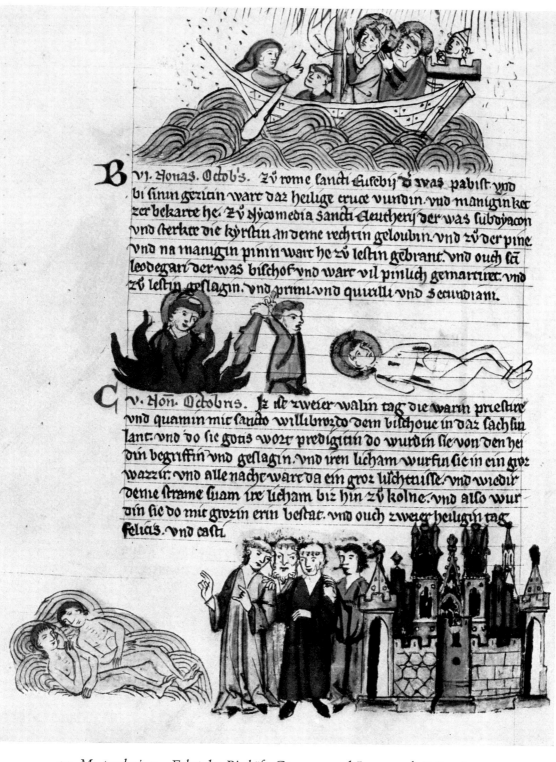

B vj. nonas octob's. Zu rome sancti Eusebij d' was pabist. vnd bi sinun gezitin wart daz heilige cruce vundin. vnd manigin ketzer bekarte he. Zu nycomedia sancti Eleutherij der was subdyacon vnd sterkur die kyrstin an deme rechtin geloubin. vnd zu der pine vnd na manigin pinin wart he zu lestin gebrant. vnd ouch san leodegan der was bischof vnd wart vil pinlich gemartirut. vnd zu lestin geslagin. vnd primi vnd quirilli vnd secundiam.

C v. non octobris. Ez ist zweier walin tag die warin priestir vnd quamin mit sancto willibrordo dem bischoue in daz sachsin lant. vnd do sie gotis wort predigitin do wurdin sie von den heidin begriffin vnd geslagin. vnd iren licham wurfin sie in ein groz wazzir. vnd alle nacht wart da ein groz luchtnisse. vnd widur deme strame swam ire licham biz hin zu kolne. vnd also wurdin sie do mit grozin erin bestat. vnd ouch zweier heiligin tag felicis. vnd casti.

55 *Martyrologium · Fahrt der Bischöfe Germanus und Lupus nach Britannien*
Mitteldeutsch, vor 1300 (Text S. 213)
55 Martyrology · Voyage of the bishops Germanus and Lupus to Britain
Central Germany, before 1300 (see p. 210)

56 *Kanonisches Recht · Widmungsbild an Papst Bonifaz VIII.*
Bologna, Anfang des 14. Jh. (Text S. 221)
56 Corpus juris canonici, VI · Presentation to Pope Boniface VIII
Bologna, early fourteenth century (see p. 217)

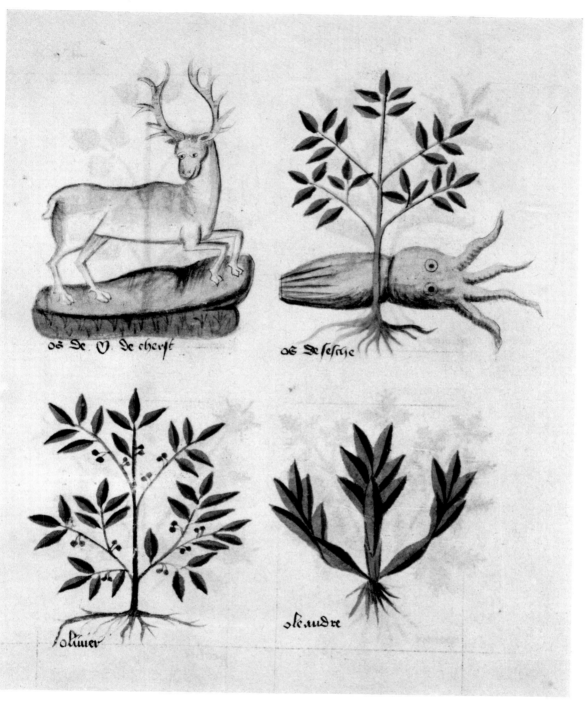

57 *Kräuter- und Tierbuch · Hirsch, Tintenfisch, Heilpflanzen*
Paris?, um 1310 (Text S. 199)
57 Codex of scientific works · Deer, cuttlefish and medicinal plants
Paris? *c.* 1310 (see p. 198)

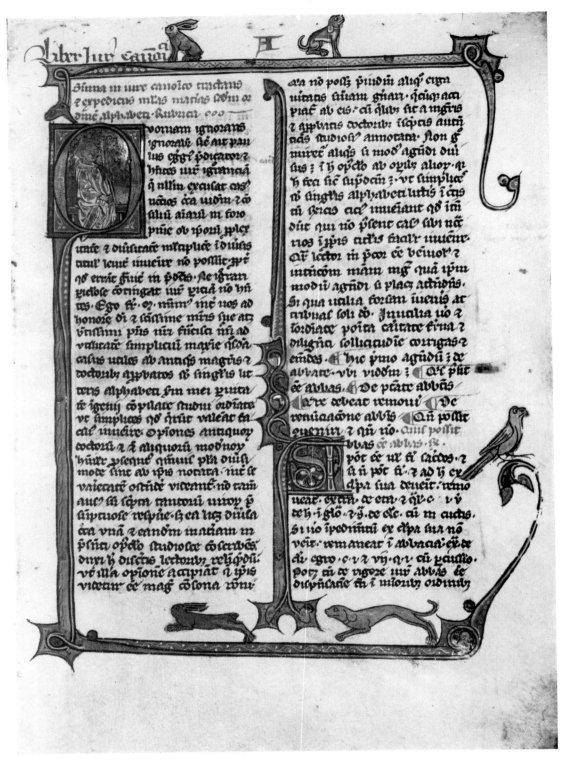

58 *Monaldus: Abriß des kanonischen Rechtes · Schmuckseite mit Initialen*
Mühlhausen?, 2. Hälfte des 14. Jh. (Text S. 217)
58 Monaldus: Summa juris canonici · Illuminated page
Mühlhausen? late fourteenth century (see p. 214)

73 *Vesperale und Matutinale · Initiale G(aude) mit Verkündigung Mariä*
Böhmisch, um 1420 (Text S. 218)

73 Vesperal and Matutinal · Initial 'G(aude)' with Annunciation
Bohemia, c. 1420 (see p. 215)

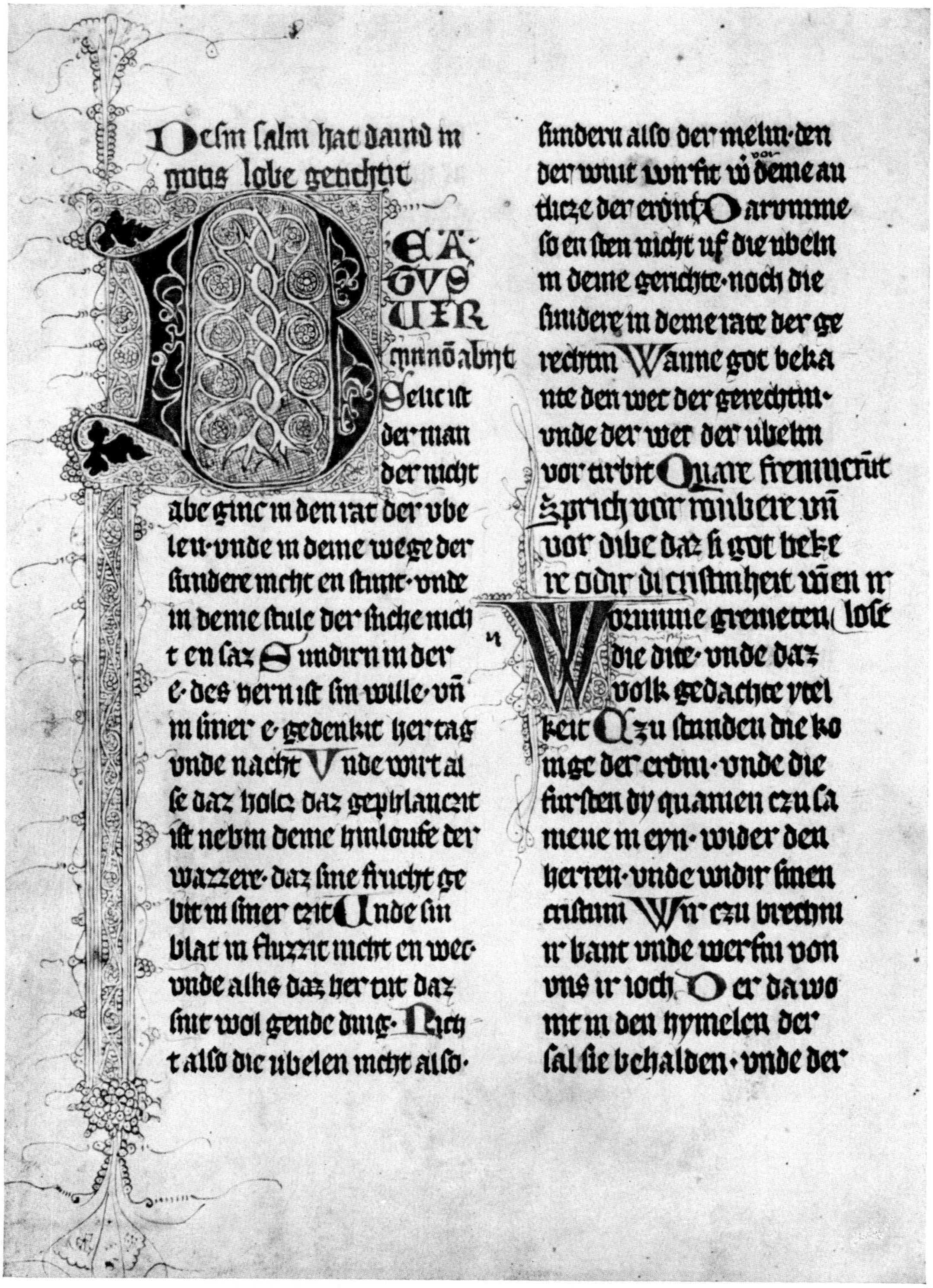

74 *Deutscher Psalter · Initiale B(eatus vir) · Deutsch, 1386 (Text S. 207)*
74 German Psalter · Initial 'B(eatus vir)' · German, 1386 (see p. 205)

75 *Gebetbuch · Schmuckseite mit Initiale H(ere)*
Niederländisch, Ende des 14. Jh. (Text S. 203)
75 Dutch prayerbook · Illuminated page with initial 'H(ere)'
Low Countries, late fourteenth century (see p. 202)

76 *Thomas de Anglia: Anmerkungen über Ovids Metamorphosen · Schmuckseite*
Oberitalien, Ende des 14. Jh. (Text S. 222)
76 Ovid: Metamorphoses, with commentary by Thomas de Anglia · Illuminated page
Northern Italy, late fourteenth century (see p. 219)

77 Jacobus de Voragine: Legenda aurea · Himmelfahrt und Erhöhung Mariä
Paris, frühes 15. Jh. (Text S. 200)

77 Jacobus de Voragine: Golden Legend · Assumption of the Virgin
Paris, early fifteenth century (see p. 199)

78 *Heilsspiegel · Christi Himmelfahrt und Jakobs Himmelsleiter*
Deutsch, um 1400 (Text S. 214)

78 Speculum humanae salvationis · Ascension; Jacob's Ladder
German, *c.* 1400 (see p. 211)

Der in sinem werke kan
Stein und kalch legen wol
Da ers von Recht legen sol
Es ist vntugent nicht
Villicht ouch nur das gesicht
Lass ich in mine gedeck es want
Ein kalch das em ander kunt
Besmitten hat bey mit schliche last
Das es yteich dem anderen ist
Darum spricht em wiser man
Wer gefüegleichen kan
Setzen ein red in sin gedicht
Die er doch hat gemachet nicht
Der hat als vil getan
Da gezweifel niemer an
Als der er von ersten nint
Der fient ist worden sin zehant
Es ist mm walte wol
Das man sin red setzen sol
Vnt andie lute wiser lov
Versmehet man es das ist uner
Hussorge nu bis des gemant
So du min buch kom ze hant
Wiskuellet die nacht dar an
Das la kestren einen man
Der doch ane wandel sy
Wer wr unstet nicht ist frey
Den salt du es nicht lassen sehen
Ein kisser man der pfleget zu spehen
Im gut red drumb mer
Das er velsche den durch ere
Der Bös man vnd die bosheit
Sullen werden hie so bereit
Das Er von minem welsche gaste
Von tugenden fliehen vaste

79 *Thomasin von Zerclaere: Der welsche Gast · Allegorische Tugenddarstellungen*
Südliches Westdeutschland, um 1400 (Text S. 208)

79 Thomasin von Zirclaria: Der welsche Gast · Allegories of the knightly virtues
South-west Germany, c. 1400 (see p. 206)

syben sacramenten Pis alles habe von mir In ynnige sele vnd volgestu der Weyßheit nach nymer sere so fingestu Wol zu prysen de den guldm tron vnd ouch mit Weyßheit zu besitzende vnd erreuch inge waz dr nutze ist zu dem ebygen lebin Amen

ber alle sere die yemant geleren kan add mag so ist daz heylige euin gelin vnd die sere vnsers lie

ben hren thu xpi Die aller hochste vnd heyligste wen got der vater hat sy vns selbir gesand durch syne em gebornen son als her spm dem ewiges. Syne lere ist nicht meyn sy ist des dr mich gesand hat Vnd ouch an eyner stad spicht vnser lire in dem ewan wer vß gote ist der hort daz wort gotis gerne vnd wen alle dmg zu gen so zuget gotis Wort nymer vnd blibet ebyg lich Diß vnd andere spruche vnde sere vnd ebysinge rey sein mich puz alden derzu Wy ich dich liphabende sele dr zu gebysen moge daz du in der schule der heilige schrifft vnd gotlicher sere lerne mogist da mit du dich fugest zu dem guldm trone Wen Sy heylige schrifft vnd gotliche sere is alles daz Wort gotis eyn Wesen vnd materie vnd wer omt fleyße sy leset vnd sie mit ernste in sein hertze schribet vnd behelt der ist selig spruchst vnser hre in dem ewan Jch vnrzeuder alde sere dich libhabende sele gotliche kunste zu lernende noch dr Weyßhat von der dich

80 *Otto von Passau: Die vierundzwanzig Alten · Der 14. Alte spricht zur Seele Leipzig?, 1446 (Text S. 215)*

80 Otto von Passau: Die vierundzwanzig Alten · The fourteenth elder and the loving soul · Leipzig? 1446 (see p. 212)

81 *Psalter · Kanonbild: Kreuzigung · Kursächsisch, um 1480 (Text S. 216)*
81 Psalter · Crucifixion · Saxony, c. 1480 (see p. 213)

82 *Graduale · Initiale P(uer) mit Anbetung des Kindes*
Zittau, 1435 (Text S. 219)
82 Gradual · Initial 'P(uer)' with Adoration of the Child
Zittau, 1435 (see p. 216)

83 *Leidensgeschichte Christi · Kreuzabnahme*
Halberstädter Gegend?, um 1450 (Text S. 211)
83 Passion book · Deposition · Halberstadt region?
*c.*1450 (see p.208)

84 *Brevier · Auferweckung der Toten*
Niederländisch, 15. Jh. (Text S. 204)
84 Breviary · Resurrection of the dead
Low Countries, fifteenth century (see p. 202)

85 *Brevier · Auferweckung des Lazarus*
Flämisch, 1440–1460 (Text S. 204)
85 Breviary · Raising of Lazarus
Flemish, 1440–60 (see p. 202)

86 *Stundenbuch · Anbetung des Kindes*
Französisch, Mitte des 15. Jh. (Text S. 201)
86 Book of Hours · Adoration of the Child
French, mid-fifteenth century (see p. 199)

87 *Brevier · Heimsuchung · Französisch,* 2. *Hälfte des* 15. *Jh.* (*Text S. 202*)
87 Breviary · Visitation · French, late fifteenth century (see p. 200)

88 *Stundenbuch · König David im Gebet*
Französisch, 2. Hälfte des 15. Jh. (Text S. 201)
88 Book of Hours · King David at prayer
French, late fifteenth century (see p. 200)

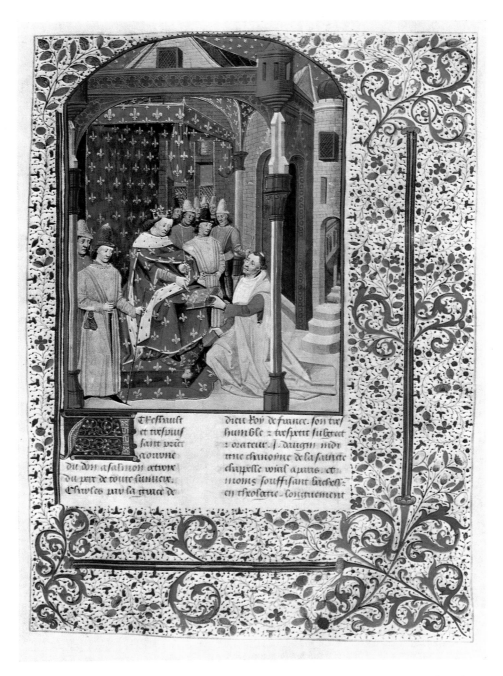

89 *Petrarca: Trostspiegel · Widmungsbild an König Karl VII. von Frankreich*
Paris, Mitte des 15. Jh. (Text S. 201)

89 Petrarch: Des remèdes de l'autre fortune · Dedication to Charles VII
Paris, mid-fifteenth century (see p. 199)

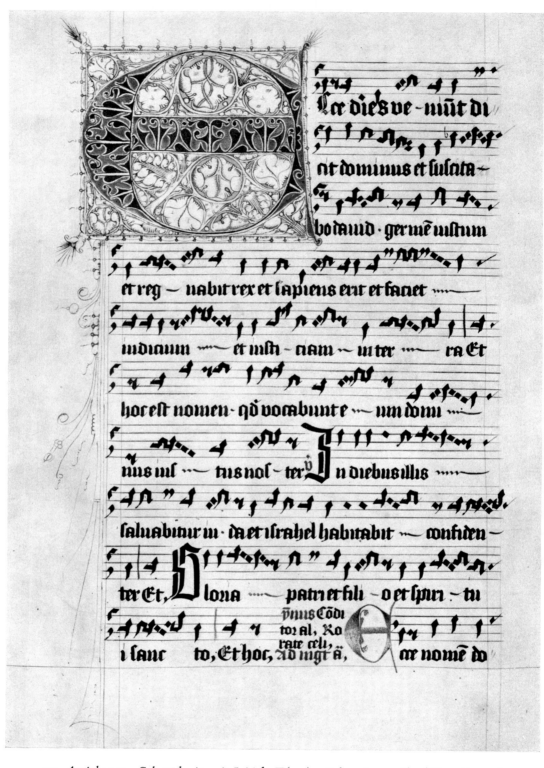

90 *Antiphonar · Schmuckseite mit Initiale E(cce) · Schwerin, 15. Jh. (Text S. 211)*
90 Antiphonary · Illuminated page with initial 'E(cce)' · Schwerin,
fifteenth century (see p. 208)

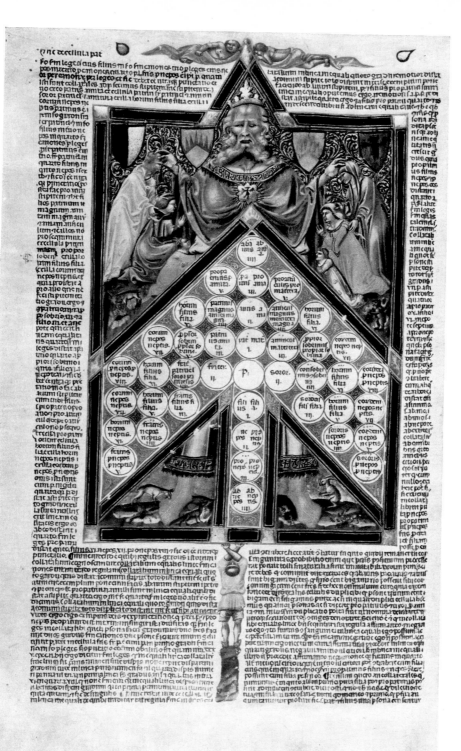

91 *Sechs Bücher Dekretalien · Stammbaum*
Italienisch, Ende des 14. Jh. (Text S. 221)
91 Book of Decretals · Tree of consanguinity
Italian, late fourteenth century (see p. 218)

92 *Antiphonar · Schmuckseite mit Initiale A(d)*
Deutsch, um 1450 (Text S. 208)
92 Antiphonary · Illuminated page with initial 'A(d)'
German, *c.* 1450 (see p. 205)

93 *Brevier · Das Pfingstwunder · Magdeburg, 2. Hälfte des 15. Jh. (Text S. 211)*
93 Breviary · The Miracle of Pentecost · Magdeburg, late fifteenth century (see p. 208)

94 *Prager Missale · Initiale A(d) mit segnendem Heiland · Böhmisch, um 1415 (Text S. 219)*
94 Prague Missal · Initial 'A(d)' with Christ blessing · Bohemia, *c.*1415 (see p.216)

95 *Sächsisches Weichbild · Schmuckseite mit Initialen G(ot) und V(on)*
Diözese Regensburg, 1453 (Text S. 218)
95 Sächsisches Weichbild · Illuminated page with initials
'G(ot)' and 'V(on)' · Diocese of Regensburg, 1453 (see p. 215)

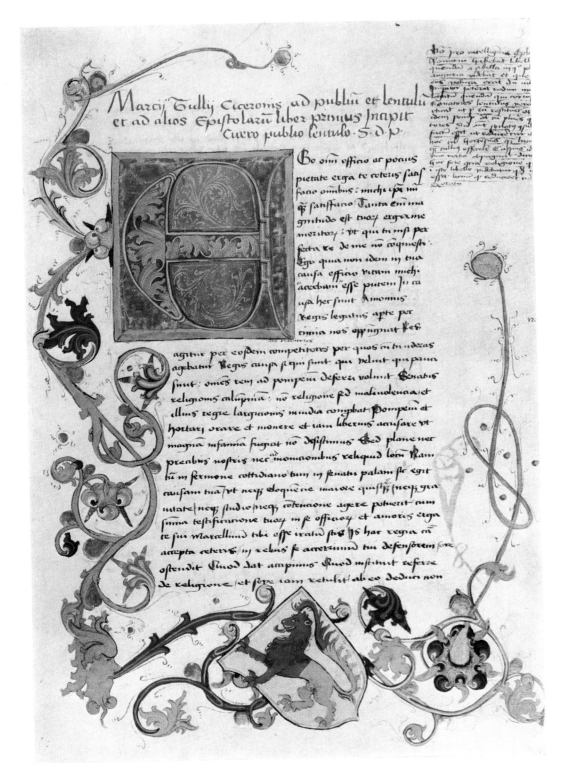

96 Cicero: Briefe · Initiale E(go) mit Randleiste
Italienisch?, 2. Hälfte des 15. Jh. (Text S. 222)
96 Cicero: Letters · Initial 'E(go)' with decorated border
Italian? late fifteenth century (see p. 219)

97 *Vouquelin: Geschichte des Königs Alexander · Geburt Alexanders*
Französisch, 2. *Hälfte des 15. Jh. (Text S. 202)*
97 Vouquelin: Histoire du roy Alixandre · Birth of Alexander
French, late fifteenth century (see p. 200)

Eth bin die tugent vond die nugent
vond vontugent hiffent an
myn gemüte stat in blüte
die wile ich mit prägen han
lachen fragen tantzen vond fpringen
dere ich fröwen vond man
fr ift waife der noch griffe
Bith mir wol gehalten kan

Sip fele wort werck vond auch den fin
Dut er daz fo wurt ime bas
wanne oba er mir valzet noch vngewin
war myn finl mit niden vuil
Dor matte ich vond tu ime fchaht
Ich wol mit lachen die lüte frölich machen
Vond doch gedancken in der finden rich
Ich bin von alter das von kalter

98 *Hugo von Trimberg: Der Renner · Titelbild · Elsässisch, 1419 (Text S. 209)*
98 Hugo von Trimberg: Der Renner · The Racer · Alsace, 1419 (see p. 206)

vm

Jin dem gezilt von ſamit
Die naht erdolte iamer zit
Alſo die Heren mit groſſer macht von
der burg einweg ritten

99 *Wolfram von Eschenbach: Parzival · Zug der Reiter aus der Burg*
Hagenau im Elsaß, Mitte des 15. Jh. (Text S. 209)
99 Wolfram von Eschenbach: Parzival · Knights leaving the castle
Haguenau, Alsace, mid-fifteenth century (see p. 206)

IVSTINI HISTORICI CLA
RISSIMI EPYTHOMATIS I
TROGVM POMPEIVM
VIRVM ELOQVENTISSI
MVM LIBER PRIMVS IN
CIPIT FELICITER

CVM MVLTI
ex Romanis etiam cō
sularis dignitatis uiri
res romanas grecco
peregrinoqᷠ sermo
ne in historiam con
tulissent: seu emula
tione glorię: siue
uarietate operis delectatus uir priscę elo
quentię Trogus pompeius grecas et totius
orbis historias latino sermone composuit:
ut cum nostra grece: greca quoqᷠ nostra lin
gua legi possent. prorsus rem magnam &
animi et corporis aggressus · Nam cum ple
risqᷠ auctoribus singulorum regum uel po
pulorum res gestas scribentibus opus suum
ardui laboris uideatur· nonne nobis Trogus

100 *Justinus: Geschichte König Philipps · Schmuckseite mit schreibendem Autor*
Italienisch, 1494 (Text S. 223)
100 Justinus: Historicae Philippicae · First page showing the author at work
Italian, 1494 (see p. 219)

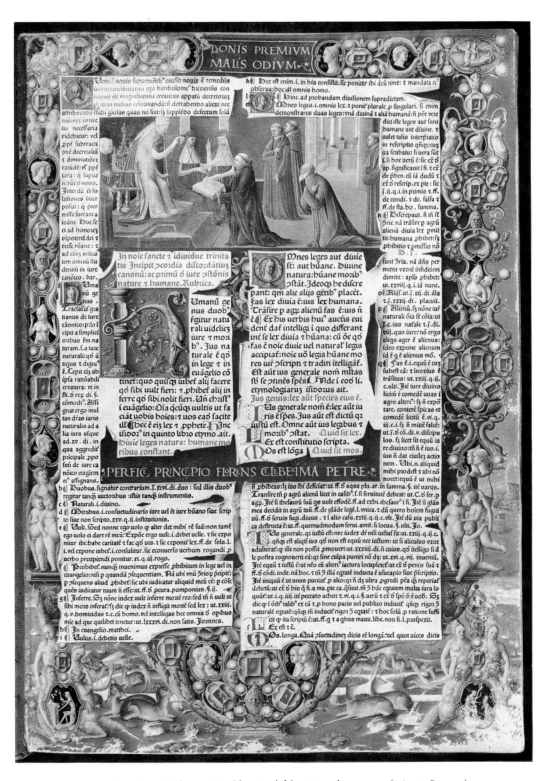

101 *Gratian: Dekret · Dedikationsbild · Venedig, 1477 (Text S. 223)*
101 Decretum Gratiani · Dedicatory picture · Venice, 1477 (see p. 219)

102 *Missale · Schmuckseite, Initiale V(enite) mit drei singenden Mönchen*
Zittau?, Mitte des 15. Jh. (Text S. 219)
102 Missal · Initial 'V(enite)' enclosing three singing monks
Zittau? mid-fifteenth century (see p. 216)

103 *Missale · Kanonbild: Kreuzigung · Schlesien?, Mitte des 15. Jh. (Text S. 216)*
103 Missal · Crucifixion · Silesia? mid-fifteenth century (see p. 213)

III

Mme kvonerbayde vnge
richte sal man vff halven
do:ff gebetv de Es sei denn
das do mait a der wnp vn
ne genotrogt sel a der geno
tiget do:yn gefurtt sei do sal
man obir richten a der ma
entredes denne mit rechte
Wirt abir do gericht vn

104 *Eike von Repkow: Sachsenspiegel · Initiale U(mme) mit Marsch von Landsknechten
zu einer Burg · Leipzig?, 1451 (Text S. 217)*
104 Eike von Repkow: Sachsenspiegel · Initial 'U(mme)'
with soldiers on the march · Leipzig? 1461 (see p. 214)

105 *Johannes von Saaz: Der Ackermann und der Tod · Die Todesernte*
Mitteldeutschland, um 1475 (Text S. 215)
105 Johannes von Saaz: Der Ackermann aus Böhmen · The harvest of Death
Central Germany, *c.* 1475 (see p. 212)

106 *Stundenbuch · Monatsbild Juli: Getreideernte*
Flämisch, 1470–1490 (Text S. 205)
106 Book of Hours · July, harvest scene · Master of the Dresden Prayerbook
Bruges, 1470–90 (see p. 203)

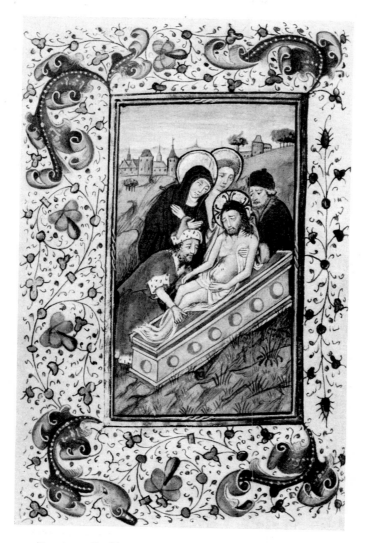

107 *Brevier · Grablegung · Lüttich, 1470–1480 (Text S. 205)*
107 Breviary · Entombment · Liège, 1470–80 (see p. 202)

Delordonnance de Cy
rus en chemyn. Et
comment il entioye

chcuaucheurs. Le ra
port dicculr. enſem
ble daucuns prisõmers

pres que Cy
rus eut ſacri
fie loſt deſlo
gia et tira
auant vng pou deſpace

puis ſavieſta ſur ſes
champs affin de don
ner loiſir aux tens dar
mes de valer querir ce
quilz y auoyent oublie

108 *Xenophon: Erziehung des Kyros · Befehl zum Aufbruch des Heeres*
Flämisch von Loyset Liedet, um 1470 (Text S. 205)
108 Xenophon: Cyropaedia · Army on the move
Loyset Liedet, Flemish, *c.* 1470 (see p. 203)

109 *Valerius Maximus: Denkwürdige Taten und Aussprüche · Tod der Lucretia*
Brügger Meister, vor 1480 (Text S. 205)
109 Valerius Maximus: Factorum et dictorum memorabilium libri novem
Death of Lucretia · Master of the Dresden Prayerbook, Bruges, before 1480 (see p. 203)

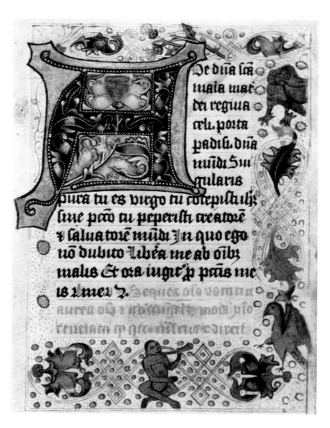

110 *Gebetbuch · Schmuckseite mit Initiale A(ve)*
Deutsch, 1471 (Text S. 208)
110 Prayerbook · Page with initial 'A(ve)'
German, 1471 (see p. 205)

HIC LIBER TERCIVS
INCIPIT. ALBERTI.
MAGNI DE MINE
R. A. L. I. B. V. S.

EMPVS AVTEM
NVNC EST CON
SEQVENTER
De metallorum naturis igre
post lapidum inuestigatum nam. Quia metallorum
genaʒ frequenter in ipis lapidibus tanq̃ lapidis
sbã sit quasi locus ꝓprius metallice egn̄onis ⸿In hoc
libro sicut et in pcedentibus Aristoᷓ tractatum nõ
undi insi per excerpta quem tamen diligent q̃sui
p diuersas mundi regiones ⸿Dicã q̃ rationabiliᷓ
aut ea quẽ a phis sunt tradita aut ea que expertũ
Exul n aliqñ factus fui uadens longe ad loca me
tallica ut expiri possem nãs metallorum ⸿Hac eñ
de cã quesiui i alkimicis transmutacoẽs metalloꝰ
ut ex hys inoteseẽt aliquatenus eorum natã et
acũa totʒ ꝓpa ⸿Est aut optimũ genus huiᷓ id sicoĩs
et certissimũ quia tunc p cãm Vniusturqʒ rei ꝓpriã
res cognoseitur & de actibus eius mie dubitatur
Nec ẽ difficile cognosce, sicut nec de lapidibi scõa
difficult inuestigat quia cãe eorum sunt maifeste
& corpora eorum non sunt diuersa sʒ omogenea

111 *Albertus Magnus: Vier Bücher über Metalle · Stahlgewinnung*
Elsaß, 1484 (Text S. 210)
111 Albertus Magnus: Quattuor libri Methavrorum · Manufacture of steel
Alsace, 1484 (see p. 207)

112 *Stundenbuch · Flucht nach Ägypten*
Nordfranzösisch, 2. Hälfte des 15. Jh. (Text S. 201)
112 Book of Hours · Flight into Egypt
Northern France, late fifteenth century (see p. 199)

113 *Stundenbuch · Der Tod und die Sterbende*
Französisch, 3. Viertel des 15. Jh. (Text S. 202)
113 Book of Hours · Death of a rich woman; initial 'D(ilexi)'
French, *c.* 1450–75 (see p. 200)

114 *Boethius: Vom Trost der Philosophie · Widmungsbild*
Flämisch, 1476 (Text S. 206)
114 Boethius: Consolation of Philosophy · Dedicatory picture
Flemish, 1476 (see p. 204)

In the illustration, partial text visible:

le prologue de ce pre
sent livre

u connoi
tre le secret
parlement
de l'homme

contemplatif a son a
me et de l'ame a l'hom
me. sur la poureté et
mendicité espirituelle
Pour apprendre a re
courir a dieu et a ses

115 *Gerson: Von der geistigen Armut · Gespräch der Seele mit dem Menschen*
Flämisch, um 1480 (Text S. 206)

115 Gerson: De mendicitate spirituali · Conversation of the soul with mankind
Flemish, *c.* 1480 (see p. 204)

116 *Brevier · Pietà · Herzogtum Bar, 2. Hälfte des 15. Jh. (Text S. 209)*
116 Breviary · Pietà · Duchy of Bar, late fifteenth century (see p. 207)

117 *Gebetbuch · Margarete von Rodemachern mit Schutzengel*
Westdeutsch, letztes Viertel des 15. Jh. (Text S. 210)
117 Prayerbook · The Lady of Rodemachern with her guardian angel
Western Germany, *c.* 1475–1500 (see p. 207)

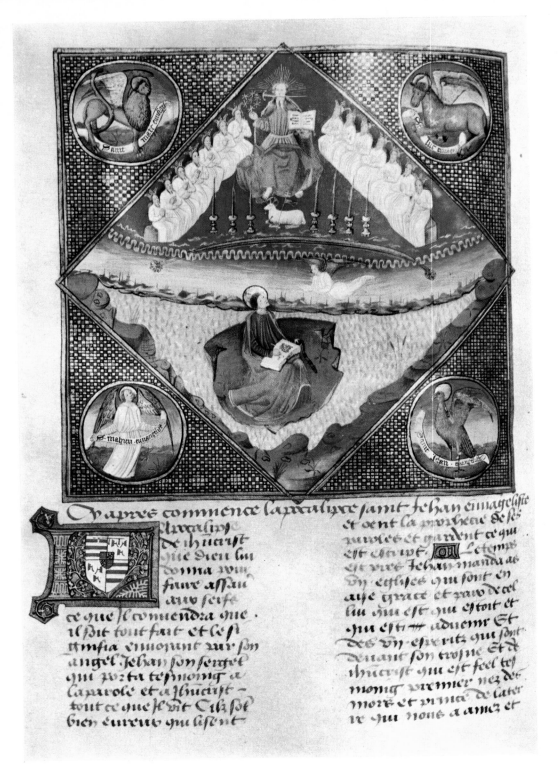

119 *Rufus: Von den Heldentaten Alexanders des Großen · Die Frauen des*
Darius vor Alexander · Flämisch, um 1480 (Text S. 207)
119 Curtius Rufus: Alexander the Great · The wives of Darius before Alexander
Flemish, c. 1480 (see p. 204)

120 *Leben des hl. Antonius · Die Heiligen Antonius und Athanasius*
Französisch, Ende des 15. Jh. (Text S. 203)
120 St Athanasius: Life of St Antony · St Antony and St Athanasius;
Initial 'C(i comence)' · French, late fifteenth century (see p. 201)

121 *Brevier · Schmuckseite mit Initiale B(eatus vir)*
Spanisch, Ende des 15. Jh. (Text S. 220)
121 Breviary · Illuminated page with initial 'B(eatus vir)'
Spanish, late fifteenth century (see p. 216)

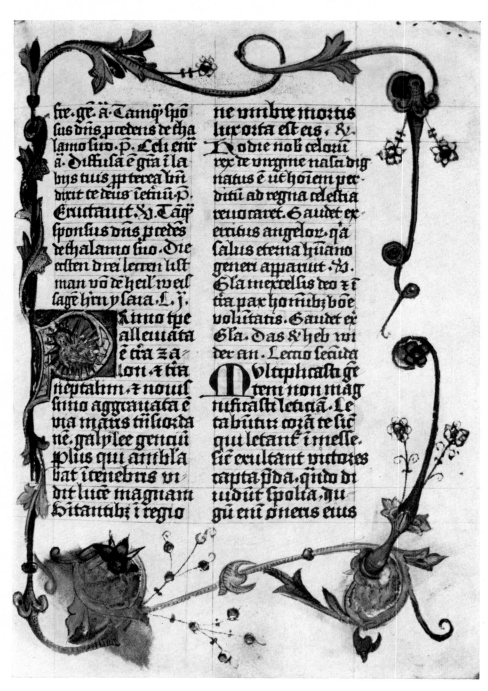

122 *Brevier · Schmuckseite mit Initiale P(rimo)*
Bayrisch, 15. Jh. (Text S. 218)

122 Breviary · Illuminated page with initial 'P(rimo)' enclosing Christ Child
Bavaria, fifteenth century (see p. 215)

123 *Brevier · Schmuckseite mit Initiale H(eir in dyn) und König David*
Niederländisch, 15. Jh. (Text S. 204)

123 Breviary · Page with initial 'H(eir in dyn)' and King David
Low Countries, fifteenth century (see p. 202)

Cy est la forme et maniere comment les Juges diseurs doibuent faire leur entree en la ville au jour que les seigneurs et aultres tournoieurs la font. Beaultmoins que les Juges diseurs doibuent mettre paine dentrer les premiers sil se peult faire

Premierement lesdictz Juges diseurs doibuent

124 *Regnier d'Anjou: Turnierbuch · Einzug der Kampfrichter in die Stadt*
Französisch, nach 1467 (Text S. 203)
124 Regnier d'Anjou: Sur les tournois · Judges entering the city
French, after 1467 (see p. 201)

125 *Geschichte von Ysage dem Traurigen · Empfang zweier Ritter*
Mittelfrankreich, Ende des 15.Jh. (Text S.203)

125 Histoire d'Ysaie le Triste · Reception of two knights
Central France, late fifteenth century (see p. 201)

Hir sendet Jacob esaw tzeghen vnde bocke myt dren knechten

Hir sendet Jacob esaw kamele myt vier knechten

Is es dynes knechtus Jacobus dynes
bruders vnde hat sie dir gesant als
syme hern her komet vns nach vnd
das besiel her on allen als tzagen
sy ym vor vnde her sleip nach die
nacht da myt syne wyben sonen
vnde meyden des morgens frue vor
tage brachte her sie ober den fort
vddrin yabec vnde her sleip gensi
ten von on vnde beitte Indeme ge
bethe qwam tzu ym eyn engil vnd
rynguste myt strencklich biß anden
morgen Als im der engil sach das
her on nicht konde obir wynden
Da rurte der engil Jacob die ruck
adde das sie dorre wart Sa myt
wart Jacob hynckene Da spricht
der engel laß mych gehen eß ist

Hir ringet Jacob myt eyne engele
das her on sal benedyen

126 *Altes Testament · Jakob sendet Geschenke an Esau, er ringt mit dem Engel*
Thüringisch, Ende des 15. Jh. (Text S. 216)
126 Old Testament · Jacob sends beasts to Esau und wrestles with the angel
Thuringia, late fifteenth century (see p. 213)

127 *Missale · Verkündigung Mariä · Italienisch, vor 1494 (Text S. 224)*
127 Missal · Annunciation · Italian, before 1494 (see p. 220)

128 *Missale · Kanonbild: Kreuzigung · Sächsisch, 2. Hälfte des 15. Jh. (Text S. 211)*
128 Missal · Crucifixion · Saxony, late fifteenth century (see p. 208)

129 *Baldus: Werke · Schmuckseite mit Initiale Q(uoniam)*
Italien, Ende des 15. Jh. (Text S. 223)
129 Baldus: Works · Illuminated page with initial 'Q(uoniam)'
Italy, late fifteenth century (see p. 220)

130 *Antiphonar · Initiale A(ngelus) mit Auferstehung*
Altzella, Anfang des 16.Jh. (Text S. 231)

130 Antiphonary · Initial 'A(ngelus)' with Resurrection
Altzella, early sixteenth century (see p. 226)

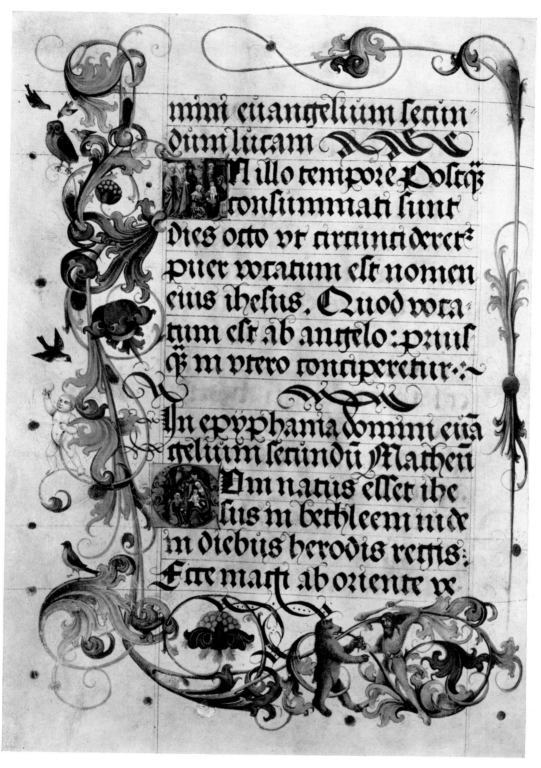

131 *Evangelistar · Schmuckseite von Jakob Elsner · Nürnberg, 1507 (Text S. 227)*

131 Evangelistary · Illuminated page · Jakob Elsner · Nuremberg, 1507 (see p. 223)

132 *Missale · Schmuckseite mit Geburt Christi und Verkündigung*
Niederländisch, Anfang des 16. Jh. (Text S. 225)
132 Missal · Illuminated page with Nativity and Annunciation to the Shepherds
Low Countries, early sixteenth century (see p. 221)

Le premier chapitre du
tiers liure contient le debat de
pourete. Commencant oula fi
premierement.
Consacucur. Et cetera.

Elcuns et au
tres voiagenrs
qui font au
cun long et
labourieux
chemin ont de coustume sor
arrester et aucunesfois torcher
la sucur de leurs visaiges et a

lautrefois mettre Jus leurs
fardeaux pour aleger le corps
et autrefois prendre le vent
fres et souef et boire ou vin
ou eaue pour oster la soif et
si ont de coustume de boire et
abuter combien ils ont fait
apres ce quilz ont tourne le
dos a aucun notable lieu dôt
Ils se sont partiz Ils recordent
entre eulx le nombre et les nôs
des chasteaulx des ruieres des
valles des montaignes et des

133 *Boccaccio: Von edlen Frauen und Männern · Landschaft mit ruhenden Pilgern*
    Französisch, um 1520 (Text S. 224)
133 Boccaccio: The Fall of Princes · Pilgrims resting by the wayside
    French, c. 1520 (see p. 221)

134 *Marschalk: Reimchronik · Das Mirakel vom heiligen Blut in Doberan Mecklenburg, vor 1513 (Text S. 229)*

134 Marschalk: Mecklenburg Chronicle · The Miracle of the Holy Blood at Doberan Mecklenburg, before 1513 (see p. 225)

135 *Antiphonale · Initiale D(um) mit dem hl. Andreas*
Altzella, 1516 (Text S. 231)
135 Antiphonal · Initial 'D(um)' with St Andrew
Altzella, 1516 (see p. 227)

136 *Antiphonar · Initiale E(cce) mit Johannes auf Patmos*
Kursachsen, 1500–1504 (Text S. 231)

136 Antiphonary · Initial 'E(cce)' with St John on Patmos
Saxony, 1500–4 (see p. 226)

137 *Missale · Kanonbild: Kreuzigung · Kirchenprovinz Bremen, 1503 (Text S. 229)*
137 Missal · Crucifixion · Province of Bremen, 1503 (see p. 224)

Wie dieser Römisch kunig seinen sun kaiser Otto den Grossen in seinem letzten willen zu einem Römisch kunig geordnet hatt.

Als nun der Römisch kunig merckt sein kranckhayt also uberhandt nemen das er seins lebens nit lenger ymd mer verhofft. fordert er alle fürsten so er die zeit bey yn Im seinem Hoer het. für yn. Vnd machet in yr gegenwortichkeyt seyn eldisten sun. Otto. zu einem Römischen kunig. Vnd vnter die andern zwen sun. Hertzog. Haınrich. vnd hertzog. Braun. taylt er die güter. Schetze. vnd Parschafft.

138 *Spalatin: Sächsische Chronik: Krönung Ottos I.*
Deutsch, 1513 (Text S. 226)

138 Spalatin: Saxon chronicle · Coronation of Otto I
German, 1513 (see p. 222)

139 *Stammbuch der Herzöge von Mecklenburg · Herzog Albrecht VII. und Gemahlin*
Mecklenburg, 1526 (Text S. 230)
139 Genealogy of the dukes of Mecklenburg · Albert the Handsome and his wife
Mecklenburg, 1526 (see p. 226)

140 *Missale · Initiale R(equiem) mit Tod auf der Bahre · Altzella, 1529 (Text S. 231)*
140 Missal · Initial 'R(equiem)' with Death on a bier · Altzella, 1529 (see p. 227)

141 *Erbbuch · Herebord von der Margariten und Gemahlin · Erfurt, 1525 (Text S. 233)*
141 Family register · Herebord von der Margariten and his wife
Erfurt, 1525 (see p. 228)

142 *Wappenbuch der Burggrafen von Nürnberg · Godefridus, Graf zu Lambogen*
Nürnberg, nach 1527 (Text S. 228)
142 Armorial of the burgraves of Nuremberg · Count Godefridus zu Lambogen
Nuremberg, after 1527 (see p. 224)

143 *Ingenieurkunst- und Wunderbuch · Zauberkünste*
Nürnberger Gegend, um 1520 (Text S. 228)
143 Ingenieurkunst- und Wunderbuch · Conjuring tricks
Nuremberg region, *c.* 1520 (see p. 224)

144 *Epistolar · Beweinung nach Dürer von Jakob Elsner · Nürnberg, 1507 (Text S. 227)*
144 Epistolary · Deposition and Entombment · Jakob Elsner after Dürer
Nuremberg, 1507 (see p. 223)

145 *Dürer: Marienleben · Anbetung der Hirten · Nürnberg, 1511 (Text S. 228)*
145 Dürer: Life of the Virgin · Adoration of the Shepherds
Nuremberg, 1511 (see p. 224)

146 *Missale · Initiale A(d te levavi) mit König David*
Altzella, 1522/23 (Text S. 231)
146 Missal · Initial 'A(d te levavi)' with King David
Altzella, 1522–3 (see p. 227)

147 *Chorbuch · Kurfürst Friedrich der Weise von Sachsen*
Niederländisch, um 1520 (Text S. 225)
147 Choirbook · Elector Frederick the Wise of Saxony; initial 'B(assus)'
Low Countries, c. 1520 (see p. 221)

Wie herodes sanct Johanns Baptisten in den kerker leit und ime
dett sin houpt abe slahen als die Jungfröwe herodiadis in vmb das
houpt batt als sii in dem sale vor dem künige tantzte die Jungfröwe gab
das houpt ir müter vff einem teller   xiiij

148 *Neues Testament · Salome mit dem Haupte Johannis des Täufers*
Westthüringen, Anfang des 16. Jh. (Text S. 232)
148 New Testament · Salome with the head of John the Baptist
West Thuringia, early sixteenth century (see p. 227)

149 *Brevier · Kreuztragung und Schweißtuch der Veronika*
Niedersächsisch, Anfang des 16.Jh. (Text S. 230)
149 Breviary · Christ and St Veronica
Lower Saxony, early sixteenth century (see p. 226)

150 *Matrikel der Universität Wittenberg · Wappen des Rektors Schilling*
Wittenberg, 1532 (Text S. 233)
150 Matricula of the university of Wittenberg · Arms of Rector Schilling
Wittenberg, 1532 (see p. 228)

151 *Pfinzing: Theuerdank · Theuerdank in Seenot · Deutsch, um 1520 (Text S. 227)*
151 Pfinzing: Theuerdank · Theuerdank's shipwreck · German, *c.* 1520 (see p. 223)

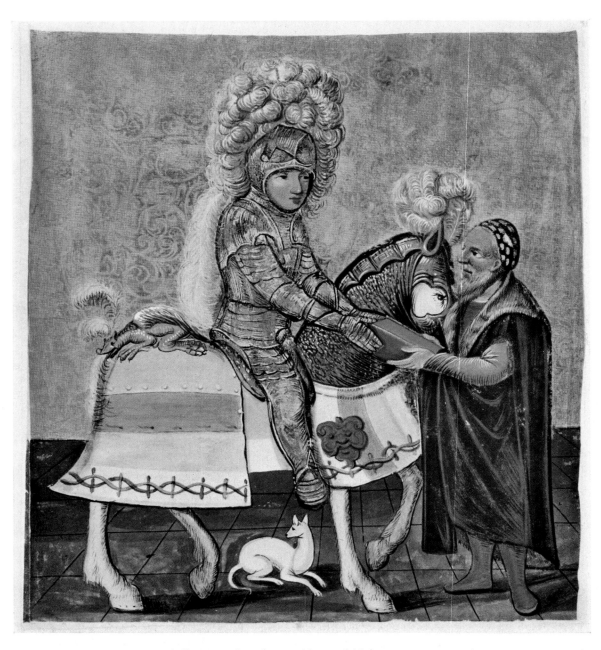

152 *Marschalk: Reimchronik · Dedikationsbild für Herzog Heinrich V.*
Mecklenburg, 1573 (Text S. 230)

152 Marschalk: Mecklenburg Chronicle · Author presenting the work to Duke Henry V
Mecklenburg, 1573 (see p. 225)

·LE·TRIVMPHE·DE·LA·MORT·

MORS·VINCIT·CASTITATEM·

arc Cupido par ma faulx romps & brise
Vice & vertu tant lung que lautre prise

153 *Petrarca: Dichtungen · Der Triumph des Todes*
Französisch, Mitte des 16. Jh. (Text S. 225)
153 Miniatures illustrating Petrarch · Death conquers chastity
French, mid-sixteenth century (see p. 221)

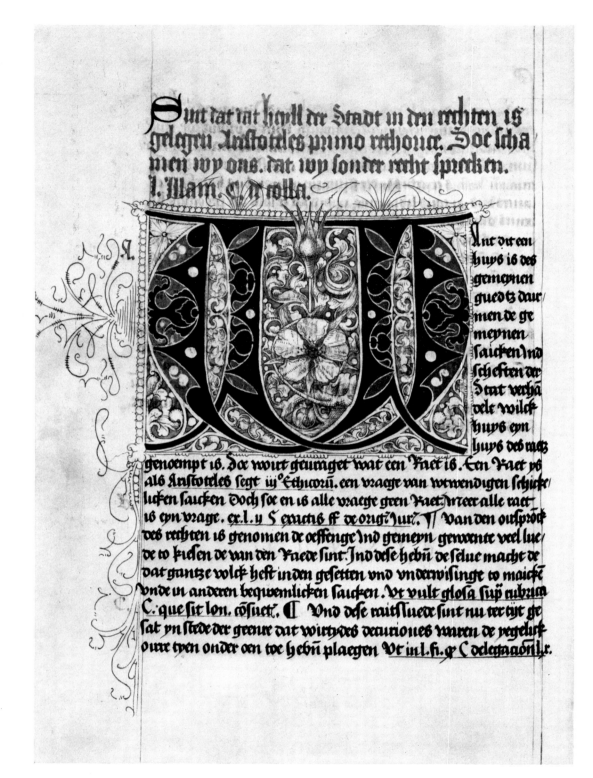

154 *Stadtrecht von Wesel · Schmuckseite mit Initiale W(ant) · Wesel, um 1530 (Text S. 229)*
154 Statutes of Wesel · Illuminated page with initial 'W(ant)' · Wesel, c. 1530 (see p. 224)

155 *Gebetbuch · Verkündigung und Anbetung der Hirten*
Deutsch, 1556 (Text S. 226)
155 Prayerbook · Adoration of the Shepherds
German, 1556 (see p. 222)

156 *Matrikel der Universität Erfurt · Der hl. Hieronymus*
Hans Brosamer, 1549 (Text S. 233)
156 Matricula of the university of Erfurt · St Jerome · Hans Brosamer
Erfurt, 1549 (see p. 228)

157 *Kurfürst Johann Friedrich Bibel · Protestantisches Dogmenbild*
Lukas Cranach d.J., 1543 (Text S. 232)
157 Bible of Elector John Frederick of Saxony · Illustration of Protestant dogma
Lucas Cranach the younger · Wittenberg, 1543 (see p.228)

158 *Kriegsbuch · Bemanntes Segelschiff · Deutsch, 1572 (Text S. 227)*
158 Kriegsbuch · Warship in full sail · German, 1572 (see p. 223)

159 Bretschneider: Einfälle für Schlittenfahrten · Der hl. Georg mit Drachen
Dresden, 2. Hälfte des 16. Jh. (Text S. 233)
159 Bretschneider: Inventionen zu Schlittenfahrten · St George and the dragon
Dresden, late sixteenth century (see p. 229)

160 *Venezianisches Geschichtsbuch · Der hl. Markus · Venedig, 1557 (Text S. 224)*
160 Venetian codex · St Mark · Venice, 1557 (see p. 220)

HISTORICAL COMMENTARY

THE EARLY
CHRISTIAN PERIOD
400–600

The oldest surviving examples of Christian illumination are the Quedlinburg Itala fragments, which are now in the Deutsche Staatsbibliothek in Berlin. The manuscript was probably written for a high-ranking prelate. The Itala was a very early Latin translation of the Bible, probably of the second century, which was in use among Christians until St Jerome's Vulgate superseded it early in the fifth century. Very little remains of the Quedlinburg Itala: four leaves of text with illustrations and two further leaves of unadorned text. A careful selection was made of passages that lent themselves to illustration, and there are four pictures on each page. The text is written in Roman uncials, a script form of large (majuscule) letters used between the fourth and eighth centuries, especially for Christian literature. The pictures are in bodycolours and gold. The bad state of preservation is due to the fact that at the beginning of the seventeenth century these leaves were used by a Quedlinburg bookbinder for binding documents.

The surviving illustrations relate to the two books of Samuel and the first book of Kings. The recto of the second leaf illustrates the fifteenth chapter of the first book of Samuel *(pl. 1)*. Top left we see King Saul, the central figure, dressed like a Roman nobleman, pouring a libation of wine on the flames. Two servants stand behind him. He is turned to face the two-horse chariot in which Samuel has come to bring him God's commands. The Roman costumes, the altar in the form of a Greek stele, and the chariot show early Christian art to have been influenced by pagan, profane art. Saul's attempt to stop Samuel leaving him by clutching at his cloak (top right), for example, is a

classical motif. The captive Agag, king of the Amalekites, is brought before Samuel (bottom left) and begs for mercy. Saul and Samuel are praying in the typical attitudes of the *orantes* who are often found on catacomb murals. In the last picture Samuel is killing Agag. The background is indicated by zones of colour: the ground is yellow, the sky is red and blue, and there are buildings in outline.

The writing on the pictures is of two kinds: the words in cursive are painting instructions and the semi-uncials are captions. We have the Quedlinburg bookbinder to thank for enabling us to read the painting instructions, which would have been painted over; he had to soak the leaves and coat them with size for his purpose. They give us some idea of how a major manuscript of this kind was made; it has been calculated that originally it consisted of eleven volumes, each of 220 leaves. First the scribe wrote the text. After consultation with the miniator he wrote the painting instructions in the spaces where the pictures were to go. When the illustrations were ready, the explanatory captions were written over them, as in these examples. This manuscript must have been prepared in one of the Italian centres of Christian manuscript art, after the year 400.

THE PRE-CAROLINGIAN
PERIOD
600–780

The Continent of Europe

The manuscript illustrated in *pl. 2*, made somewhere in the north-eastern part of the Frankish empire in about 725, is a very good example of the period. The initial letter and the first few words stand out in coloured uncials, while the rest of the text is written in semi-uncials. The upright stroke of the initial is decorated with a heart-shaped ornament and terminates in a fishtail, while the curved stroke encloses a stylized fish, decorated with a figure of eight. The fish was a very early symbol for Christ, and was a typical pre-Carolingian motif. While early Christian illumination had preferred subdued shades, the tendency now was to bright, strong colours. The green and yellow heart-shaped ornaments have red centres, and the same colour scheme is used for the whole of the top line. The balance between the heading, the ornate first line and the rest of the text lends the page as a whole a unified appearance.

Representational figures are very rare in this calligraphic decoration. One exception is the primitive figure of Christ in the margin of a fragment which contains the books of Isaiah and Jeremiah *(pl.3)*. The scribe's intention was to underline the Messianic prophecy of the text. This manuscript may tentatively be dated at the end of the eighth century and was made in the vicinity of Chur, in the Grisons canton of Switzerland. The text is written in small letters, the pre-Carolingian minuscule, and the figure in the margin stands in no decorative relation to the text. In spite of its lack of realism, it is not without expression. The right hand raised like an orator's, the left hand holding a book, the suggestion of movement in the way the trunk and head are seen full on, while the legs are turned sideways, the thoughtful expression still visible on the face in spite of the poor state of preservation, all add up to an effective whole. The effect is strengthened by the colouring: green, vermilion and yellow.

During the same period Irish monks developed a totally independent style of illumination, which was vastly superior to the Continental style in richness and imagination. The scriptoria were in the monasteries founded by Aidan and his successors in Northumberland; manuscripts written in Ireland itself are of a later date. This style combined Celtic, Germanic and late classical elements. The so-called Salaberga Psalter is a very fine example *(pl.4)*. It is named, erroneously, after Salaberga (d.665), the first abbess of the convent of St Jean in Laon, where the manuscript was kept for some years during the twelfth century. In psalters the first psalm, *Beatus vir* ('Blessed is the man'), is customarily written very elaborately, with no failing in invention over the centuries. The initial 'B' of this psalter has the single curved stroke usual at this early date. The letter is decorated with bands of two alternate ornaments ending with two herons which support the top. The elongated bird's head enclosed in the letter is a characteristic device of Irish illumination. The whole letter is outlined by fine red dots. The following 'e' is fused with the 'a' in an original way, and the words that follow stand out in coloured majuscules. The initial 'Q(uare)' of the second psalm is also in the form customary at the time. The Irish scriptoria not only had their own kind of ornamentation, but also their own kinds of script. The imaginative decoration, the composition of the page, the range of colours all make a sumptuous impression.

Another Anglo-Irish manuscript, now in Gotha, is less rich but shows the same stylistic traits *(pl.6)*. The use of dots, both inside letters and round their outlines, is typical. The 'Q' has the same form on both manuscripts *(pls. 4, 6)*. But the 'Q' of *Quoniam* as the first word of the whole text is more elaborate than that of *Quare*. The second letter, 'u', is also decorated with a criss-cross pattern inside it and has the same colouring. The Irish monks were inexhaustible in their invention of new forms of braiding patterns and fantastic zoomorphic devices. Since the initial comes at the beginning of St Luke's Gospel, the evangelist is symbolized by the figure of a calf, in accordance with Revelation 4:7. The tip and foot of the upright stroke are different. The black, orange and purple which recur in the smaller initials give the whole page a festive appearance.

THE CAROLINGIAN PERIOD
780–900

Italy

Northern Italy was incorporated in the Frankish empire by Charlemagne in 774. Verona became an important centre of illumination in the time of Bishop Egino (d. 802), whose name was given to a codex, now in Berlin, which was made for the library of Verona cathedral. The style is closely related to that of Aix-la-Chapelle, where the artist must have received his training. There are four whole-page miniatures which depict two Fathers of the Church, one of them St Ambrose *(pl.5)*, and two popes. St Ambrose, an important ecclesiastical statesman, who compelled the Emperor Theodosius to do public penance, was born in 340 and was bishop of Milan for twenty-four years until his death in 397. He is shown writing in the same conventional attitude as the evangelists in early manuscripts. His assistant sits behind him, lost in thought. The saint is inspired by the youthful Christ whose head appears above him in the rounding of the arch. This miniature represents a deliberate reaction against the purely abstract ornamentation of the pre-Carolingian period, and a return to the classical and early Christian practice of depicting human figures.

The Anglo-Frankish School

Things developed differently in the north-western territories of the empire. The influence of British and Irish missionaries was so strong that the term Anglo-Frankish has been coined for the style. Pure ornament continued to be used; ornate initial letters and opening lines of the text were still part of the decorative scheme. A page from a gospel book, now at Merseburg, has all the characteristics of Anglo-Saxon illumination *(pl.7)*. The initial 'L(ucas)' is framed by dots, and the decoration of the letter itself is simple; the principal components are a figure of eight and a fan-shaped motif, and there is no sign of the complex, entwined ribbons of Carolingian miniators. If the script did not show the manuscript to date from the first half of the ninth century, the initial could be pre-Carolingian. The colouring, in strong black, blue, red and yellow, is also typically British.

A gospel book, now in Halberstadt, is far more splendidly decorated. The opening page of St Mark's Gospel *(pl.8)* is beautifully composed. The initial 'I(nitium)' fills the left-hand side of the page; the rows of dots, the involved braiding, the animals' heads, are new variations on older Anglo-Irish models. The text to the right of the initial is written in two different scripts. The very first words are in capitals, and the rest in uncials, but in the same colours as the capitals and the initial. This page is the work of an artist of great ability.

The School of Tours

One of the most important centres of Carolingian illumination is Tours, particularly the monastery of Marmoutier, founded by St Martin in 375. A life of the saint by Severus Sulpitius is in a manuscript now at Halle. The copyist also gives his own name: he was Adalbaldus, a presbyter, who completed the manuscript before 834 on the orders of the abbot Fredegisus. The first page of the text is richly illuminated *(pl.12)*. Two of the first five lines are emphasized by being written in gold on a crimson ground, while the other three are written in red. The initial 'I(gitur)' fills only two-thirds of the height of the page, and is divided into two strips of gold and three of blue, with gold braiding. The arrangement of the two kinds of script and the initial shows great technical skill.

Minor Carolingian Schools

Canons were a usual feature of gospel books even in the Carolingian period. They were a tabular arrangement of references to passages from all four gospels which covered the same subject matter. They were first drawn up by Eusebius, bishop of Caesarea, around 330. He divided the gospels into sections, and numbered each gospel separately. Using these numbers he drew up ten tables of concordance, which he called canons. They were written in Greek, and first occur in Syrian manuscripts. Eusebius described his method in a dedicatory letter to his friend Carpianus. Although the canons have no liturgical significance, they were included in gospel books and even in St Jerome's Vulgate. The custom of framing the tables with pillars and arches goes back to Ptolemaic tables. The artists of the Middle Ages seized upon the

opportunities offered by this convention and gave full rein to their imagination. The example I have chosen comes from a gospel fragment of which one half is in Weimar *(pl.9)* and the other in the Munich Staatsbibliothek. It must have originated in the region of Mainz under influences from Sankt Gallen. The two large arches rest on three columns, each with the same ornamentation. The blue field between the outer arch and the two inner arches is filled with gold tendrils. Animals, or, as in this case, birds, appear in the spandrels. The lavish use of gold and silver creates a sumptuous effect. This is one of the finest examples in Germany.

A gospel book in the Sächsische Landes-bibliothek in Dresden appears to have been influenced by the so-called 'palace school', which was connected with the court of Charlemagne at Aix *(pl.11)*. Against a green background St Mark the Evangelist is shown bent over his work, wearing a close-fitting white robe, spotted with gold. Above him is his symbol, the lion, painted in red on a silver ground, and the scroll establishes the connection between the saint and the symbol. There are stylistic similarities to the gospel books of Aix cathedral and the Vienna Schatzkammer, the two most important examples of the palace school. Although this is an original work the miniator must have known them or others like them, from which we may deduce that the Dresden manuscript originated somewhere along the Rhine.

THE EARLY ROMANESQUE
900–1100

Reichenau

During the Ottonian period the most important centre of manuscript illumination was the Benedictine abbey on the island of Reichenau on Lake Constance, which had been founded in 724. The artistic quality of the manuscripts produced there was far above that of any others. An evangelistary of *c*. 970 will illustrate this *(pl. 20)*. A whole page devoted to the name of the Virgin has a frame of acanthus leaves in four colours. The initial 'M' fills the centre and obtrudes across the frame on either side. The actual letter is decorated with a braiding pattern, and the spaces it encloses are filled with gold and silver tendrils on a green back ground. The other letters are written in gold capi tals on purple, above and below the initial. In the very centre is the hand of God, extended as it were protectively over the Mother of his Son, and reaching symbolically from heaven towards earth, reminding men of the presence of the Godhead in the world. The composition and execution of this page make it one of the finest of surviving manuscripts.

Sankt Gallen

The Benedictine abbey at Sankt Gallen was set up in 614. In the tenth and eleventh centuries what is now Switzerland was part of the duchy of Swabia. Sankt Gallen had been a leader in art and learning in the ninth century. The monastery was sacked by Hungarian invaders in 926; the library was destroyed except for some treasures sent to the sister foundation on Reichenau for safe keeping. These include a grammar by Priscianus, a teacher of Latin in Constantinople in the reign of Ana stasius (491–518). This secular manuscript served an important ecclesiastical purpose, as all church services were, of course, held in Latin. The manu script, now at Halberstadt, was made around 900 and has some very fine initials *(pl. 10)*. In the example, entwined tendrils grow out of the upright

stroke of the 'T' in a symmetrical pattern. The letter itself is yellow and the tendrils are silver, edged with vermilion, the total impression being one of great richness.

The initial 'T(e igitur)' from a Merseburg sacra mentary is similar in style although this manuscript was written a hundred years later, at the beginning of the eleventh century *(pl. 19)*. The initial is executed in gold and silver with red edges, and the capital letters on the page are in the same colours. As in the previous example, the ends of the cross stroke and the foot of the upright are exactly alike. The ornament at either side is a feathery fan in stead of tendrils, and encloses an inscription in the hand of Thietmar, bishop of Merseburg (d. 1018): *Sacerdos dei, reminiscere thietmari, con fratris tui, peccatoris et indigni* ('Priest of God, re member Thietmar your brother, an unworthy sinner'). The manuscript must have belonged to this notable bishop, to whom we owe the impor tant chronicle of the Ottonian emperors.

Fulda

The Benedictine abbey at Fulda was already an important scriptorium in the Carolingian period. Founded by St Boniface in 744, it enjoyed a cer tain prestige from being directly under the author ity of the pope. It was an important centre of learning, putting into practice the precepts of Alcuin, Charlemagne's adviser, and a scriptorium was a natural adjunct of scholarship.

This tradition was still alive under the Ottonian emperors; one fine example of the later Fulda school is a gospel book from Enger, near Herford, known as the Codex Wittekindeus and traditionally sup posed to have been given by Charlemagne to his godson Wittekind, prince of the Saxons. The manuscript was found in the church where Witte-kind was buried, but the date of his conversion and baptism was 785, while the manuscript was in fact written in Fulda around 975. Among other illuminated leaves, the manuscript includes por-traits of the four evangelists. The best of these is that of St Matthew *(pl. 15)*. The figure of the saint and that of the angel, his symbol, form the central axis of the composition. An interior is suggested by the frame of pillars and of masonry at the top. The turbulent folds of the evangelist's garments are in contrast to the peaceful, thoughtful expression on his face. He is listening to the words of the angel, which can be read on the scroll. They are the opening words of the Gospel according to Mat-thew: *Liber generationis Jesu Christi* ('The book of the generation of Jesus Christ'). The enthroned evangelist is rather a majestic figure, the angel above him graceful and gentle. The symbols of the other evangelists, the lion, the bull and the eagle, are included in the upper frame. The effect of this miniature is completed by the subtle colouring. The pale violet and green masonry and acanthus frame are set off against a purple background. The same shades are used for the garments of Matthew and the angel. The hair and the beard are brown, the gold halo is edged with red. A pink chair and dark green pillars add the final touches to the unique colour scheme. The composition is based on a model from the Aix-la-Chapelle palace school.

The Anglo-Frankish School

The further development of the style which had evolved in the north-west of the Frankish empire during the Carolingian period can be seen in a gospel book which is now in Halle *(pl. 13)*. The chain of dots round the initials and the birds'

heads are typically Anglo-Irish. On this page at the beginning of St John's Gospel the initial 'I(n)' stands centrally, within an oblong frame with squared rosettes at the four corners. The frame is formed of gold edges on either side of a delicate ribbon pattern which is repeated in the body of the initial. The lavish use of gold and silver is one reason for the page's rich appearance; another is the clarity of composition. A comparison with the Cologne Gospels supports the supposition that this manuscript originated in the region of Cologne in the early part of the tenth century.

A fragment of a sacramentary in Leipzig also shows Anglo-Frankish characteristics. The re-presentation of the Crucifixion *(pl. 14)* is reduced to its essentials: the figures of Christ on the cross, Mary and John. These two seem to float in space and the cross does not stand on the ground but penetrates the frame at the top and bottom. Natu-ralism is completely neglected in favour of expres-siveness. The three figures are drawn but left un-coloured. The rough-hewn green cross stands against a purple background. It forms the com-positional axis, slightly left of centre. In mediaeval colour symbolism, purple represented the blood of Christ and therefore the Passion. A green cross expressing the hope of paradise and eternal life for believers occurs again in a French psalter of the first half of the eleventh century, which also shows the figures floating; evidently it was quite a com-mon convention. The way Mary wipes her tears with a corner of her cloak also occurs frequently in many different forms. Her slim figure is right against the frame of the picture and turned towards the cross. Her robe is wrapped closely round her with many folds. John is turned a little more to the front. His hands are extended towards Christ and he looks down with an expression of anguish. Both John and Mary have green haloes with red and white rims. Christ is already dead. His head is sunken, his hair hangs round his shoulders, his body slumps heavily. The feet are supported by a board and a green snake with a white head twists round the base of the cross. At the top is a plaque with the inscription *Hic Nazarenus rex Iudaeor(um)* ('This is the Nazarene, king of the Jews'). The picture is surrounded by a frame in three colours, vermilion, blue-grey and crimson, and its total effect is striking.

Saxony

The duchy of Saxony gained in political and cultural importance in the Ottonian period, the century following the accession of Henry I to the imperial crown in 919. Scriptoria in the northern part of the duchy followed Anglo-Frankish models, as can be seen in a Leipzig gospel book containing miniatures which bear a close stylistic resemblance to the sacramentary fragment illustrated in *pl.14*. The title-page of the Gospel according to St Matthew *(pl.16)* is rich in artistic invention. The words are written in gold capitals on a purple ground. The frame has braided ornaments in the corners and clover leaves in the middle of the long sides, with strips of braiding in different colours in between. In addition to the magnificent title pages, the manuscript has illuminated initials at the beginning of the text of each gospel.

A single surviving leaf from a Gospel book, portraying St Luke the Evangelist *(pl.17)*, was probably executed in the west of Saxony. The attitude and the head show the influence of the Carolingian palace school. The tiled background is very rare at this early date: other examples are in an Alemannic manuscript in the library of Innsbruck university (Cod. 484) and in a Cologne Crucifixion of *c.*

1200. The box of parchment rolls is an interesting reminder of the laborious task of building up a codex, writing one leaf at a time. The text written in golden letters across the back wall reads *Lucas per vitulum XPI fert pontificatum* ('Luke bears the apostolate through the calf of Christ'). The evangelist's symbol, the winged calf (or bull), is framed by a gabled roof. Its fore-hooves hold a parchment book with the text of the gospel. The room resembles a temple: the cross on the gable and the line of the writing desk form a central axis. The evangelist is wearing a long green tunic under a gold cloak. The feet and hands are unusually expressive. The head is reminiscent of classical art. The golden frame is embellished with a graceful ornament. The reverse side of the leaf is splendidly gilded with the words *Incipit evangelium secundum Lucam* ('Here beginneth the gospel according to Luke').

What is now Westphalia was also part of Saxony in the eleventh century. A sacramentary made in Minden during the episcopate of Bishop Sigebert (1022–36) shows the high standard reached by this school. There must have been close and lively contacts between various schools. This manuscript is related to the Reichenau school and is no less impressive than its models. One of the miniatures shows the women at the tomb of Jesus *(pl.21)*. The central axis is formed by the building with the empty coffin. To the right of it sits the angel on the tilted stone. His wings rise up sharply as they do in Reichenau miniatures. He is speaking to the four frightened women who stand on the other side with boxes of balm and incense in their hands. The foreground contrasts with this calm group. The guards are asleep on an extremely rough piece of ground. Their limbs and clothes are as lumpy as the clods of soil. They cannot hear the angel's message; they belong to a different world.

The contrast is extraordinarily effective and indicates a great artist who understood how to imbue external events with a spiritual significance.

Hainault

The county of Hainault, now a province of Belgium, lay in the furthest western corner of the Holy Roman Empire. It was there in the second half of the eleventh century that a psalter was made, in Soignies, with pages of illuminated text as well as miniatures. As in the Salaberga psalter, the opening words *Beatus vir* receive particular attention *(pl. 24)*. The initial 'B' is surrounded by a rectangular frame which has circular devices in the corners and rosettes in the middle of the sides. The letter is outlined and uncoloured on a crimson background, but its internal spaces are filled with spirals and foliate tendrils. The other letters are arranged to the right of the 'B' in red capitals. The page is marked by the contrast between the rectangular frame and the involved curves of the inner decoration.

Bavaria

A gospel book now in the Landesbibliothek in Dessau appears to have originated in the diocese of Freising, between Landshut and Munich. At all events the first page of St Matthew's Gospel *(pl. 18)* exactly resembles a Munich gospel book (Cod. lat. 6204) which is known to have come from Freising cathedral library. The Dessau copy is unfinished, the illumination being drawn but not painted; the design is the same, with the 'I' beside the initial and the angel, the evangelist's symbol, in the middle of the spiral. Before the Reformation the Dessau manuscript was in the library of the

Benedictine abbey at Nienburg on the river Saale. Perhaps there was a Bavarian miniator, or Bavarian manuscripts, in the Nienburg scriptorium. The resemblance to the Munich gospel book is so great that its Bavarian origin is beyond dispute. The initial 'L' occupies three-quarters of the page. The body of the letter is very slim and it encloses a complex ornament. The division into three spirals, branching out of each other, and the central emphasis given by the head of the angel, argue a considerable talent. The last of the three lower letters and the frame are given only in outline.

THE LATER ROMANESQUE
1100–1250

Bavaria

An important characteristic of manuscript illumination in the later Romanesque period is the widening range of subject matter. The monks began to copy secular texts, such as universal chronicles, which told the history of the world in a continuous narrative, based on the historical parts of the Bible. The earliest versions are to be found in manuscripts of the twelfth century. When Frederick Barbarossa became emperor in 1152 his uncle Otto, bishop of Freising, sent him his history of the world from the creation to 1147 in eight volumes. The part dealing with the author's own lifetime is an extremely valuable historical source. Otto was a member of the Cistercian order and died in 1158 when he was about forty-four years old. His concept of the world is based on Augustine's *City of God*. The library of Jena university owns a copy of the original manuscript of his chronicle, illustrated with pen and ink drawings. The leaf we have reproduced *(pl. 23)* shows, above, the creation of Eve and the expulsion from Eden and, below, Noah's ark. Goethe, who included the post of university librarian at Jena among his many offices, wrote in 1820 that 'the artist was able, with a clear, sure hand, to give his figures and their actions sufficient significance and mobility; a certain naiveté of expression is completely successful in its effect'. To avoid any possible misinterpretation, key words have been written on the drawings: *arca, columba, corvus* (ark, dove, raven), the last being a symbol of death. The ark is built like a church, with the occupants looking out of the windows. The writing in the frame tells what is happening.

Swabia

A martyrology, a list of martyrs with their feast days and biographical details, was one of the liturgical books of the early and mediaeval church. A single leaf from one is glued to the cover of a gospel book, two hundred years older, in the university library in Jena *(pl. 37)*. It depicts the martyrdom of St Lawrence. The surface of the picture is divided into nine squares and rectangles, of which six serve as ornament. In the middle the saint is shown on the gridiron over leaping flames. He is being prodded with pitchforks by two executioners. This brutality is allayed by the angel descending from heaven to comfort the martyr and receive his soul. On the left the emperor Decius sits on his throne under a canopy watching the grisly scene. On the right there are two servants, one fetching wood and the other fanning the flames with a bellows. Houses are indicated in the background and there is a close interrelationship between the picture and the ornamentation, which makes the miniature attractive in spite of its horrific realism.

Echternach

During the Ottonian period the Benedictine abbey at Echternach had been second only to Reichenau. Founded in 698, it had become a centre of missionary work under St Willibrord and was rich and powerful enough to acknowledge no secular authority other than the emperor. The style of illumination characteristic of Echternach developed from the Treves (Trier) school. The scriptorium produced its best work at the end of the tenth century and the beginning of the eleventh, but some notable works of art from a later period have also survived. They include a codex, now in Gotha, which contains a number of works, among them the *Flora* of Abbot Theofrid (d. 1108). The author is depicted *(pl. 25)* in a black habit with a bowl of flowers in his right hand. With his left hand he is holding his *Flora* which lies open on a lectern. He looks down thoughtfully, almost anxiously. This noble figure stands against a blue background and is enclosed by a gold frame and a frieze of gaily coloured palmettes. This is one of the finest of all German miniatures.

Cologne

There are no known Carolingian manuscripts from the archbishopric of Cologne, but there are some Ottonian examples of a very high standard, such as the Hitda Gospels in Darmstadt. In the first half of the twelfth century, in the Benedictine abbey of Sankt Martin in Cologne, a copy was made of the *Ecclesiastical History of England* of the Venerable Bede, who died in Jarrow, County Durham, in 735. In addition to a picture of dedication, the codex contains a Christ in majesty, surrounded by the signs of the four evangelists, the angel, the lion, the bull and the eagle *(pl. 22)*. As well as the outer frame there is an inner frame of green around the blue background. The figure of Christ, his throne and the four symbols are drawn in pen and ink and uncoloured. Christ on the central axis is linked to the figures in the four corners by scrolls, each of which bears the opening words of the appropriate gospel. Christ faces straight forward, his right hand touching St Matthew's scroll, his left pointing downwards. His feet rest on a globe, on which are marked the names of the three continents, Europe, Africa and Asia. Asia bears the star seen by the three Wise Men. Christ's tunic and cloak are wrapped closely round him, following the contours of his body. He wears a golden halo, as do the four symbols. He is shown as a young man, his hair parted and falling to his shoulders, his eyes gazing into the distance. According to mediaeval colour symbolism, the blue background signifies heaven and the green frame hope. Both the drawing and the colouring are lively and attractive.

Saxony

One of the most important centres of illumination in Saxony during the later Romanesque period was the diocese of Halberstadt, which was founded early in the ninth century. Surviving manuscripts indicate the existence of some major scriptoria in the diocese. The museum of Halberstadt cathedral still holds a lectionary written and illuminated by the prebendary Marcwardus, who died in Halberstadt in 1148. A comparison of the Halberstadt Christ in majesty *(pl. 29)* with the Cologne version *(pl. 22)* reveals considerable differences in composition as well as in style and colouring. Marcwardus uses a clearly defined geometrical framework, placing his central group within a mandorla.

The Cologne artist allows himself greater freedom, turning the scrolls and the wings of the four symbols to ornamental purposes. The Saxon artist decorates his border with a meander or key pattern, while the Cologne miniator chooses a clover leaf. In the Halberstadt manuscript the evangelists are depicted in an unusual fashion, as human bodies with animal heads. Christ is supported by the apostles Peter and Paul, whom he is commanding to found the Church and preach the gospel. Both are shown as young men. Peter is holding the key and a scroll which reads *Tu es Christus, filius Dei vivi* ('Thou art the Christ, the Son of the living God'). Christ is seated on a rainbow and rests his feet on the globe. His right hand is raised in benediction, his left hand holds a book open at the words *Ego sum A et O* ('I am Alpha and Omega, the beginning and the end'). His serious face is framed by auburn hair, and he is looking straight out of the page. By comparison, the Cologne Christ looks young and unconcerned. The garments and the background are also treated quite differently. The gold symbolizes Christ's kingship, while the blue of heaven is confined to the spandrels. These two treatments of the same subject are very revealing of regional differences.

Another work of the Halberstadt school is a bible of the Augustinian monastery at Hamersleben in the diocese. The monastery church was dedicated to St Pancras, who was beheaded in Rome when only fourteen years old *(pl. 27)*. He is shown standing and holding a sword, to indicate the manner of his death, and a palm leaf as a symbol of his martyrdom. Two monks lie at his feet, holding an open book. On either side of him members of the order, in groups of three, are gazing at him in veneration. His figure is five times the size of theirs, as a sign of his greater importance. His fair hair and features are typically north German. His dress is that of a mediaeval prince, a green shirt of chain mail and a red cloak. The buildings in the background are in a contemporary style. The two founders stand below the tower on the left, holding a model of the church, which was started in 1112. The manuscript must date from about 1170.

The chapter library of the cathedral of Brandenburg includes, among other things, two illuminated codices whose stylistic resemblances suggest that they were made in the same scriptorium. The script places them between 1200 and 1240. Both were written in the region of Magdeburg for the Premonstratensian canons of Brandenburg cathedral. The lectionary fragment *(pl. 34)* has the same spirals and fronds on initials as the other, an evangelistary. Even the bands on the upright strokes have the same cruciform device on them.

The lectionary has no representational illustrations, but the evangelistary has nineteen whole-page miniatures as well as numerous figures in initials and in the margins. One picture, of the Entry into Jerusalem *(pl. 36)*, clearly demonstrates the characteristics of the Brandenburg artist, which combine Byzantine and Saxon elements. The figure of Christ should be compared with one in a lectionary in the Panteleimon monastery on Mount Athos; the similarity of the heads is astonishing. Byzantine manuscripts must have been known to the Brandenburg artist. He has, however, a very distinct personality of his own, able to give precise forms to the creatures of his imagination. The composition of the picture, the distribution of the figures about the surface, the concentration on essentials, the expressive power of individual figures, argue an unusual artistic ability. Young men are spreading their garments under the hooves of the she-ass in the foreground. The youth in the act of pulling off his garment is

a traditional motif in Byzantine illumination, but not in that of Saxony. Jesus is raising his right hand in blessing, holding the reins in his left. He is riding side-saddle. Behind him to the left the disciples are coming into view, led by Peter, John and James. To the right there is a stylized palm tree, from which two men are cutting branches of welcome. On the right-hand side of the picture, the people of Jerusalem are coming out to welcome Christ, wearing the conventional tall hats. Their words: *Benedictus qui venit in nomine Domini* ('Blessed is he that cometh in the name of the Lord') are written on a scroll which forms a diagonal link between the central figure and the minor ones. This vivid scene is made even more lively by the choice of colours.

A missal was written in the scriptorium of Halberstadt cathedral for the provost, Semeko (d. 1254). One page has an initial 'P(uer)' which encloses a Nativity scene *(pl. 42)*. The manger has the form of an altar, symbolizing Christ's sacrifice of himself, commemorated in the mass. The ornamentation of the upright stroke of the 'P' resembles the 'F' of a Halberstadt lectionary which embraces the apostle Paul *(pl. 38)*. Both manuscripts use a gold background as a symbol of divine wisdom. Paul is dressed in a blue tunic and red cloak. The turbulent folds are characteristic of the age. To judge by the script, which crowds the letters closer together, the lectionary must be of a later date (mid-thirteenth century) than the missal. On the latter the neumes, an early form of musical notation, are interesting. The symbols derive from Greek accents and show the rise and fall in pitch of the melody. Neumes are found in manuscripts from the eighth to the thirteenth century, when they were replaced by stave notation. The spacing of the script is excellent on both leaves. The lectionary has red ink for headings and black for the text. The missal employs different sizes of script for separate passages.

There is another bible in the cathedral library at Halberstadt which dates from the early thirteenth century. The very first words of Genesis, *In principio creavit deus coelum et terram* ('In the beginning God created the heaven and the earth'), are written on the gold background of the initial 'I' *(pl. 35)*. God the Father appears on the 'I' as a young Christ. The world was created by the word of God, which became flesh in Christ. The cross on the halo leaves no doubt that this is intentionally a Christ-figure, the embodiment of the creative Word. He holds the blue cloak over his red tunic with one hand while the other points to the opening words of the story of the Creation. The face is framed by fair hair and beard; unfortunately the eyes are now faded. The cloak falls from his shoulders in angular folds. It is a divine figure of great dignity and grace.

This initial has a stylistic resemblance to a picture of Moses standing beside the burning bush on Mount Horeb, which is in a psalter belonging to the Cistercian convent of Sankt Marienthal, near Zittau *(pl. 43)*. The figure of Moses fills the right-hand half of the picture, dressed in a cloak and tunic which fall in sharp folds. The head, surprisingly, is ringed by a halo. With his left index finger Moses is pointing to the bramble bush, which burns but is not consumed by the flames. Behind it appear the head and shoulders of a Christ-like God the Father in a cruciferous nimbus. He is pointing to a scroll which bears his command to Moses *Descende in egyptum* ('Go down into Egypt'). Over him hangs an unnatural but impressive cloud. God appears behind Moses so that he is heard but not seen, although in Exodus 3 : 6 Moses is said to have hidden his face, 'for he was afraid to look upon God'. The folds in Moses'

garments resemble those in God the Father's in the Halberstadt bible, while his head is of the type of the Brandenburg evangelistary. The manuscript therefore probably originated in Saxony.

The Thuringia-Meissen school

Scriptoria were founded during the later Romanesque period in the marches of Meissen and Zeitz, which had been annexed under the Ottonians. The Benedictine abbey at Pegau, founded in 1091, produced a manuscript copy of Rufinus' translation of the homilies of Origen on the first four books of the Pentateuch. The Greek theologian Origen (184–254) lived first in Alexandria and later in Caesarea. His writings, which were later banned by the Church, gave a great stimulus to the formulation of dogma, and some were translated by the Latinist Rufinus (345–410). The Pegau manuscript has an illuminated leaf for the opening words of Genesis, *In principio...* *(pl. 28)*. The initial 'I' depicts the seven days of Creation in seven circles, with God the Father among the cherubim and seraphim at the top and resting on the seventh day at the bottom. The circles are surrounded by heart-shaped ornaments. The text is in several colours on a purple ground. A coloured frieze of palmettes provides the frame.

Another Pegau manuscript contains St Bernard of Clairvaux's commentary on the Song of Songs. At the beginning there are two whole-page miniatures, of which one *(pl. 33)* shows Christ in a mandorla between two angels with scrolls in their hands, all in the upper half of the picture. The scrolls read *S(an)c(tu)s, s(an)c(tu)s, s(an)c(tu)s: d(omi)n(u)s d(eu)s sabaoth* ('Holy, holy, holy, Lord God of Sabaoth'). Christ, like the angels, is richly clad; he wears a beard and his head is ringed by a cruciferous nimbus. The lower part of the picture represents a building divided by four pillars into three arched niches. Above them, over the roof, is written *Adolescentule: sponsa: Salomo* ('Youth: bride: Solomon'). In the left-hand niche stand a youth holding a scroll in both hands, a fair-haired maiden who holds a ring before her breast, and behind them a third figure, of whom only the head is visible. The bride under the central arch is the most richly dressed of all the figures; she wears a crown and long golden ear-rings. On the right sits Solomon, author of the Song of Songs, on his throne, with a sceptre in his left hand and a book in his right, in which can be read *Canticum cantico(rum) canto* ('I sing the song of songs'). The symbols of the four evangelists appear in the corners of the multi-coloured frame. This miniature is quite different in style from the illumination of the Origen manuscript. The general composition and the heads in particular are more typical of Saxony. Either there was a Saxon miniator in the Pegau monastery, or the manuscript was acquired from another scriptorium for use as a model.

Another manuscript from Thuringia-Meissen contains the homilies of Pope Gregory the Great (540–604) on Ezekiel. It must date from the end of the twelfth century, and was in the library at Altzella, but originated elsewhere. It has an un-finished pen and ink drawing *(pl.26)*, which shows Gregory sitting on a throne, listening to the Holy Ghost, in the form of a dove. Perhaps he is thinking of his famous *regula pastoralis*, for centuries the guiding rule for the clergy. He is wrapped in a voluminous robe but the position of the thighs and knees makes it clear that he is seated. A young monk is sitting on his left, taking dictation. The drawing is coloured in only a few places: the curtain is green, the capitals of the pillars are red. It is regrettable that the colouring was not completed.

The library of the Benedictine monastery at Posa, near Zeitz, was transferred in 1573, by an order of the elector, to the Landesschule, Schulpforta, founded in 1543. By this move it escaped the fate of the manuscript collection of the former Cistercian monastery at Schulpforta, which was almost entirely lost. The Posa scriptorium produced a number of illuminated manuscripts which enable us to make a thorough study of the Posa style. The scriptorium must have been very active in the period just before and after 1200, and appears to have provided manuscripts for other monasteries, particularly Cistercian ones, both in the immediate vicinity and further afield. Its masterpiece is the copy of St Augustine's *City of God*. Each of the twenty-two books begins with an illuminated initial, decorated with animal and plant motifs; the codex also contains two full-page miniatures of the City of God, and of cities of this world in six different epochs. The latter *(pl.32)*, like a modern strip cartoon, starts in the top left-hand corner with a picture of Lucifer, crowned as an angel, watching Lamech kill Cain and Tubal Cain (Genesis 4 : 22–4). In the background is the city of Enoch as the archetypal earthly city. The next picture, to the right, shows the foundation of Nineveh by King Ninus and the god Baal. Outside the city, in the left foreground, stands Nimrod with his bow and quiver of arrows (Genesis 10 : 8–9). The left-hand picture in the second strip shows the third epoch: the kings are Aeneas, whose kingdom of Latium was the forerunner of Rome, and Cecrops, the founder of Athens; the huntsmen are Isaac and Esau. The picture on the right shows Goliath and Pharaoh Nechoh (2 Kings 23 : 29) on either side of the stylized city, in which are the kings Abia and

Jeroboam. The fifth age is symbolized by more kings and galloping horsemen, and the sixth picture shows Herod Antipas and Herodias (Matthew 14 : 3–11) while the scene inside the arch depicts some event in the life of a saint. The bottom strip shows five figures of non-biblical antiquity, including Plato and Vergil. The frame of the whole miniature is a wall encircling the temporal city, ornamented with twenty medallions of Roman gods, with Jupiter in the middle at the top, wearing a crown and holding a sceptre. This miniature illustrates the great learning of the Benedictines, which enabled them to give Augustine's work an artistic gloss. The costumes and architecture are of the twelfth century. The composition is extremely accomplished.

To judge by the style, a manuscript given to the Cistercian monastery at Altzella by Hermann, a deacon of Meissen, also came out of the Posa scriptorium (pl. 30). It contains the epistles of St Paul with the *collectanea* of Petrus Lombardus, the scholastic theologian and bishop who died in Paris in 1160. The initial 'P(rincipia)' shows typical characteristics of the Thuringia-Meissen school: the projections around the outline, the arrangement of the tendrils, and the use of mythical creatures and human figures as ornaments. Paul himself stands in the upright stroke, holding on to the curved stroke. He is dressed in a green cloak and a blue tunic with red sleeves and his hair and skin are fair. He is looking into the distance. The initial lies against a blue background, and the inner space is gold. The tendrils and leaves are red, blue and green. The arrangement of the initial and the text is very skilful; the left-hand column is wider than the right and gives greater emphasis to the dominating initial. The words *Liber Celle* at the bottom of the page relate to the fact that the manuscript belonged to the Altzella monastery.

The initials of the Mildenfurt bible, now in Jena, also show the influence of Posa. The Premonstratensian monastery of Mildenfurt lay to the north-east of Weida in Thuringia. Only the refectory, the chapter house and the south side of the cloisters remain of the former buildings. The initial 'H(ec)' at the beginning of Exodus is particularly fine (pl. 31). We find here the same convolutions, the same divisions, the dragon motif, the curled leaves that are typical of other Posa manuscripts. The red letter stands against a gold ground inside a blue and green frame. The dragon is beige, the tendrils are blue, red and green. This gorgeous colour scheme and the lively draughtsmanship make a sumptuous impression.

A bible in the library of Merseburg cathedral must also have come from Posa. The story of Joseph (Genesis 37–50) is illustrated in the first volume of this bible in a single-page strip (pl. 45), resembling the miniature of the six temporal cities in the Schulpforta *City of God* already discussed (pl. 32). The narrative runs from the top left corner to the bottom right and each strip is divided into two scenes, with alternate use of gold and dark blue as the background. The initials are also very similar in both manuscripts. The differences point to the passage of sixty years between their dates of origin (1180 and 1240), during which different techniques had evolved. The drawing in the later manuscript is more naturalistic; the camel, for instance, is amazingly real. Facial expressions, attitudes and gestures are extremely vivid. The top strip shows Jacob sending Joseph out to his brothers, who are at that very moment plotting to kill him. Below we see Joseph being sold to the Ishmaelites and his bloodstained coat being shown to Jacob. In the third row Joseph is seen, first, running away from Potiphar's wife, and then interpreting the dream of the baker. In the bottom strip he receives Pharaoh's ring and drives through Egypt as ruler. These lively scenes are enclosed by a meander frame. The styles of clothes and architecture, the fair and red-haired people, are typical of central Germany in the thirteenth century.

Yet another mid-thirteenth century manuscript from Posa, still in the library of the Cistercian convent of Sankt Marienthal, is a copy of the Rule of St Benedict, which was observed by Cistercians and Benedictines alike. The beginning of the prologue is adorned with a remarkable initial 'A(usculta)' (pl. 44). St Benedict sits above the cross stroke, instructing a monk at his side in the obligations of the order. Below the cross stroke the space enclosed by the letter is filled with six coiled tendrils. The way they intertwine, the shape of the leaves, the stepped frame following the outline of the letter and edged in vermilion, are as characteristic of Posa as the way in which the initial is allowed to spread into the margin.

A manuscript formerly in the possession of the Cistercian monastery at Altzella, though not written there, is a copy of the works of Gregory the Great. His definitions of vices and virtues stimulated the imagination of mediaeval miniators. The Tree of Virtues (pl. 39) is a pen and ink drawing, highly coloured. The female figure at the root represents Humility, counterbalanced by the figure of Christ, the 'new Adam', at the top. The individual branches each represent one of the seven cardinal virtues, and the heart-shaped leaves branching off them also have minor virtues written on them, so that the whole system of Christian virtues is displayed. The illustration of ethical concepts by this kind of picture was very popular in the Middle Ages.

A perpetual calendar, now in Dresden, probably came from somewhere in the northern part of Thuringia. Besides the leaves of the calendar the manuscript has seven whole-page miniatures, including one depicting the Resurrection (pl. 41). Christ is seen stepping out of the tomb with the banner of the cross in his hand. Two soldiers in full armour are crouching, asleep, in front of the tomb. The miniator has restricted the content of his picture to the absolute minimum – no angels, no women – in order to stress the salient fact: Christ is risen from the dead. He achieves this emphasis by simplicity.

There is a striking similarity between the perpetual calendar and a psalter in the Cistercian convent of Sankt Marienstern in Lausitz. A comparison of the Risen Christ (pl. 41) with King David playing his harp (pl. 40) shows the head, the treatment of the hair and the facial expression to be exactly the same in both. The figure of David and the initial 'B' surrounding it are equally simple. No rich ornamentation, no restless foliage. Both pictures have a gold ground, as was customary in the later Romanesque period. King David is absorbed in his playing. He is wearing a golden crown on his thick black hair. He radiates a certain charm. Even the folds of the garments fall in a similar manner in both pictures; there can be no doubt that they come from the same scriptorium.

THE GOTHIC AGE
1250–1500

France

The reigning house of France took an unusually keen interest in manuscript illumination. For example there is a codex composed of works on medicine and hygiene, made in Paris for Philip IV, the Handsome (1285–1314) and his nephew

197

Philip VI. The most famous medical school of the Middle Ages was that at Salerno, which was the fountainhead of all medical science in Europe, and the source of the most up-to-date textbooks. The Paris manuscript contains pictures of plants, minerals and animals with medicinal properties; the captions are written in Latin or French. Our illustration *(pl.57)* has pictures of a deer, a cuttle-fish and medicinal plants, all drawn realistically. Drawings of plants were already known in By-zantine illumination of the fifth century (the Vienna *Dioscurides*). Interest was re-awakened in the Gothic period and this particular manuscript tells us about the state of medical knowledge in Salerno at the beginning of the fourteenth century.

Another Parisian manuscript is a copy of Guyart Desmoulin's *Bible historiale*, a free version of bible stories in the vernacular. Such bibles were primarily intended for instruction and were often illustrated. Desmoulin's work was one of the most popular French versions. The copy in question, now in Berlin, includes, among others, illustrations of the Creation *(pl.64)*. The decoration of a page of text with a light, elegant marginal ornament is typically Gothic; the chequer board background to the miniatures is typically French. On the left God the Father, a Christ-figure with cruciferous halo, is walking on the face of the waters, divid-ing them from the firmament; on the right he is creating the sun and the moon. Both pictures have similar blue and red borders, but the backgrounds are different: vermilion on the left and green on the right. There is an initial 'D' under both illustrations, so that both columns of text are similar in appearance. The difference between the positions of the miniatures in the two columns makes the total effect of the page more lively.

The miniator of an encyclopaedic work by Bartholomaeus Anglicus held different views on the arrangement of a page *(pl.69)*. He put all four of his illustrations at the top, leaving space for text and initials at the bottom. The whole is sur-rounded by a most delicate pattern of foliage and enlivened by a picture of a hound chasing a rabbit. Three of the four miniatures are devoted to the creation of the sun and moon, of birds, and of plants and animals; the fourth shows the presen-tation of the work to Charles V. The encyclo-paedia is chiefly concerned with the natural sci-ences. It was written around 1260 and was translated into French by Jean Corbechon, an Augustinian monk and theological scholar, by order of King Charles V, in about 1372. Charles, surnamed the Wise, reigned from 1364 to 1380. In the dedicatory picture he is seated on his throne, with crown and sceptre. The translator is kneeling before him, presenting his work, watched by two courtiers. The pictures are realistic and attractive and the colouring is very fine. The patterned back-grounds are typical of French illumination. An entry in the manuscript gives us the scribe's name. He was Fremin de Reuelle, who was also em-ployed by Jean, Duke of Berry (1340–1406), the first modern bibliophile in the grand manner.

Another manuscript of the same period con-tains a history of the ancient world written in French by Henri Romain. Our illustration *(pl.68)* shows the foundation of Rome. The divi-sion of the page is asymmetrical, the left-hand mar-gin being wider than the right. There is no margin at all at the top, where the border of the picture touches the edge. The miniature fills more than half the body of the page. The text begins with a fine initial 'P(our ce quil est)'. Participating in the foundation of Rome are a number of people in mediaeval dress, walking round inside the limits of a city wall. Romulus, labelled by a scroll, stands outside the gate, towering over it, and over the tiny masons working at his feet. In the background the scene is enclosed by a landscape. This became an increasingly important feature of later Gothic art, achieving beauty of its own, independent of the subject of the foreground. The artist is striving for realism in this miniature, though he has not solved the problems of perspective and of the relative sizes of people and buildings.

The *Golden Legend* was one of the most famous books of the Middle Ages. Jacobus de Voragine, a Dominican monk who became bishop of Genoa in 1292, compiled this collection of legends between 1263 and 1272. It was translated into many European languages. One copy, made in Paris but showing signs of Italian influence, has sixty-six miniatures, including one of the Assumption of the Virgin Mary *(pl. 77)*. In the upper part of the picture Christ and Mary are sitting under a canopy supported by four angels, against a chequered background. Christ's right hand is raised in a gesture of speech, while his left rests on the globe. The lower part of the picture is packed with a throng of apostles and early Christians. One of the central figures is John the Evangelist, and another apostle is holding the branch of palm brought to Mary by an angel before her death. The effect of the picture is unfortunately somewhat spoiled by the deterioration in its condition.

The works of Petrarch were also widespread throughout Europe, but nowhere so much as in Italy and France. His *De remediis utriusque fortunae* ('Of the remedies of both sorts of fortune') was much read. The Sächsische Landesbibliothek in Dresden has a mid-fifteenth-century manuscript copy dedicated to Charles VII of France (1422–61). It contains a number of gilded initials and two whole-page miniatures. One shows the translator, Jehan d'Augin, presenting his work to the king *(pl. 89)*. The canopy and the king's ermine

robe are covered with fleur-de-lis. The dedication is written below, beginning with the initial 'A (Tres hault)', and establishes the place and date of origin. The execution of both miniature and marginal ornament is exquisite and provides a superb example of the high quality of French manuscript illumination.

The Book of Hours was a new kind of prayer book which emerged in the first half of the fourteenth century. Usually written in the vernacular rather than Latin, it begins with a calendar, which offered miniators plentiful opportunities for pictures portraying the different months, the signs of the Zodiac and the saints whose feasts fell throughout the year. Elsewhere in the book there are miniatures of such standard subjects as the Passion, the childhood of Christ and the life of King David. Marginal ornament plays an important part in the Books of Hours, whether in the form of tendrils and foliage or of a solid frame decorated with animals, flowers and precious stones. Books of Hours were made in large numbers, and many magnificent examples have survived. A manuscript now in the library of Leipzig university includes a Nativity scene *(pl. 86)*. The main accent is on the foreground where the Infant Jesus lies in a ray of light from heaven, worshipped by his parents, and by the ox and the ass. At the back the stable opens on to a hilly landscape. The miniature and the text are surrounded by an illuminated border on three sides; two dragons lurk in the foliage, providing a sinister contrast to the tender scene in the stable, which is made glorious by a lavish use of gold.

The Flight into Egypt is another subject frequently treated in Books of Hours. A Berlin manuscript has a charming version *(pl. 112)*. Joseph is leading the ass on which Mary is riding, holding her Child with both hands. The setting is a European landscape with flowering trees; Jerusalem appears as a mediaeval city. The little miniature, which has four lines of text and a magnificent initial 'D(eus)' below it, is surrounded by delicate tendrils. The page was clearly conceived and composed as an artistic whole.

The penitential psalms were always included in the Books of Hours, so that scenes from the life of David were always among the illustrations, inviting comparisons between Books of Hours and psalters. A manuscript in Leipzig shows David at prayer in the middle of a landscape *(pl.88)*. The king is richly dressed in an ermine cloak, and his harp lies at his side. He is looking up to God, who appears in a ring of fire. An angel stands on a mountain peak as an intermediary between the king and his God. This whole-page miniature is a genre scene in a delicate border.

The Book of Hours was for the use of laymen, while priests and monks had breviaries, which one might suppose would not be so richly decorated. In fact a considerable number of illuminated breviaries of the fifteenth century have survived. The illumination is similar to that of the Books of Hours: a picture, text with an initial and a graceful border, making their effect as a single unit. *Pl.87* shows the Visitation from a breviary in Rostock. The Virgin Mary and St Elizabeth are meeting in front of the house, Elizabeth curtseying before Mary, who holds out her hand in greeting. She is accompanied by a servant. The background consists of the usual landscape and mediaeval city. There is a subtle interrelationship between the ornamentation and the picture, both in forms and colour.

The prayers to be said for the souls of the dead appeared at the end of the Book of Hours, providing a special stimulus to the imagination of miniators. A Book of Hours in Gotha shows the death of a noblewoman as Death thrusts his spear into her heart *(pl.113)*. A serving woman stands in the foreground, taking a candle from the hand of the dying woman. On the other side of the bed a priest approaches, followed by her husband or son. The brown panelling of the room forms a contrasting background to the blue canopy of the bed. This interior fills most of the picture apart from a narrow strip of landscape at the right. The border, which contains a centaur, birds and other animals, is almost gay, and certainly lively, by comparison with this sombre scene; such contrasts are not uncommon. There are the usual four lines of text, with an illuminated initial, below the miniature.

A subject which recurs frequently in the literature of the Middle Ages is the life of Alexander the Great. There were historical works about him, such as the one by the Roman historian Curtius Rufus, and numerous literary and popular epics, of which every country had its own vernacular version. A lavishly illustrated manuscript of the second half of the fifteenth century, now in Gotha, contains a French version by Jean Vouquelin. The depiction of Alexander's birth, in a mediaeval setting, was particularly popular *(pl.97)*. The foreground is almost filled by the bed of his mother Olympia, with the bath tub at its side. Beyond it stands a group of noble ladies in mediaeval dress; the midwife is holding the child, already swaddled. The father, Philip of Macedon, in an ermine robe, stands at the foot of the bed, engaged in conversation with Aristotle. The magician Nectanabus, whom the queen summoned to interpret the seven stars in the sky and foretell the fate of the new-born child, stands in the doorway. This genre scene occupies half the page. There are an initial and twelve lines of text below it. The border is a different width on each side, and is interrupted altogether by the curved top edge of the picture. This arrangement is common in Books of Hours.

The story of Alexander was one of those that were popular throughout Europe, but there were others which were known in only a few countries. One such was the French prose romance *Ysaie le Triste*, the story of the son and grandson of Tristan and Iseult. There exist only two manuscript copies, in Gotha and Darmstadt, and there are also two extant copies of an edition printed in Paris in 1522. The Gotha manuscript has a large number of illustrations, including at least one which is of interest to social historians *(pl. 125)*. The clothes, the headdresses, the style of interior decoration, are those of the late fifteenth century. There are five people carrying on an animated conversation at the table. The fair Orimonte in the middle is asking her father who the two knights are, who are coming through the door on the left; two women offer them a cup of wine in welcome. The gaily dressed figures move about on the pale brown floor in realistic attitudes; the bright colours enliven the scene. It is not only the rarity of this manuscript but also the image it reflects of its age that make it of inestimable value.

A most refined example of manuscript illumination in the late fifteenth century is provided by a life of St Antony (d. 356). The title page *(pl. 120)* is bordered with exquisite tendrils in which nestle birds, fruits, a mask and a portrait. There is a frame on three sides between the border and the body of the page, which falls into two parts: a miniature and an initial and text. In front of a checked background we see the saint, Christianity's first hermit, leaning on the T-shaped cross named after him, with his attributes, a censer and a begging-bowl, in his hand. His right hand is raised in a rhetorical attitude. The figure kneeling

before him is St Athanasius (293–373), a Greek and one of the Fathers of the Church, who was probably the author of a Life of St Antony. Both in its draughtsmanship and its colouring, this miniature is a typical example of Gothic illumination at its peak.

The number of illuminated manuscripts on secular subjects increased steadily throughout this period. Books were produced on every subject that interested fifteenth-century society. The part played by tournaments and jousting in life at court is recorded in a book by Regnier d'Anjou, Duke of Lorraine. A manuscript of this work, now in Dresden, contains thirty-two miniatures, one of which has a mediaeval city, hills and groups of trees in the background *(pl. 124)*. In the foreground the judges of the tournament are riding towards the city gates. The procession is led by trumpeters and heralds, followed by the king-at-arms, whose surcoat has jousting knights embroidered on it. One of the horsemen wears the fleur-de-lys on his cloak. All of them are wearing hats of the style fashionable in the latter part of the fifteenth century. The scene is quite realistic in its presentation and is complete in itself, not linked in any visual or compositional way to the text at the bottom of the page. This development continued in the sixteenth century, as well known painters, not trained miniators, undertook commissions to illustrate books and the art of illumination merged into painting.

The Low Countries

Dutch illumination of the fifteenth century was confined to the diocese of Utrecht and neighbouring areas. It was all produced in monasteries, and so the bulk of the material consists of liturgical books. A late fourteenth-century prayerbook, now at Greifswald, contains several illuminated pages *(pl.75)*. The arrangement is asymmetrical, the border being widest at the bottom and narrowest at the left-hand side. The border, the initial and the text are interrelated. The flowers inside the frame of the initial are taken up again in the border. The harmonious effect derives from the proportions, the relationship of the initial to the text and of both to the border. The dove of the Holy Ghost is a remarkable device, plunging out of a bell-shaped heaven, and placed centrally for emphasis. The shift of accent to the initial at the left-hand edge of the page is effective and charming. The background is gold and the body of the initial sea-blue. The branches are green and the flowers are blue and red. The border is also red, blue and green, so that there is an overall effect of splendour.

There is a very similar page in a breviary in Weimar *(pl.123)*. The initial 'H(eir in dyn)' is also surrounded by the text to the right and below; the border is more delicate and is an excellent example of the finest 'filigree' work. This expression, taken from metalwork, in the context of illumination means ornamentation with very fine lines, speckled with dots of gold and silver. The accent of the border does not fall in the middle of the bottom edge, but on the right-hand side, on the figure of King David, surrounded by a scroll. He is depicted as the author of the seven penitential psalms which begin on this page. The ornamentation of the page is all in blue, red and gold.

A Rostock breviary marks the beginning of the penitential psalms with a picture of the resurrection of the dead *(pl.84)*. Christ, his bleeding wounds clearly visible, sits on the rainbow with the orb between his feet. Two angels hover on either side of him, blowing their trumpets to call mankind to judgment. The graves are giving up the dead. A mediaeval gate on the left is the entrance to para-

dise and on the right are the jaws of hell. The figure of Christ and his robe emphasize the central axis. The border is conventional with tendrils, flowers and two strawberries, which symbolize earthly desires.

Flemish illumination has earlier origins than Dutch. Manuscripts from Ghent and Bruges began to appear at the beginning of the fourteenth century, but the art came to maturity with the brothers Hubert and Jan van Eyck, who collaborated on the Turin-Milan prayerbook for Jean, Duke of Berry, between 1415 and 1417. Flemish prayerbooks spread throughout Western Europe, and the quantities which have survived indicate that they existed in enormous numbers. The move of the Burgundian court to Flanders in the fifteenth century was also of importance to the development of illumination. The dukes of Burgundy were art-lovers and commissioned works from the great Flemish masters. New studios were established to cope with the increased demand.

A breviary by the Master of the Privileges of Ghent and Flanders, dating from between 1440 and 1460, is now in Gotha *(pl.85)*. The Raising of Lazarus, as narrated in John 11 : 32, is depicted on a page with a fine broad border. Lazarus, still in his grave-clothes, is kneeling in front of Christ, who is speaking to him, his right hand raised. Mary, Martha and their companions stand further back, some outside the burial chamber. Christ's attitude and facial expression are 'troubled'. There is a superb view of hills and trees and the city of Jerusalem. The peacock in the border on the left symbolizes immortality and resurrection.

A miniature of the Entombment in a Liège breviary is arranged on the page in the customary manner, leaving one margin rather wider than the other *(pl.107)*. The scene is set in a meadow in a Flemish landscape. There is no sign of the sepulchre hewn out of the rock of which we read in the Bible. Joseph of Arimathaea and Nicodemus are carefully lowering Christ's body into a stone coffin. The counsellor is wearing a rich red robe trimmed with ermine, and Nicodemus is wearing blue. Mary and John are watching, grief-stricken. The sadness of the scene is in contrast to the green summer landscape. In the background Jerusalem can be seen as a mediaeval city.

The calendar of saints' days is an important part of the Book of Hours, and the inclusion of local saints is often of great help in ascertaining a manuscript's place of origin. Calendars were decorated with the signs of the Zodiac or with series of pictures of the twelve months, such as the harvest scene representing July in a prayerbook from Bruges, now in Dresden *(pl. 106)*. It shows peasants at work in the field in the foreground, with trees, hills and buildings further back. The zodiacal sign of Leo is seen at the top in the red disc of the sun. Yellow and green are the principal colours. The miniature is surrounded by the usual kind of border. Unfortunately the manuscript has been spoilt by damp; the colours have faded and details have been obliterated.

The same artist, known as the Master of the Dresden Prayerbook, was responsible for a magnificent manuscript in the library of Leipzig university. It consists of two volumes containing the *Factorum et dictorum memorabilium libri novem* ('Nine books of memorable acts and speeches of the Romans') by Valerius Maximus, a writer in the reign of Tiberius (14-37 A.D.), with a French translation. It is a collection of anecdotes illustrating abstract concepts, such as friendship, gratitude and happiness. Each of the nine books begins with a whole-page miniature of high artistic merit. The sixth of these shows the death of Lucretia *(pl. 109)*. Lucretia, the wife of Collatinus, com-

mitted suicide after she had been raped by Sextus, the son of Tarquin the Proud, an act which made her the classic example of chastity. The miniature sets the scene in a mediaeval hall. Lucretia kneels in the centre. She has already thrust the sword into her breast, and is surrounded by a group of horrified and weeping men and women in rich clothing. As always in Flemish painting of this date, there is a view, through open doors, of a landscape, in which horsemen can be seen approaching down a road. The miniature, the border and the text form a unified whole.

The classical authors were never entirely forgotten during the Middle Ages, and in the Gothic period they began to appear in vernacular translations. A French translation of Xenophon's *Cyropaedia*, for instance, has survived in a Flemish manuscript of the second half of the fifteenth century. The style shows the miniatures to be the work of the Fleming Loyset Liedet of Bruges. One of them depicts an army on the move, with cavalry, infantry and cannon *(pl. 108)*. The whole scene is mediaeval: the armour, the landscape, the city in the background, are all of the artist's own times. There is deliberate realism in the treatment both of the details of the horses, armour and cannon, and of the general view of the castle, the city walls, the gates and the church in the background. It is not the army of Cyrus, king of Persia, but of a fifteenth-century king of a European country, and the miniature is of interest to the historian for that reason.

As well as ancient history, mediaeval scholars were interested in Greek philosophy, usually through the medium of the Roman statesman Boethius (480–524), who translated the works of Aristotle, Ptolemy and others into Latin and wrote commentaries on them. The *Consolation of Philosophy*, which he wrote in prison while awaiting execution, is his best known work. Margaret, the sister of Edward IV of England and wife of Charles the Bold of Burgundy, commissioned a French translation of this work from Jean de Meun; the manuscript, illuminated by a Bruges artist, contains a dedicatory picture of the duchess receiving the work from the translator *(pl.114)*. The ceremony appears to be taking place in a courtyard or street. Margaret and her ladies in waiting are wearing the elegant court dress of the age (1476). The colouring, the draughtsmanship and the composition show this to be the work of a great artist.

Mysticism, which sought to place the human soul in direct contact with God, flourished in the later Middle Ages. Its leading exponent in France was the Parisian theologian Jean Charles Gerson, who attempted to fuse scholasticism and mysticism. Gerson (1363–1429) was chancellor of the university of Paris, and played an important part in the Council of Constance (1414–1). A manuscript of one of his tracts, *De mendicitate spirituali* ('Of spiritual poverty'), is now in Gotha. The first page has a miniature depicting the soul as a naked, winged woman, with a mendicant's purse and staff, conversing with a monk and a nobleman wearing the order of the Golden Fleece *(pl.115)*. Five other men are listening to the conversation, which is taking place in a Gothic chamber with the view of a landscape through the tall windows. Comparison with the dedicatory picture in the Boethius manuscript *(pl.114)* makes it seem probable that the two artists were both working in Bruges at the same time, possibly even in the same studio. The meticulous concern for every detail, whether in the floor, the walls and the windows or in the facial expressions and gestures, is the mark of an artist of the same high quality.

The popularity of Guyart Desmoulin's *Bible historiale* is proved by the number of surviving manuscript copies of it. It is interesting to compare the Parisian codex of 1368 *(pl.64)* with a Flemish copy of between 1460 and 1480 *(pl.118)*, which came from the library of Duke Charles de Croy, a member of a noble Belgian house. Friedrich Winkler has attributed the illumination to the Master of *Girart de Roussillon*, the miniator of the manuscript copy of the old French epic of that name, made for Philip the Good. Although a hundred years separate the two copies of the *Bible historiale*, the treatment of the background and of the figures is similar in both. The difference lies in the greater refinement of detail. The Flemish manuscript shows John with an open book on his knees, listening to the angel whose words he is writing down. Above him are the seven candlesticks and the Lamb, and above them God in majesty, a sword in his mouth and the book with seven seals in his right hand. Fourteen – not four and twenty – elders sit on either side of him, dressed in white robes, with gold crowns on their heads (Revelation 1; 4; 5). This picture is enclosed by a square lozenge. The symbols of the four evangelists with scrolls bearing their names occupy the spandrels. This geometrical construction of one square within another is unusual and effective. Each part is separate yet linked to the others. There is no further ornament in the margins.

Another popular work of which there are many Gothic manuscript copies is the life of Alexander the Great by Curtius Rufus. One copy, now in Jena, is of a French translation by Vasco Gomez de Lucena. Each of the nine books opens with an illuminated page *(pl.119)*. The language of the text is a long way from Quintus Curtius Rufus, a Roman historian of the first century A.D., and the illustrations are even further from Asia Minor of the fourth century B.C. Alexander and the wives of Darius are wearing mediaeval court dress and their expressions might have been drawn from life. The composition and the execution testify to the talent of the unknown artist, a pupil of Phillippe de Mazerolles.

Germany in general

The generic term German has to be used in the absence of evidence to ascribe manuscripts to specific regions of Germany. Among this group we have a fragment of a German translation of the Old Testament, of the second half of the fourteenth century. The last page of the Book of Numbers *(pl.63)* shows Moses presenting the Ten Commandments to the Children of Israel. He sits on a brown chair, wearing a blue tunic and a red cloak, listening to the voice of God from above. The book of the Law is open on a brown lectern. Five of the Israelites, in red and blue robes, are standing beyond two hills, labelled as *filii Israhel* ('Children of Israel'). The wave-like contours of the ground are repeated in the red and blue tendrils in the sky above. This picture, done in watercolour and apparently in a hurry, is not without expression, particularly in the figure of Moses.

A German psalter of the same period has a delicate filigree initial at the beginning of the text *(pl.74)*. Only two colours, red and blue, have been used; the beauty of the letter lies in the exquisite grape motif which not only fills the interior of the letter itself but also continues down the margin. This delicacy of draughtsmanship was a characteristic of the Gothic feeling for style.

Many manuscripts required not only the skills of illumination and writing but also a knowledge and understanding of music. The Church played a decisive role in the development of musical notation. The oldest musical symbols of the Christian Middle Ages are neumes, which were replaced by the four-line system invented by Guido d'Arezzo in 1025. The use of clefs to give the pitch developed around 1200, and later mensural notation came in, to indicate the duration of notes. This system enabled texts to be prepared specially for the use of choirs, and they too were illuminated. We illustrate *(pl.92)* a page of an antiphonary in Bautzen cathedral library. The chant is written above the text and the page is ornamented with a graceful border and an initial 'A(d)' in brilliant colours. The body of the letter is patterned with leaves and encloses two bunches of flowers. Details such as the strawberry beside the initial are executed with care and skill, and the script and the notation are both extremely clear.

Prayerbooks were numerous in Germany as elsewhere. Miniatures apart, the main sections of the text were also illuminated. An example of this is taken from a manuscript in Halle, which is small and easy to carry about the person *(pl.110)*. The page has a border on three sides in which we see an owl, a raven and a monkey blowing a horn. All three are part of the symbolism of the seven Deadly Sins: the monkey represents avarice, the raven avarice and gluttony, and the owl anger and sloth. The initial 'A(ve)' is decorated with leaves and the text is crammed into a small space. The various different kinds of ornament derive their full effect from the colouring.

Western Germany

Every new period in the history of manuscript illumination sees changes in subject matter. The typical manuscripts of the early Romanesque period are the great gospel books, while it was the

Book of Revelation which attracted Gothic miniators. A page from a manuscript made in Lorraine in the fourteenth century *(pl.52)* shows, in the bottom left corner, the seven-headed beast of blasphemy (Revelation 13 : 1–2) and two armoured men outside a fortress, whose occupants, visible above the walls, are presumably the saints. It is said of this beast that 'his mouth (was) as the mouth of a lion', which inspired the miniator's other picture. The four fantastic heads, set round the corners of a square to form a single fiery gullet in which the head of a fifth beast can be seen, are more like lions than anything else, but two of them are horned and a third is a brilliant blue never seen on any feline. They are manifestations of the same delight in the grotesque as appears in Gothic gargoyles. These two square pictures are separated by a narrow building from which St John (presumably) is looking out. They are of different sizes which makes the two columns of text of different lengths. The miniator was obviously a man of strong and idiosyncratic imagination.

Another manuscript from the southern part of western Germany contains *Der welsche Gast* ('The Italian stranger'), a Middle High German didactic poem by Thomasin von Zirclaria. Thomasin was a native of northern Italy, born in Friuli, who died a canon in Aquileia before 1238. His poem is a moral tract on the knightly virtues, depicted allegorically as actual knights in the miniatures. The top picture in our example *(pl.79)* shows *tugend* (virtue) enthroned, commanding four armed knights, who represent *staet* (constancy), *mazze* (moderation), *recht* (justice) and *milt* (mercy), to 'be manful'. The middle picture shows a fight between *staet* and *unstaet* (treachery). Naturally *unstaet* is vanquished and put to flight. The tapestry background betrays French influences. The bottom picture shows the victory of *mäzz* (moder-

ation) over his opposite, *unmäzz*. The pictures are brightly coloured but crude. Their function was instructional, not artistic.

Contemporary interest in the literature of mediaeval Germany is shown by the popularity of a work like Wolfram von Eschenbach's epic poem *Parzival*, of which no less than seventy manuscript copies survive. It appeared in print as early as 1477, in Strasbourg. A Dresden manuscript probably comes from the studio of Diebold Lauber in Haguenau in Alsace *(pl.99)*. Lauber was active between 1427 and 1467. His medium was pen and ink, and he developed an unmistakable studio style which enables us to follow his progress. His illustrations were accompanied by captions in red. On this example it reads 'So the lords rode away from the castle with a large company'. The picture shows five noblemen, who appear to be engaged in lively conversation, with the castle they are leaving in the background. The chief colours are blue, grey and brown. There is a conscious striving for realism. The individual heads and their facial expressions have obviously been carefully differentiated. This is collective work from a studio which hoped for widespread distribution and good sales.

Another manuscript from Alsace, now in Leipzig, is of *Der Renner* by Hugo von Trimberg, another lengthy didactic poem, an allegory of the Seven Deadly Sins. Hugo von Trimberg (1253 – 1313) was rector of the monastery school in Theuerstadt, on the outskirts of Bamberg. He wrote *Der Renner* ('The Racer') between 1290 and 1300. The title-page *(pl.98)* of this copy illustrates the lines *Renner ist ditz buoch genannt | Wanne ez soll rennen durch diu lant* ('This book is called the Racer, for it shall race throughout the land'). The Racer is shown dressed in lilac and grey riding a horse at full gallop, with a staff in his right hand. The horse is wearing protective armour with a green and lilac vizor. A man in blue and lilac is running alongside, crying the praises of the work. This simple drawing is extremely lively; the Racer really is racing along.

Ecclesiastical manuscripts were still of a higher artistic quality than secular ones. A breviary from the duchy of Bar on the upper reaches of the Moselle, at that time part of the Holy Roman Empire, is so richly illuminated that it must have been intended for a high-ranking cleric. It contains thirteen miniatures of which the *pietà* is one of the most beautiful *(pl.116)*. The subject of Mary mourning over the body of Christ, laid in her lap, at the foot of the cross, first occurs in German art in fourteenth-century sculpture, and not until the fifteenth century in miniatures. In sculpture it is usually restricted to the single group of Mother and Son, with no background or other figures. In painting there are normally the two additional figures of John and Mary Magdalene and the scene is set in a landscape. The empty cross towers unnaturally tall above the group. John, on Mary's right, is supporting Christ's head, while Mary Magdalene is preparing to anoint his body. The hills and trees of the landscape are German. The cross and the two tall trees emphasize the vertical. The faces of the three mourners express the deepest sorrow. The decoration in the border is still and tranquil, with foliage and flowers on a grey background. The strawberry plant in the middle at the bottom symbolizes the earthly passions which caused the tragedy. The peacock beside it is an image of immortality and resurrection. The man whose head can be seen in the bottom left-hand corner is probably the artist. The skilful asymmetrical composition of the page, and the glowing colours, show him to have possessed great artistic powers.

At least one female patron of the fifteenth century is known to us by name. Margarete of Nassau-Saarbrücken, Lady of Rodemachern in her own right, had a prayerbook made which contains her portrait on the page dedicating the work to her *(pl.117)*. She is kneeling at a prie-dieu. Her guardian angel, with splendid multi-coloured wings, stands behind her, holding her head, with his right hand raised in blessing. In the top left-hand corner Christ appears in a cloud as the Man of Sorrows. The nine coats of arms round the edge of the picture are those of the many branches of Margarete's family and of her feudal overlords. The two figures form a central axis. The trust and intimacy of the relationship between the lady and her guardian angel lend the picture charm. A Flemish influence is unmistakable.

One of the pioneers of the interest in natural sciences felt in the later Middle Ages was Albertus Magnus (1193-1280), who not only wrote a commentary on Aristotle's scientific works which did much to make them more widely known, but was also extremely learned in physics, chemistry and mechanics. A Dominican, he taught at the university of Paris, then directed the new faculty of *studium generale* at Cologne, where Thomas Aquinas was among his pupils. He became Dominican provincial of Germany and bishop of Regensburg. He spent the last years of his life in Cologne, where he was buried. One manuscript copy of his work on minerals, from Alsace, depicts fifteenth-century mining and firing techniques *(pl.111)*. Over this scene at the bottom of the page, the sun rises above a rocky landscape in the right-hand border. The border on the left is filled with a pattern of flowers. The scroll at the side of the initial 'T(empus)' contains the scribe's name and the date: M(agister) Forest(us) 1484. An illustration of a technological process is very rare in mediaeval manuscripts.

Mecklenburg was one of the territories east of the Elbe that were conquered and converted during the early Middle Ages. By the mid-fourteenth century the dukes owed allegiance only to the emperor. In 1378 Ernst von Kirchberg, a native of Thuringia, came to the court of Mecklenburg at Schwerin and was commissioned by Duke Albert II to translate the *Chronica slavorum* of Helmold into High German verse, and to continue the narration up to 1337. The title page of the manuscript depicts the duke and his son, Albert III, who was king of Sweden from 1364 to 1389 *(pl.65)*. The old duke, wearing an ermine robe, holds the banner of Mecklenburg, the bull's head and the golden griffin, while his son holds the Swedish banner, the three golden crowns. As the picture was painted during their lifetime, these are probably authentic portraits. The cut of the beards and the clothes must certainly be in the fashion of the time. The two figures are enclosed by an oval frame, within a rectangular frame. Attention is immediately focused on the dukes.

The diocese of Schwerin was the centre of religion in Mecklenburg. An antiphonary of Schwerin cathedral has been preserved. An antiphonary consists of three sections: the gradual, the responsorial and the antiphonary proper. Later the gradual was made separate. The antiphonary proper is in three parts: the *antiphonarium diurnale* with the canticles sung at the daytime offices throughout the year, the *antiphonarium vesperale* with the parts of the breviary sung at Vespers, and the *antiphonarium nocturnale* with the canticles for the night-time offices. The first page of the Schwerin antiphonary is illuminated *(pl.90)*. The initial 'E(cce)' is decorated with formalized leaves, coloured in red, blue and green on a ground the colour of the

parchment. The music and text are evenly distributed on the page. The manuscript consists of the *pars hiemalis*, the antiphons sung between the first Sunday in Advent and March 25.

A psalter, probably from the diocese of Hildesheim, contains both Latin and Low German texts *(pl.72)*. The first psalm, *Beatus vir*, is the most richly ornamented, as is usual in illuminated psalters. David sits playing his harp inside the initial 'B'. The 'jigsaw' frame outlining the letter is curious. Its four-leaved clover motif is repeated in the centre of the stars that are distributed round the border. The text is written in alternate lines of Latin, in black, and Low German, in red. The initial is completely hemmed in by the text on two sides and the border on the other two. This arrangement is quite unusual.

A Crucifixion from a Halberstadt missal is simpler but equally effective *(pl.128)*. The cross and the two figures stand against a gold background which symbolizes divine wisdom and is in contrast to the uneven ground, rough clumps of earth and tree trunks. Mary and John are deep in prayer, and the same calm radiates from the stiff body and dead face of Christ. The utter simplicity of this miniature renders it all the more effective.

A Passion book, now in Dessau, ornamented with eight whole-page miniatures, is probably also from the region of Halberstadt. The portrayal of the Deposition is reduced to the essentials *(pl.83)*. The centre of the picture, which immediately holds the attention, is the broken body of Christ. The left arm is held by Nicodemus who has climbed a ladder to loosen the nails. The body is supported from below by Joseph of Arimathaea. The pincers, nails and inscription lie at the foot of the cross. The background is a formalized wood, more like a piece of tapestry. The individual faces express alarm, grief and effort. At first glance this picture seems primitive but we must admire the power of its expression.

A Magdeburg breviary, also in Dessau, contains a whole-page picture of the miracle of Pentecost (pl.93). Mary, surrounded by the twelve apostles, is sitting in a Gothic chamber. Above her, in the central axis of the picture, hovers the dove of the Holy Ghost. The golden rays from the dove turn to flames on the heads of the apostles. The background is gold, symbolizing divine wisdom. The apostles are praying, ready to receive God's commands. Two benefactors of the cathedral kneel at the front, holding a scroll. The statues on the pillars are of St Maurice, holding the *labarum*, and St Katherine with a sword and palm leaf as symbols of victory. Magdeburg cathedral was dedicated to these two saints, which confirms that this manuscript did originally come from there. The many fires in the city's history seem to have destroyed nearly all the works of art made for the archbishops and the cathedral. The symmetry of the composition, the colours and the execution make this a work of distinctive originality.

The Thuringia-Meissen School

The monastic scriptoria of Thuringia and the Meissen marches continued to pursue their own style. A bible in the Zwickau Ratsschule shows close stylistic connections with the Benedictine abbey of Posa, near Zeitz. The manuscript is decorated with some fine initials. The first page of the Epistle to the Hebrews (pl.51) has two: the 'E(pistola)' is purely ornamental while the 'M(ultifariam)' encloses a figure of the apostle Paul, which forms the central stroke of the 'M' as a dragon forms that of the 'E'. The two coloured initials stand against a gold ground and are filled with twisting

foliage. The Zwickau bible is an example of what Ernst Kloss has called the Saxon provincial style, which had a decisive influence on Silesian illumination.

A psalter which once belonged to Altzella and from there came into the possession of the daughter foundation at Sankt Marienstern came from another Benedictine scriptorium in central Germany. It contains a picture of the Visitation (pl.46) which places Mary and Elizabeth in an architectural frame under two decorative gables, crowned with fleurons. That the encounter is taking place out of doors is indicated simply by the presence of a tree. The cousins are embracing, and evidently have plenty of questions to ask each other. The gold background once again symbolizes divine wisdom, whose intentions both women are helping to fulfil. The significance of the heads in the four corners of the frame is unknown, nor have two coats of arms at either side been identified. The miniature is quite complete in its simplicity and its gay colours are charming.

Two other manuscripts, a missal and a breviary, still in the Cistercian convent of Sankt Marienstern, are so similar in style that they must have come from the same scriptorium at very much the same time. They were probably made in one of the great Benedictine abbeys of Thuringia or Meissen in or around 1300. They would have been acquired by Altzella, which had no scriptorium of its own at that date, and then handed on to Sankt Marienstern. Both pages are so original in their composition and in their details that it is hard to find anything comparable. The missal (pl.48) depicts the Nativity inside the curve of the initial 'P(uer)', with six praying angels in the upright stroke. The manger is shown as an altar, symbolizing Christ's offering of himself, commemorated in the mass. The star of Bethlehem shines above the two animals. The roof has Gothic gables. Two angels hover above the initial with a scroll, announcing Christ's birth: *Gloria in excelsis deo et in terra pax hominibus bonae voluntatis* ('Glory to God in the highest and on earth peace to men of good will'). The letter is mainly gold, with a decorative rim. The physical characteristics of the people are north German and bear a slight resemblance to the faces in the Brandenburg Evangelistary *(pl.36)*. The sumptuous colours, principally red and gold, make a rich impression.

The Resurrection depicted in the breviary *(pl.49)* gets more space than the Nativity, leaving room for only seven lines of text. Text and picture are enclosed in an ornamental frame. Christ occupies the central position in the picture, sitting on the edge of the tomb, wearing a magnificent star-studded robe. The vermilion of the background is picked up in the headings in the text above. The border has an unusual combination of geometrical and plant ornaments, and the freedom of the leaves attached round the edge is particularly curious. The page – border, text and miniature – was conceived as a single artistic entity, and this is the source of its effect.

An inexhaustible supply of material was provided by the lives of saints and martyrs. The martyrology began as a calendar of the feasts commemorating the deaths of martyrs and then came to include accounts of their lives as well. Passages were read from it at Prime. The library of Jena university owns a German version, dating from about 1300, which is of great value to philologists as the major existing work in the dialect of Thuringia and southern Saxony at the end of the thirteenth century. It is a Christian didactic poem, a kind of rhymed lamentation. The text is illustrated with primitive pen and ink drawings, which were coloured at a later date, with the narrative following each picture. Our example *(pl.55)* shows, at the top, the voyage of the bishops Germanus and Lupus to Britain, during which they were overtaken by a storm. The ship is struggling against huge waves while Germanus admonishes the wind. In the centre we see two martyrdoms: St Eleutherus at the stake and St Leger, bishop of Autun, being clubbed. The bottom row illustrates the story of two priests who accompanied St Willibrord to Saxony. They were put to death and their bodies thrown into the river. According to legend they were carried downstream as far as Cologne, where they received Christian burial. The miniator's intention was to record significant events; he was not concerned with realism for its own sake. The proportions, for example, are quite irregular: people are as tall as buildings. The martyrology was an educational book; the purpose of text and illustration alike was to drive home the story.

Breviaries lent themselves to a wide range of decorative ideas. Brilliant colours and especially gold were lavished on them. An illuminated page from a Weimar manuscript is a good example *(pl.53)*. The initial 'H(odie)' is formed by a chain, as the upright stroke, and a dragon, as the curve. The dragon's head hangs in one of the links of the chain and its tail fans out like a leaf. The wings are multi-coloured. The same chain motif is used in the second initial, 'V(irgo)'. The bottom and right-hand margins are decorated with a representation of the Stem of Jesse, beginning with a star which encloses the Infant Jesus and is surrounded by eight birds. Jesse in Jewish dress stands holding on to the root of the tree which grows upwards through King David and the Virgin and Child, and ends with the Holy Dove perched on its top. This marginal ornament is an original idea.

A Revelation, also in Weimar, shows a quite different style of ornamentation, dominated by figurative illustrations which take up whole pages. One of the most impressive of these miniatures depicts the fight of St Michael with the dragon, watched by St John *(pl.61)*. The archangel is standing on the beast's back and thrusting his lance into its fiery jaws. He is looking down at the effects of the blow, while John looks up trustingly, his raised forefinger expressing his faith. Michael wears a green robe under a white cloak and John is dressed in blue and green. The beauty of this miniature lies in the noble attitudes of the two saints, in its asymmetrical construction, which finds room for a few short lines of text in the top left-hand corner, and in its allegorical force.

The Gothic age is characterized by a thirst for education, which was promoted not only by the new universities but also by the Church. A product of this is the kind of picture bible which originated in a Benedictine monastery somewhere in Bavaria or Austria for the instruction of lay-brothers. These bibles are known, rather misleadingly, as *bibliae pauperum* ('poor men's bibles'); a better name might be *bibliae parabolicae* ('parable bibles'). The French term *bible moralisée* is also often used. Events in the Old Testament were shown to have an allegorical or prophetic significance by juxtaposition with comparable events in the gospels, an interpretative process known as typology. It was a work typical of Benedictine scholarship, intended to make bible stories more widely known by the use of illustrations as well as words. The *biblia pauperum* enjoyed great popularity and a large number of manuscripts and early printed copies have survived. A handsome example in Weimar puts two sets of parallel events on one page *(pl.60)*: at the top the burial of Christ is depicted in association with Joseph being

lowered into the pit by his brothers and Jonah being thrown into the sea. The central picture is surrounded by four smaller circles containing David, Solomon, Jacob and Isaiah. Originally these supporting figures were always prophets, but there were later alterations to the original scheme. The lower group centres on Christ's descent into hell. The typological parallels are David's fight with Goliath and Samson's with the lion. This time the four smaller circles portray David, Hosea, Isaiah and Jacob. The various figures are named for the sake of certainty. The pictures are pen and ink drawings, coloured principally in shades of green, red and yellow. Both sets of pictures are skilfully set in the text. Even where the lines vary in length the total appearance of the page is not spoiled.

The other important work of mediaeval typology is the *Speculum humanae salvationis* ('The mirror of human salvation'), compiled in or about 1324, probably by a Strasbourg monk, Ludolf von Sachsen, who, although a Dominican to start with, later became a Carthusian. The book consists of forty-five chapters of typological comparisons of biblical events, and even uses some profane stories. The difference between the *biblia pauperum* and the *Speculum* is that in the former the chief emphasis is laid on the pictures, while in the latter it is on the text: the pictures play a subordinate role. Both Latin and vernacular versions of the *Speculum* circulated freely up to the end of the fifteenth century. No less than 350 manuscripts, and a large number of printed copies, have survived to the present day. The copy in Gotha is illustrated with primitive pen and ink drawings *(pl.78)*. The typological parallels to the Ascension are Jacob's ladder and, on the facing page, the Good Shepherd and Elijah being carried up to heaven in a fiery chariot. The portrayal of the

Ascension consists merely of six disciples who have fallen on their knees to pray, and the feet of Christ as he disappears into the clouds. The other illustration is equally simplified. Jacob lies asleep on the ground, propping his head on his hand. Two angels are climbing up the ladder which rises beyond him. Much the larger proportion of the page is given over to the text, which is more important than the drawings.

Works were written which attempted to under-pin the gospel truths with a philosophical base, such as the *Speculum virginum* ('maidens' mirror'). A manuscript in Leipzig has a vivid illustration of the tree of wickedness with its spreading branches *(pl. 70)*. Its roots lie in the Scarlet Woman, 'Babylon the Great, the mother of harlots and abominations of the earth' (Revelation 17 : 5), who holds a golden cup *(aureus calix)* and wears a golden crown. Two serpents are entwined round the trunk, and two dragons are sitting among the branches. The branches hold a total of fifty-four golden, heart-shaped leaves, each of them inscribed with the name of a vice. The branch and twig arrangement allows minor, related vices to be seen to grow from the major vices. All the pictures in this manuscript are coloured with equal brilliance. With the trunk of the tree as the central axis, the many branches are spread out against a back-ground of restless checks. This tangle of lines and the garish colouring show the miniator to have possessed a vivid imagination.

The Gothic age was an age of mysticism, and the Franciscan order developed their own particular mysticism of suffering. One of the teachers of the order, Otto von Passau, wrote a book called *Die vierundzwanzig Alten oder der güldene Thron der minnenden Seele* ('The four and twenty elders or the golden throne of the loving soul'), in Basle in 1386. It is a guide to the Christian life, which leads to union with God. The four and twenty elders come from Revelation 4. Otto's book was clearly very popular and later went into a number of printed editions. In 1446 Nikolaus Kürssener of Pirna translated the text into the dialect of Saxony for Prince George I of Anhalt. The manuscript contains twenty-two miniatures, of which our example *(pl. 80)* shows the fourteenth elder in cardinal's robes in conversation with the loving soul, a young, fair-haired maiden. The red and the white figures stand out against the black back-ground with sculptural clarity. The initial 'U(ber)' forms a link between the tendrils in the left-hand and bottom margins. The harmonious arrange-ment of text and ornament on the page is exem-plary.

One of the important works of early humanist literature in German is *Der Ackermann aus Böhmen oder der Rechtsstreit des Menschen mit dem Tod* ('The Ploughman of Bohemia, or Man's dispute with Death'). Written in about 1400, it is generally attributed nowadays to Johannes von Saaz. This human complaint against God for allowing death sprang from the author's own anguish at losing his young wife in childbirth. After a long debate, in a final prayer he accepts the divine order of things. It was the first New High German book, and was widely read. Albert Pfister in Bamberg printed two editions illustrated with woodcuts, in 1460 and 1463. Both in text and illustrations they conform to the Jena manuscript, the only one in all the libraries covered in this book. Our illus-tration *(pl. 105)* reproduces the Harvest of Death. In the foreground Death mercilessly cuts down two people with his scythe, while in the back-ground he takes aim at an unsuspecting horseman with bow and arrow. The meaning is clear: Death strikes down everyone, rich or poor, by one means or another. The work appealed to a wide public, not just to theologians, by its treatment of a universal theme. The rather naive illustrations are immediate and sincere.

The most important miniature in any missal is the picture of the Crucifixion, with Mary and John, which always lies opposite the canon major, the very heart of the Mass, which covers the Transsubstantiation. There is a fine example in a Berlin manuscript *(pl.103)*. The light brown cross stands against a black background with gold tendrils. Christ is already dead; his head has fallen. Mary and John stand on either side, in attitudes of dignified restraint. Flowers are growing around their feet. Mary holds her right hand out towards the cross, while John clasps his gospel. Mary is wearing a red dress and dark blue cloak, John wears a green cloak over his blue tunic. The frame is in the same colours. Outside the frame on three sides, there is a border of green tendrils with red and gold ornaments. The colours are subtly matched.

A picture of the Crucifixion was also always included in a psalter. The Dessau psalter *(pl.81)* is of a later date (c. 1480) than the Berlin missal and the loincloth is tossing in the wind, as often occurs in contemporary sculpture. The turbulent folds of the garments are also characteristic of the art of the period. John is looking up to heaven, holding out his hands, as if to protest his innocence of any part in the crime. Mary's hands are crossed, her face is grief-stricken. Christ's eyes seem to be looking down at her in the last agony. The red background, speckled with black strokes, symbolizes Christ's blood and mourning at his death. The green ground symbolizes the hope given to mankind by the Resurrection. The miniature makes an extremely vivid impression.

A German Old Testament of the late fifteenth century, now in Dessau, is richly illustrated *(pl.126)*. The artist was clearly concerned to make his figures as realistic as possible; only in the case of the camels does he seem to have lacked satisfactory models. Men and beasts are drawn in perspective. The pen and ink drawings have been painted in watercolour. The three pictures on this page illustrate the events narrated in Genesis 32. In the top and centre we see Esau, on horseback, receiving conciliatory messages and gifts of goats and camels from Jacob's servants. The bottom picture is the most vivid, showing Jacob wrestling with God in the form of an angel. They clasp each other in a fierce embrace and God's face is hidden. He has a grip on Jacob's hip. 'And the hollow of Jacob's thigh was out of joint, as he wrestled with him.' One can almost hear the desperate cry 'I will not let thee go, except thou bless me.' The landscape is composed of a path, a tree and a grotesque rock. The miniator's concern was to illustrate the text. There is no superfluous ornamentation, and the text is compressed into a very small space.

Some of the finest illuminated manuscripts of the fourteenth and fifteenth centuries were legal books. The works of learned lawyers were called *specula judicialia* ('judicial mirrors'), to distinguish them from the codes and statute books issued by legislatures. The most important of these works is the *Sachsenspiegel* ('Saxon Mirror'), written, initially in Latin, in 1220 by a Saxon knight, Eike von Repkow, who subsequently himself translated it into Low German. It contains the laws of Saxony relating to land and feudal tenure, and the laws which were common to all the German territories. The Dresden *Sachsenspiegel* manuscript is generally acknowledged to be the most valuable of all the illuminated copies. Unfortunately it was so severely damaged during the war that it is now impossible to reproduce it adequately; we have been obliged to use a Leipzig copy instead. In addition to one very good initial it contains three miniatures, one of which depicts eight soldiers and a knight marching towards a castle (pl.104). The castle stands on a rock at the top of the picture, the central axis emphasized by the tower, and is separated from the foreground by a ditch and trees. The knight is carrying a red banner with the black German eagle on it. This little genre picture is contained within the green initial 'U(mme)', the body of which is decorated with a leaf pattern. Among the tendrils in the border stands a peacock displaying his tail feathers as a symbol of pride. Lower down there is a green parrot which signifies good luck. The brilliant colours play an important part in the effect made by this page.

Besides the *Sachsenspiegel*, which is a work of major importance, there are a number of manuscripts which contain the laws of individual towns, such as the Zwickau statute book of 1348. The text is illustrated by small coloured pen and ink drawings. One page (pl.59) has four drawings which depict various kinds of punishment. At the top a criminal is broken on the wheel, in the middle another is beheaded, and at the bottom others are hanged and flogged. This codex is of great value to historians since it not only exemplifies the process of the law in the fourteenth century but also shows how the sentences were carried out. The primitive drawings are coloured in a uniform style throughout, green, yellow, blue and red being the colours principally used.

In addition to civil and criminal law there were books of church law, all based on the *Corpus juris canonici*. The oldest part of this collection of church law is the *Decretum Gratiani*, written by the jurist Gratian in Bologna in about 1150. It was introduced in the German dioceses during the second half of the twelfth century. When the Franciscan order entered Germany in 1221 it took upon itself the propagation of canon law. Glossators were continuously at work on the *Decretum Gratiani*. One of these versions is the *Summa juris canonici*, otherwise known as the *Summa Monaldini* after its compiler Monaldus of Capo-distria, who was the Franciscan provincial of Dalmatia, in the early fourteenth century. One of the surviving manuscript copies of his work is at Mühlhausen. This Monaldus was often confused in later years with an archbishop of Benevento and a bishop of Melfi, both of whom were near contemporaries and bore the same name. For this reason the author is portrayed in his episcopal vestments on the first page of the Mühlhausen manuscript inside the initial 'Q(uoniam)' against a gold background (pl.58). The two columns of text are separated by an ornament and surrounded by a frame, decorated at the top by a hound and a hare with their backs to each other, while at the bottom the hound is chasing the hare. It is not clear whether these animals are meant to provide light relief or whether they have some symbolic significance. The simple layout of this page is enriched by imaginative colouring.

Southern Germany

There are very few south German manuscripts of the Gothic period in the libraries drawn on for this book. The Gotha Landesbibliothek owns a book on courtly manners entitled *Die Blumen der Tugend* ('The Flowers of Virtue') written in 1411 by a Tyrolean nobleman, Hans Vintler. He lists both virtues and vices, among which he includes witchcraft (pl.71). The verses and pictures record mediaeval customs which would otherwise have been lost. A love-potion will only be effective if the woman digs up a particular herb at night, we see her digging up a flower with a kind of spear. Silver and gold increase if left out in the light of the new moon; this picture has the immediate, simple appeal of a children's book. The two-storied house is barely taller than the man who gazes hopefully up at the moon, waiting for the magic to operate. The manuscript is arranged so that the verse precedes the relevant illustration, which as it were brings the text to life.

An early fourteenth-century treatise on the courts and jury system of Magdeburg, based on the *Sachsenspiegel*, became well known throughout Germany. This study of jurisdiction in one particular town in Saxony is known as the *Sächsisches Weichbild* (see the Glossary). In a manuscript copy written in the diocese of Regensburg the scribe has mistakenly involved Eike von Repkow *(pl.95)*, whom he depicts sitting in the initial 'V', wearing a white cloak and a dun-coloured jerkin and holding a book in a red satchel. A scroll with the name 'Ecke' leaves no room for doubt on who the figure is meant to be. The right-hand column lies between two rather weedy tendrils, while the left-hand column is embellished by a decorated initial 'G'. The manuscript is not very richly illuminated and was probably intended for the use of students.

A Bavarian illuminated breviary which contains notes on the conduct of services is now in Halle *(pl.122)*. The text lies within a simple border of tendrils and leaves. The Christ Child lies inside the initial 'P(rimo)', bathed in golden light. The codex has unfortunately been affected by damp which has spoiled part of the border. The balance of text and decoration is nicely calculated.

Most of the best examples of Bohemian illumination are today in Prague and Vienna, but there are a few in Bautzen and Zittau. One of these is a collection of theological and philosophical reflections, written in Czech by one Thomas of Stitni. The first page is ornamented with a miniature and a border *(pl.54)*. A father is instructing his three sons who are on their knees listening to him. The garments, the facial expressions and the colouring in this genre scene are skilfully treated. The black background is relieved by a pattern in gold. The miniature is surrounded by a narrow brown frame. The painting of the tendrils at the bottom of the page was not quite completed. This decoration is conventional and has no inherent connection with the page as a whole.

Another Bohemian manuscript, in Zittau, contains a vesperal and a matutinal. Like antiphonaries, these books were very bulky and between 65 and 75 cm. tall; when in use they stood on tall desks so that a number of choirmen could use the same copy. This particular example is richly decorated with patterned borders and figurative initials. On the page reproduced *(pl.73)* the space inside the initial 'G(aude)' is filled with an Annunciation. The angel approaches Mary in a mediaeval walled town. Standing beside a prayer stool, she has crossed her hands over her breast and is listening to his message in an attitude of humility. The Holy Dove hovers over her. Two other angels are holding a scroll over the roof with the words *Sanctus, sanctus, sanctus dominus*. Behind and above the starry heaven has opened and God the Father is revealed among the angels with the Christ Child already burdened with his cross. This entire scene is framed by the initial which in turn is set inside a square frame. The spandrels are occupied by four of the prophets: Isaiah, Daniel, Hosea and Zechariah. The words of their Messianic prophecies are written on the scrolls they hold. The colouring is rich and pleasing and the total effect is quite charming.

The centre of Bohemian illumination was Prague, the place of origin of an early fifteenth century missal, now also in Zittau. It is embellished with a whole-page Crucifixion and pages of illuminated lettering. One of these depicts Christ seated on a draped throne within an initial 'A(d)' *(pl.94)*. The beautifully drawn folds of his pale robe are shaded with a reddish tinge. Generous folds of this kind are typical of contemporary carving. The slim right hand is raised in blessing, in the left he holds an orb as a symbol of redemption from original sin. (An orb and an apple are the same shape, so the one symbolizes mastery over the other.) A greying brown beard and long curling hair frame a thin rosy face with solemn far-seeing eyes. The blue background is divided by fine white lines into squares, decorated with stars and gold spots. The green letter which surrounds this figure is decorated with foliage which is taken up again in the margin. This foliage is coloured beige, red, pink, green, blue, lilac and brown and is very finely drawn. The reproduction even of only one corner is enough to convey the sumptuous impression made by the whole page.

From 1412 onwards Zittau belonged to Oberlausitz, which in turn, after many vicissitudes, belonged to Bohemia; it was not ceded to Saxony until the Thirty Years War. For this reason a gradual written in Zittau in 1435 shows Bohemian stylistic traits *(pl.82)*. In script and ornament it resembles the Bohemian vesperal *(pl.73)*. The blue leaves on the initial 'P(uer)' are very like those on the initial 'G', and the tendrils of both borders are also alike. Certain differences appear, however, in

the treatment of the figures. The heads are round instead of oval. Instead of the loose robe with long folds, Mary's dress fits closely; the wide hem falls untidily. The stable buildings look more Oriental than the mediaeval city of the Annunciation. The composition is far simpler and includes only the essential figures. Nevertheless this picture exercises the same appeal as the other.

Another Zittau manuscript, also still in its place of origin, is a missal with a fine illuminated page *(pl.102)*. Inside the initial 'V(enite)' three monks are singing in front of a desk, on which a book lies open. The background is blue with a gold pattern. The body of the letter is decorated with beige leaves and surrounded by a gold frame. On three sides of the music and words there is a border coloured green, grey, beige, blue and red, with birds, bears and monkeys among its tendrils. In the bottom left-hand corner there is a second picture in which the Man of Sorrows appears to a man at prayer, probably the missal's owner. St Bartholomew stands behind him. Below this group there is a coat of arms which includes a book bound in pigskin. The detail which we have reproduced illustrates the style in which the missal is decorated.

Spain

We have unfortunately not been able to include any examples of early Spanish illumination in this book. The earliest Spanish manuscript I found is a late fifteenth-century breviary in Gotha, once the property of Ferdinand of Aragon (1479–1516) and Isabella of Castile (1474–1504). The Oriental influences brought to bear on Spanish art in earlier centuries are still apparent in the Moorish style of the frame of our example *(pl.121)*. The diamond pattern is also found in the lion and myrtle courts of the Alhambra. The initial 'B(eatus vir)' encloses a picture of David in the robes of a Spanish king, praying in an ornate Gothic palace. The initial is set in a square box but encroaches on the left-hand border. Smaller initials are scattered over the whole page. Gold is used lavishly, and this breviary is one of the most magnificent of its kind.

Italy

The Italian illuminated manuscripts of the thirteenth, fourteenth and fifteenth centuries which survive include works of classical literature and law as well as devotional and liturgical texts. The works of Aristotle, for instance, were evidently widespread. A manuscript now in Erfurt depicts Aristotle teaching, in the interior of an initial 'P(ostquam)' *(pl. 50)*. With the index finger of his right hand he is pointing to a globe, while his left hand rests on a volume of his works. He sits on a low bench with an expression of deep thought on his face. Two pupils sit at his feet drinking in the master's words. This concentrated little picture receives its finishing touches from the colouring, gold, pink, blue and white.

There is considerable doubt as to the place of origin of a psalter, which can be dated at about 1330 or 1340. It employs the 'strip cartoon' form of earlier manuscripts. Our example *(pl. 47)* shows two separate events in the upper strip, the Annunciation and the Visitation. The figures are shown against a bare, gold background, some of which has unfortunately peeled off, with no scenery whatever. The dramatic impulse comes from their gestures and facial expressions. The heads have been drawn but not painted, and they are German in type, not Italian. The same is true of the Nativity in the lower strip. The inclusion of only the chief protagonists, and the absence of buildings or landscape, concentrate the power of expression of the individual figures. The patterned frame also separates the two levels of the miniature.

The *Decretum Gratiani* was the most widespread of the legal texts. Gratian lived in the twelfth century; he was a Camaldolite monk of the monastery of San Felice. He can be regarded as responsible for establishing ecclesiastical jurisprudence on a separate footing from theology. In about the year 1150 he assembled the canons of church law from all the various separate sources, with a certain amount of connecting text of his own, to form a companion to his lectures on the subject at the university of Bologna. The *Decretum Gratiani* is the most substantial volume of the *Corpus juris canonici*, the complete collection of church law, and innumerable manuscript copies of it have survived; the students at Bologna alone would certainly have needed a large number of copies.

Pope Boniface VIII added a sixth volume to the *Corpus juris canonici* by having a selection made of papal decrees published after 1234. A manuscript copy of this *liber sextus* is preserved in the archives of Erfurt cathedral. It opens with a dedicatory picture *(pl. 56)* in which the pope receives the book from a kneeling monk in the presence of prelates and monks. An interior is indicated by two small alcoves and some draped curtains. The pope is seated on his throne in the left foreground with the codex open on his lap. A second presentation is being made on the right, so there is a certain degree of symmetry in the composition. The heads and the brilliant colouring are typically Italian. There is no frame round the picture. The text begins immediately underneath it with an initial 'B(onifatius)' and this is finished off with a vignette. The closely written outer text, which in fact forms a frame to both miniature and text, consists of commentary.

The university of Jena has a copy of the *Decretum Gratiani* of which we are fortunate enough to know the miniator's name, as it appears under the table in the foreground of our example *(pl.67)*. Niccolò di Giacomo di Nascimbene (1330–1402) is the dominant figure in Bolognese illumination of the second half of the fourteenth century. His depiction of the trial of a bishop in the papal court, with the pope himself, five cardinals and an archbishop sitting in judgment, has all the characteristics of Italian art: delight in colour for its own sake, vivid gestures, realistic variety of facial expressions, and clarity of composition with a strong central axis. The court is sitting in a semicircle on raised, canopied seats. The semicircle is completed by a table in the foreground at which a number of clerks are sitting. One of them is standing, reading from a document. The public are crowding in on either side. The defendant is kneeling to the left of centre, trying to hand the pope a document. The picture is well set off by the surrounding text which contains several decorated initials.

Another manuscript collection of decretals contains a tree of consanguinity *(pl.91)*. The founder of the family stands in the centre against a background of coats of arms, blessing his children and grandchildren. Most of his body is concealed by the table of genealogy which gives the degrees of relationship in the circles. It is supported from below by a man standing outside the frame so that the page is divided in two. The foot of the picture is enlivened by small animals. The text is set fairly symmetrically on either side of the picture. The two *putti* at the top are early forerunners of Renaissance ornaments. The page is coloured with the usual strong Italian shades.

The history of Alexander the Great was as popular in Italy as it was elsewhere. A Leipzig manuscript contains an illustration of Alexander's battle with King Porus of India *(pl.62)*, whose archers and javelin throwers fought from howdahs on the backs of elephants. Curtius Rufus tells, in chapters 47–9 of Book 8, of how Alexander loaded wagons with bronze statues which were heated in the fire, and drove them towards the elephants. As they burnt their trunks they ran wild and broke the Indian battle lines. The presentation is primitive, although the elephants are quite realistic. The colours are sober: the elephants are dark grey, the armour is bluish, and the wagon is blue. The only bright colours are the red and green of the towers. The bronze figures are beige, and the horse is a grey. The lower part of the page depicts a cavalry skirmish involving the two kings. This group is enlivened by gold swords, shields and vizors. Very nearly every page in this manuscript is illustrated in the same way, leaving very little room for the text.

Italy was above all others the country which preserved and kept alive the literature of the Romans. Many copies of Livy have survived, including one in Leipzig, the first page of which depicts the building of a castle *(pl.66)*. Six workmen are busy on the roof, watched by a king, with sceptre and crown, on horseback. A man and a woman are riding towards him; they too seem to be interested in the building. Another, smaller picture above the second column of the text shows four carpenters at work. This delight in the portrayal of everyday activities is typical of Gothic art. The illustrations are wider than the text but are balanced by the border at the bottom of the page, which had to be omitted from this reproduction. It includes in the centre the arms of the house of Sansimone for whom this manuscript was made.

Among other works of Latin literature, Ovid's *Metamorphoses* were particularly suitable for illustration, offering the imagination of the miniator a wide scope. One fine example is a Gotha manuscript which is prefaced by a commentary, *Ovidius moralizatus*. The *Metamorphoses* had been given a Christian interpretation since the time of the early Church Fathers, and some of the characters were conventionally associated with biblical figures: Apollo and Daphne, for instance, with Christ and Mary. The first page of this codex has a portrait of the commentator, dictating to two monks. All the illustrations are small, with between two and five on a page, and a number of them were not finished, which enables us to study the process of illumination. Spaces were left free by the scribe in which the drawing was sketched, first in pencil, then in black ink. The frame was painted first, then the background and finally the figures. The first page of Ovid's text is particularly ornate *(pl.76)*. In addition to the border decoration which includes coats of arms, there is a small miniature in each of the columns of text. The one on the left shows Deucalion and Pyrrha asking Zeus how they are to repopulate the earth after the Flood. We see people forming from the stones they throw over their shoulders. On the right Apollo is shown killing the monster Python. In the foreground he is struck by Cupid's dart and inflamed with love for Daphne who runs away from him. The strong colour contrasts of black and red make both the miniatures and the margin particularly vivid.

The works of Cicero were widely read. The cathedral library at Zeitz contains a manuscript copy of his letters. On the first page of the text the border is filled with a design of tendrils *(pl.96)*. Emphasis is obtained in the middle of the lower edge by a coat of arms, and on the left side by the initial 'E(go)'. The ornament on the letter matches that on the border. The text is indented

below the initial, giving rise to an asymmetry of composition. This page is a competent but by no means outstanding piece of work.

With the spread of printing in the second half of the fifteenth century, it was those books which were in greatest demand which were printed first. One of the earliest editions of the *Decretum Gratiani*, printed in Venice in 1477 by Nicolas Jenson, a copy of which is in Gotha, is a superb example of the transition from the illuminated manuscript to the printed book with coloured illustrations. The text and commentary are printed, the initials, border and dedicatory picture on the first page are painted by hand *(pl.101)*. The text proper, with two initials 'H(umanum)' and 'O(mnes)', is set below the picture in red and black, and is surrounded by the commentary, in a smaller type size and with smaller initials. The whole page is framed by a painted Renaissance border of extreme opulence. Cupids, nudes, portraits, a landscape with animals, crowd upon each other, with precious stones scattered among them. The style and spirit of the composition, the love of life and earthly beauty, are characteristic of the Renaissance which had begun in Italy in the early fifteenth century, nearly a hundred years before it flowered north of the Alps.

The thirst for learning included the study of ancient history. A life of Philip of Macedon by the third century Roman historian Marcus Junianus Justinus is preserved in a Gotha manuscript. The first page is decorated with a magnificent Renaissance-style border *(pl.100)*, in which a tortuous pattern of strapwork twists around cherubs, animals and, at the bottom, the arms of the future Pope Pius III. This kind of convoluted ribbon motif is very common in late fifteenth-century manuscripts from all parts of Italy. The frame encroaches on the text to include the initial

'C(um)' with a portrait of the author. In spite of the different width of each of the four sides of the border, the page as a whole creates an effect of harmony and balance. Another typical Renaissance feature is the six-line heading in golden capitals; the text below is written in Renaissance minuscule. The medallions are ringed by red laurel wreaths and the initial by a green one. There is a very careful coordination of the individual ornaments, and the colours are also skilfully matched, creating a rich and very satisfying page.

The same is true of a copy in Stralsund of the works of the lawyer Baldus de Ubalis Baldeschi. Born in Perugia in 1327, he taught Roman and canon law at Bologna, Perugia, Florence and Pavia, where he died in 1400. The first page of his commentary on the Digests, or summary of Roman Law, is embellished with an ornate border *(pl. 129)*. In this case the principal element in the design is a pattern of leaves, not strapwork. There are three coats of arms in the middle of the left, bottom and right sides, the last of which bears the word *Libertas* ('liberty'). The initial 'Q(uoniam)' grows out of the border in the top left corner. It is followed by seven lines in a larger script than the rest of the page. The colours stand out brilliantly against a gold background. Only Italy produced miniatures of such radiance.

A missal in Leipzig also stems from this transitional, early Renaissance period. Its style and colouring are unmistakably Italian. It contains an Annunciation *(pl. 127)* which shows Mary, wearing a red dress and blue cloak edged with gold, sitting at a desk on which lies an open book. She is listening, in an attitude of humility, to the angel's message, her hands raised. Golden rays fall from Gabriel on to her. She is sitting in front of a Renaissance building with blue pillars, its entrance hung with green curtains. The picture is surrounded by a blue and red frame ornamented in gold. It is marked by a peculiarly Italian grace. The bright blue of the cloak is found only in Italian painting. We can only lament the deterioration in the manuscript's condition as a result of damp.

THE HIGH AND LATE RENAISSANCE
1500–1600

Italy

Italy continued to lead the development of Renaissance styles in the sixteenth century. A very fine example of Italian manuscript illumination of the late Renaissance is found in Dresden *(pl. 160)*. This manuscript comes from Venice and is dated 1557. It is the proclamation of the appointment of Nicola Marcelo as mayor of Bergamo, by Lorenzo Priolo, doge of Venice. The frontispiece portrays St Mark, the patron saint of Venice, standing reading on an altar which is adorned with the doge's arms. In the background is a scene of buildings, hills and trees. This picture is set in an oval frame, leaving room in the spandrels for allegorical figures representing hope, love, wisdom and strength. Their sepia colouring forms a distinct contrast to the rich green, ochre and blue of the miniature. Our attention is focused at once on the saint, who holds the centre like a Roman statue. The composition and the colours, which are glowing but not bright, create an impression of classical restraint.

From Italy the Renaissance spread north. In France the works of the Italian poets were well known, and translated into French. A fragment of a French translation of Boccaccio's *The Fall of Princes* is now in Dresden; the manuscript has an illuminated page at the beginning of each of the four books. Our example *(pl.133)* is framed, like the others, by a Renaissance archway and shows pilgrims resting at the edge of a wood, with a town and a castle visible in the background. The figures and the landscape are executed with artistry and skill right down to the last detail. Each of the pilgrims is an individual, characterized by attitude, gesture and facial expression. One is taking a long, cool drink, the others are conversing eagerly, while one wipes the perspiration from his face. The landscape also accommodates two columns of text without strain; what would have been a separate frame in a Gothic manuscript is here part of the miniature. The text is treated as part of the composition, with little pretence that it has any independent significance. The name of the artist responsible for this highly original work is unknown.

The enormous influence exercised by Petrarch (1304–75) on his contemporaries and on posterity is evident in illuminated manuscripts. There is in Berlin a French manuscript of the mid-sixteenth century with eighteen miniatures illustrating his poems. Six of them relate to the work of his old age, *The Triumphs*. This poem in twelve cantos presents allegories of love, modesty, fame, time and eternity. Two cantos are concerned with the triumph of Death, whom no one can escape, not even Laura, the poet's beloved. A miniature *(pl.153)* shows her lying under Death's feet, still alive and clasping a broken column, but looking up in horror at the grisly spectre who triumphs over her with scythe, spear and the victor's palm leaf in his hands. The smiling landscape of trees and meadows, and the blue sky behind them provides a contrast between the beauty of the world and grim death. The miniature could really be a painting in its own right, and the connection with the four lines of text in different scripts seems merely incidental.

The Low Countries

Dutch and Flemish illumination continued to flourish in the early part of the sixteenth century. A missal of this period has an illuminated page with a border composed of figurative scenes *(pl.132)*. The top half of the border is given over to the Annunciation to the Shepherds. God the Father and three angelic musicians fill the sky, and below them Gabriel unfurls a scroll bearing the words *Gloria in excelsis deo*. In the bottom right-hand corner we see the birth of Christ. While Joseph worships the Child, Mary is looking earnestly at the swaddling cloth she is holding. Is she foreseeing the time when she will use it as a shroud? The lower left-hand corner of the border is decorated with a design of strawberries, the symbol of earthly desire, flowers and a coat of arms. The two initials 'P(uer)' and 'G(loria)' are in a pure Renaissance style, the parts of the letters being shaped like vases. The text is interrupted by a line of music. This page is a fine example of harmony of text and appearance.

The great esteem in which Flemish illumination was held led many of the German princes to commission work from artists in Flanders. Frederick the Wise of Saxony, for instance, had a choirbook made. On one page *(pl.147)* he is portrayed, in the same attitude as the Lady of Rodemachern *(pl.117)*, kneeling in prayer, with his patron St Katherine behind him. Other contemporary portraits prove that this is a realistic likeness. For this reason it has been suggested that it was added by Lucas Cranach the elder when the book reached Wittenberg, but there is no proof. The initial 'B(assus)' shows typical Renaissance traits; instead of being smothered in leaves and tendrils, the letter itself is composed of vase-like ornaments on a plain ground. The frame is a different width on each side and decorated with foliage, flowers and birds. The music is written on the five-line stave. The total impression, compared with illumination of an earlier date, is of clarity and simplicity.

Germany in general

In Germany too the new age was stirring. The sixteenth century saw some of the greatest geniuses in German art: Dürer, Holbein, Grünewald, Cranach, to name but a few. Their work gave a new stimulus to manuscript illumination. Where they did not themselves work as miniators, their engravings and woodcuts served as inspiration. The religious turmoil of the first quarter of the sixteenth century did not quench the demand for devotional and liturgical books. The monastic scriptoria continued to function until secularization closed them for ever.

The pen and ink drawings of a Dresden prayer-book were clearly influenced by Dürer's Little Passion. In the Adoration of the Shepherds *(pl.155)* the architecture of the stable is extended so that the kneeling shepherds are almost inside. The ox and ass have been added. In the background the Annunciation to the Shepherds is

drawn on a larger scale than in the Dürer woodcut. The attitudes of Mary and Joseph, and of the shepherd kneeling on the left, are the same, and the group of the crib, the Child and the Angel is also similar. The landscape in the background is, however, quite different.

In the course of the centuries a situation had arisen whereby the scribe and the miniator of a manuscript no longer worked in the same place, as they had done in the monastery scriptoria. Manuscripts were sent to famous artists for illumination after the text had been written, or even before.

This is probably what happened in the case of the *Sächsische Chronik* of Georg Spalatin, the illustrations of which clearly reveal the influence of Hans Burgkmair the elder (1473–1531). It seems likely that the manuscript was written in Wittenberg but illuminated in Augsburg. Spalatin (1484–1545), whose real name was Burckhardt, studied in Wittenberg and then became tutor and secretary to Frederick the Wise. He was a friend of Luther and Melanchthon and played an important part in the Reformation. He was both a theologian and a historian. He completed his history of Saxony in 1513. After the death of Frederick the Wise in 1525 he went to Altenburg. The Weimar copy of the chronicle is illustrated with innumerable coloured pen and ink drawings, one of which portrays the coronation of Otto I by his father Henry the Fowler *(pl.138)*. The nobles have assembled in a Renaissance hall and are dressed in the fashions of the early sixteenth century, despite the fact that the coronation in question took place in the year 936, and indeed after the death of Henry. He is shown sitting beneath a canopy, placing the crown on his son's head, watched approvingly by the nobles. They form a group on the right of the throne, while the foreground is left clear to focus attention on the act of coronation. This picture demonstrates how dependent on other graphic art book illumination became towards the end.

The dependence of illumination on printed books is shown by a manuscript copy of *Theuerdank* made after the publication of the first edition in Nuremberg in 1517. *Theuerdank* is an allegory of Maximilian I's courtship of Mary of Burgundy, written at least in part by Maximilian himself. The type face of the first edition was designed by Vinzenz Rockner: it is an early German black letter *(Fraktur)*. The illustrations were the work of three Augsburg artists, Leonhard Beck, Hans Burgkmair the elder and Leonhard Schäufelin. An unknown painter and scribe undertook the task of copying the book and reproducing the woodcuts in watercolour. One of the best shows Theuerdank in danger of shipwreck *(pl. 151)*, based on a woodcut by Schäufelin. Unfalo the evil spirit, disguised as a scholar, stands on the shore and gives Theuerdank the disastrous advice to cut away his sail. The turbulent sea, the frightened men on the ship, the scenery, are impressively depicted, the use of watercolour allowing quite different effects from those made by the woodcut.

A Dresden manuscript of 1572, one of the many books on warfare, contains a vivid picture of a ship on a stormy sea *(pl. 158)*. The brown ship sails over the green and blue waves under a full spread of white canvas; the barrels of a number of cannon protrude from her sides and the crew can be seen on her deck. The picture is interesting for the idea it gives of how a warship of the late sixteenth century looked and was armed.

Nuremberg was an important centre of artistic and cultural activity at the beginning of the sixteenth century. Painting was represented by Dürer, sculpture by Adam Krafft, Veit Stoss and Peter Vischer, to name but a few. The poet Hans Sachs, scholars like Pirckheimer and Regiomontanus all lived in the Imperial Free City. The most original of the artists, although he was to some extent influenced by Dürer, was Jakob Elsner *(d.c. 1517)*. In 1507 he was commissioned by Pope Leo X to illuminate an evangelistary and an epistolary which the pope was to give to Elector Frederick the Wise of Saxony. Elsner painted one miniature, of the Saviour, with his hand raised to bless, on the front cover of the evangelistary, under glass. Inside the book he painted two magnificent electoral coats of arms, a Crucifixion and several pages with illuminated initials and borders. Our example is one of these *(pl. 131)* in which Elsner turns the initials 'I(n)' and 'C(um)' into minute pictures of the Circumcision and the Adoration of the Kings. In spite of their size the composition and the colouring are so clear that there is no difficulty in recognizing the subjects. The style is still Gothic in many ways; Elsner belonged more to the fifteenth than to the sixteenth century.

On the front cover of the epistolary Elsner painted the apostle Paul, and inside it the Deposition and Entombment *(pl. 144)*. The composition is clearly inspired by Dürer's Great Passion, but the details are original, not only of the landscape, but of the garments, attitudes and facial expressions. The anguished face of the Mother of God, who has taken her son's hand, and the head of John are quite different from Dürer's. Elsner has also composed an original frame incorporating the arms of the elector and a host of angels holding the various sacred articles connected with the Passion and the Crucifixion. The medallions in the corners hold four of the Church Fathers. This striking picture has unfortunately suffered some deterioration in the bottom left-hand corner.

Manuscript illumination made one last attempt to defend itself against the advance of the woodcut by the painting of series of woodcuts that appeared in books. A beautiful example of this is the Dresden copy of Dürer's Life of the Virgin, printed in Nuremberg in 1511. It is very possible that the painting was done in Dürer's own studio. The tenth woodcut in the series represents the Adoration of the Shepherds *(pl.145)*. Dürer's monogram AD can be seen on a slab of stone in the centre foreground. In addition to the colouring of the woodcut the page is decorated with an original border, with foliage and flowers on three sides and a bear-baiting scene at the bottom. This has no connection with the Nativity, of course, but may have been included at the wish of the unknown person who had the copy coloured. This combination of the ancient techniques of illumination and the new ones of the woodcut is extremely successful; this book can hold its own with the finest mediaeval manuscripts.

An heraldic book of the burgraves of Nuremberg was probably also produced in the city in the first half of the sixteenth century. It opens with a full-page portrait of Count Godefridus zu Lambogen *(pl.142)*. He is dressed in the costume of his day, bluish armour under a pale blue cloak, a helmet with yellow, red and blue plumes over his greying hair. He holds a staff in his right hand grasps his sword with the left. Beside him on the green floor stands au escutcheon, two black lions on a pale background quartered with a device in red and yellow. A blue and yellow cartouche over

his head gives his name and titles. It is a formal portrait; the manuscript, now in Halle, is an extremely valuable historical source.

To judge by the linguistic evidence, the Weimar *Ingenieurkunst- und Wunderbuch* ('Book of engineering and magic') was also written in the region of Nuremberg. The manuscript is a compilation of a number of parts, begun in 1430 and not completed until 1520 or later. The first ninety-seven leaves contain military and constructional drawings, eighty-one of which are taken from Conrad Keyser's *Bellifortis* of 1405. The rest consists of scenes of everyday life in about 1520, with a strong emphasis on magic and witchcraft. One of the sepia drawings *(pl.143)* shows two fairground magicians at work, leading people by the hand and showing them women's heads in different numbers and positions in mirrors. The people are drawn from all different social classes, including a noblewoman, a nun and a scholar, whose true characters are revealed by their reaction to the 'magic'. The nun is frightened, the scholar astonished and credulous, and the noblewoman engrossed. This drawing is an interesting document of social history: people of all degrees of wealth and education were taken in by conjurors' tricks. The costumes show the fashions of the day. Books about magic were widespread in the Middle Ages, in spite of the Church's disapproval. Magic was a means by which man attempted to overcome the fearful and mysterious forces of nature.

Western Germany

A missal now in Greifswald, which was made in the ecclesiastical province of Bremen, in north-western Germany, has an unusual and attractive Crucifixion *(pl.137)*. The cross stands against a

224

pale sky full of stars, with both sun and moon shining above the cross beam. Christ's loincloth and Mary and John's cloaks all have the same pattern on them. A sword is thrust into Mary's heart as a symbol of her grief. She and John are both thin and strained; John's face is particularly striking in its sorrow. The haloes are ringed with the same lacy pattern as the frame of the whole.

A manuscript from further west contains in its first eleven leaves the statutes of the town of Wesel on the Rhine (pl.154). The text is written in Latin and Low German and decorated with a number of handsome filigree initials. The miniator is concerned to establish the equilibrium of text and ornament that existed in earlier times. He uses script of different sizes and in different colours: the heading, for instance, is red. He takes exactly half the depth of the text for the initial. The left-hand margin is decorated with a design drawn in red ink. The initial is magnificent, coloured red, blue and green on the neutral background of the uncoloured parchment. Flowers and foliage abound within the curves, but the body of the letter itself is decorated sparingly. Using contemporary motifs this manuscript revives older traditions.

Northern Germany

The dukes of Mecklenburg seem to have had a hereditary interest in their own history, ordering the writing of chronicles which closely followed the fortunes of the ruling house. Just as Duke Albert II had commissioned a rhyming chronicle from Ernst von Kirchberg in the fourteenth century (pl.65), Duke Henry V, the Peaceloving (1503–52), ordered a continuation from his counsellor Nicolaus Marschalk, who later became a professor at Rostock. Twenty-one copies of the work have

survived, in addition to the original manuscript at Schwerin and an illuminated copy in Rostock. The Schwerin manuscript is decorated with half-page pictures painted in body-colours. One depicts the miracle of the Holy Blood at Doberan (pl.134). This legend, already recounted in Kirchberg's chronicle, tells of a shepherd who concealed the Sacrament in his crook, with the result that no wolf dared approach his sheep. The illustration shows the peaceful scene of the grazing sheep with the shepherd and his crook. But in the margin we see the villain of the piece, clinging to a pillar and racking his brains as to how to get hold of the crook. He hides it in his house, but blood flows from it, betraying him to the monks and the sheriff. The little genre scene is excellently drawn and coloured. The white sheep in the green and brown countryside beneath the blue sky and white clouds are the epitome of rustic simplicity.

The Schwerin manuscript of Marschalk's chronicle must have been completed before 1513, whereas the Rostock copy was made sixty years later, in 1573. Its frontispiece shows the author presenting the book to Duke Henry (pl.152). Since Marschalk died in 1525 and Henry in 1552, it is doubtful whether there could be any real resemblance, but the figures have been plausibly characterized. Marschalk is shown as an elderly man, wearing a fur-lined academic gown. He has the appearance of an intellectual, a scholar fully competent to perform the task he was given. He stands so close to the horse that it appears to be nuzzling him. The duke is a young man and takes the book with a faraway expression on his face. The gold background with its tapestry pattern has unfortunately deteriorated, but the artistic and historical value of the picture is none the less undeniable.

For our last example of illumination in Meck-lenburg we have yet another history, the ducal genealogy which is now in the *Land* archives in Schwerin. Our illustration *(pl.139)* shows Duke Albert VII, the Handsome, and Anna, daughter of Elector Joachim I of Brandenburg, whom he married in 1524. They are standing in front of a splendid Renaissance building, he in armour, she in the fashionable dress of the 1520s, large feathered hat and brocade dress with puff sleeves. At their feet are their respective coats of arms, Mecklen-burg's crowned black bull with silver horns and Brandenburg's red eagle with golden claws. The captions below give the names and styles of the ducal couple. The picture is interesting for its portrayal of the physiognomy and dress of the early sixteenth century.

Lower Saxony received its name when Maxi-milian I created the Lower Saxon province between Wesel and the Baltic in 1512. We have a breviary from the region with twelve whole-page miniatures. One *(pl.149)* depicts the apocryphal encounter, on the road to Calvary, between Christ and St Veronica, who received an imprint of Christ's face on her kerchief when she wiped his brow with it. In this miniature Christ has fallen beneath the weight of the cross. Veronica kneels beside him, holding up the cloth as if to display the miracle to the onlooker. Her dress is that of a well-to-do German woman of the sixteenth century. There are two rough soldiers behind them, one with his club raised as if to strike. The end of the cross is held by a cowed-looking Simon of Cyrene, 'him they compelled to bear his cross'. In the background the last houses of Jerusalem and the beginning of the country can be seen with John and the two Marys coming through the city gate. Preparations are being made for the Crucifixion on the hill on the right. This im-

pressive scene is enclosed in a yellow frame, with flowers and animals creating an idyllic contrast to the cruelty of men.

Saxony and Thuringia

Manuscript illumination in the monasteries of Saxony and Thuringia reached a final peak in the early years of the sixteenth century. One example from this period is an antiphonary in eight vol-umes, made between 1500 and 1504 for the cathe-dral chapter in Meissen, and now the property of the cathedral chapter in Naumburg. Appalling as it may seem, in the nineteenth century visitors to Naumburg cathedral were allowed to cut out and take away initials as souvenirs, so that the work survives only in part today. One of the finest of the remaining initials is an 'E(cce)' with a picture of St John on Patmos *(pl.136)*. The saint, a noble figure, sits in the foreground writing the book of Revelation. The generous folds of his garments are typical of the sculpture and painting of the time. The whole page is embellished with a superb marginal ornament; the large format of the manuscript (78 × 54 cm.) made it desirable to reproduce only a detail.

The most important scriptorium in Saxony at the beginning of the sixteenth century was the Cistercian monastery of Altzella, near Nossen, under Martin von Lochau, abbot from 1493 to 1522. A page of an Altzella antiphonary has an initial 'A(ngelus)' which contains the figure of the Risen Christ, sitting on the tombstone *(pl.130)*. The artist has accomplished the whole with only four colours: a gold background, a wine-red initial picked out in white, a vermilion cloak and a blue-grey tomb. The initial is not placed at the very top of the page but below three lines of script, which relaxes the formal composition of the page. The border consists solely of tendrils and small flowers in the usual colours, blue, green and red.

Another Altzella antiphonary of 1516 is unusually informative, containing statements that it was written by the monks Johannes de Fribergk and Johannes Helbig and illuminated by Roswinus Andreae for Elisabeth von Temritz, abbess of Sankt Marienstern from 1515 to 1523. In our example *(pl. 135)* the initial 'D(um)' on the lower half of the page encloses St Andrew with his symbol, the cross saltire. The blue letter stands out stylishly against a black background with gold tendrils. The saint stands in front of a pale green wall in a green robe and brown cloak, holding a book in both hands. The pattern in the border is more thickly entwined than in the previous example but is formed of the same elements and colours. These two antiphonaries create a very impressive idea of the style of the Altzella scriptorium in its last years. The monastery was secularized in 1540.

Brother Johannes Helbig copied another missal for Abbess Elisabeth von Temritz in 1522–3. The page we reproduce *(pl. 146)* is typical of its style. The initial 'A(d te)' contains a picture of King David kneeling, while God appears in a cloud above. The contrast between the king's red robe and the dark blue letter is very effective. The text and music are framed by a border which includes the arms of Sankt Marienstern, a star, supported by two *putti*. This is a Renaissance element which has managed to penetrate the monastery walls in spite of its secular nature, while the rest of the border is in the Gothic tradition. The composition of the page is superb.

The second volume of this missal was not completed until 1529 and was presented to Elisabeth's successor, Abbess Margarete von Metzecraden. The beginning of the Mass for the Dead is impressively decorated *(pl. 140)*. The initial 'R(e quiem)' is in a typical Renaissance style, with its vase and mask ornaments. A comparison of this 'R' with the 'A' from the first volume *(pl. 146)* serves to demonstrate the transition from Gothic to Renaissance ornaments. The miniator has devised a striking image of the power of death. A monk lies dying on the ground, the inevitability of his death illustrated by the skeleton on the bier above him. The angle focuses attention on it: the monk cannot escape and is in need of the mass which starts on the right of the initial. The theme of death is underlined by the three skulls in the border, in the place of a coat of arms, but does not concern the two *putti* playing on the left-hand side. Such contradictions were common, even in a religious book. The composition of the page matches that of the first volume.

Luther's translation of the Bible had several predecessors in the fifteenth century. The first printed German bible appeared in Strasbourg in 1466, and went into seventeen editions. Manuscript copies were also made, such as a codex now in Weimar, decorated with coloured drawings. One of these depicts Salome with the head of John the Baptist *(pl. 148)*. Salome is wearing the dress of a German noblewoman of the early sixteenth century, with the usual rich folds, and a fashionable headdress. She stands to the left of centre with a tree behind her, and symmetrically balanced on the right by the figure of the headsman in front of a building. The emphasis builds up from the sides and centres on the head of John the Baptist. The presentation is naturalistic and clear.

The Reformation had meanwhile been gaining ground. In 1543 the Cranach studio in Wittenberg produced a pictorial summary of Protestant dogma. Three versions of it are known to us, and it also occurs as a miniature on the cover of the John Frederick bible, in the library of Jena university *(pl.157)*. It is divided down the middle by the Tree of Life, which is withered on the left and green on the right. Scenes of contrasting significance from the Old and New Testaments are placed in the two halves. On the left, Adam and Eve stand under the Tree of Knowledge in the background. In the front Adam, as naked humanity, is pursued by death and driven into hell. At the foot of the Tree of Life, Moses is explaining this with the tables of the law to the Elector John Frederick the Steadfast. God the Father appears as judge in the heavens above. On the right-hand side mankind is led to the cross of Christ by John the Baptist. The Risen Christ stands on a skeleton as a sign of his victory over death. In the background we see the path taken by Redemption: the serpent on the cross in the desert and the Annunciation, where the Christ Child appears to Mary bearing the cross. This interesting picture is an attempt to express the basic tenets of the new faith in an artistic form. Mankind stands between the law and the gospel of salvation. The law condemns to death and hell. Christ means redemption and life. Only a great artist like the younger Cranach could have achieved this illustration of Christian dogma in pictorial terms. Explanatory verses from the Old and New Testaments are set above and below the picture.

Finally we have some examples of secular illumination in the sixteenth century. A register of the property of an Erfurt patrician family, that of Von der Margariten und Lewenburg, has an ornate frontispiece *(pl.141)*. The border consists of the coats of arms of eight related families, linked by decorative tendrils. In the centre is a picture of Herebord von der Margariten in full armour and his wife in the dress of the 1520s. They are holding up their own coat of arms. A picture like this is of great value to genealogists.

In the many new universities it became the custom for a new rector to sign his name on a fresh page in the university's matriculation book *(matricula)* and then to have it illuminated with a design composed partly of the rector's family arms or crest, partly of religious genre scenes and partly of initials and a border. The following pages contained the names of all the students who matriculated during his tenure of office. The *matriculae* of the university of Erfurt, founded in 1392, have been preserved and we reproduce a page from the second volume, which bears a watercolour painting of St Jerome and his lion *(pl.156)*. According to legend, St Jerome was approached one evening, in the monastery at Bethlehem of which he was abbot, by a lion with a thorn in his paw. After Jerome had extracted the thorn, the lion stayed with him and became quite tame. This was a favourite subject of artists, who never failed to include the lion in pictures of St Jerome. This miniature is signed H B 1549 in the bottom left-hand corner, showing it to be the work of a professional artist, who has been identified as Hans Brosamer. The rector was the 283rd of the university, Magister Joannis Ellingerott of Göttingen. His arms and those of his wife are shown at the bottom of the page with a bullfinch between them. This kind of illumination developed further in the albums which were widespread in academic circles in the seventeenth and eighteenth centuries.

We also still have the illuminated *matriculae* of the university of Wittenberg, founded in 1502. In 1532 Ulrich Schilling of Cannstatt was rector. He had his page *(pl.150)* decorated with his canting arms, a golden can, and medallions of Luther, Melanchthon, Jonas and Bugenhagen, who were the four most distinguished teachers in the university at the time. Luther had been professor of Exegesis since 1512. Melanchthon was made professor of Greek in 1518, at the age of twenty-one. Justus Jonas, a faithful friend of Luther's, had been teaching since 1521. Johann Bugenhagen came to Wittenberg as parish priest in 1521 and joined the university staff in 1525. The rector felt grateful and indebted to his colleagues, whose fame reflected on himself. The portraits are ascribed to Lucas Cranach the elder. A rector owed it to the dignity of his office to engage a major artist for the work.

Illumination sometimes also found a place in a less rarefied world. A Dresden manuscript is given over to ideas for decorated sledges for processions and parties. The artist not only painted horses with all shapes and sizes of sledges, but also mythological beings and Christian heroes, such as Neptune with his trident, Diana on a hart and St George killing the dragon (pl.159). While the driver, elegant in black court dress, struggles to control the rearing horse, St George plunges his lance into the dragon's jaws. The pictures are painted in body-colours. The ground is grey, the sledge red and blue, the white horse wears blue and yellow harness. The saint wears blue armour and a red cloak. The dragon is blue and yellow.

NOTES ON THE PLATES

Bibliographical references are given here in an abbreviated form. Full titles and descriptions will be found in the Bibliography.

Plate 1

Berlin, Deutsche Staatsbibliothek. Ms. theol. lat. fol. 485. Quedlinburg Itala fragments. Central Italy, after 400. Parchment. 6 leaves. 30·5 cm. × 27·5 cm. Fol. 2 r.: Illustrations to 1 Samuel 15.

The leaf reproduced illustrates four scenes: (1) 1 Samuel 15 : 12–15. Samuel comes to Saul, to bring him God's commands. (2) 1 Samuel 15 : 27. Saul attempts to seize Samuel by the cloak, as the prophet leaves him. (3) 1 Samuel 15 : 30–2. Agag, king of the Amalekites, is brought to Samuel as he and Saul are praying. (4) 1 Samuel 15 : 33. Samuel slays Agag.

In 1865 the Magdeburg archivist Von Mülverstedt discovered leaves 3 and 4 of the Itala fragments in the binding of an account book of the Quedlinburg monastery, bound in 1618 by Asmus Reutel. Leaves 1 and 2 were discovered in 1869 by Burgomaster Brecht, in the binding of a Quedlinburg police edict of 1624. A fifth leaf came to light in 1887 and a sixth later. They at once aroused the attention of scholars all over the world and were acquired for the royal library in Berlin in 1875–6, in exchange for a collection of seals. The manuscript came, via Sankt Gallen, into the possession of Emperor Otto I, who gave it to the monastery of Quedlinburg. In their important work on the fragments, Degering and Boeckler advanced the theory that the manuscript originated from the same scriptorium as the Vatican Vergil (Vat. lat. 3225), in Rome, in about 380. De Wit draws other conclusions. He leaves the question of place of origin open and dates the

Vergil in about 420. The script is the most obvious difference between the two manuscripts. The Itala, like all Christian literature, is written in uncials, while the Vergil is in *capitalis rustica*. Kirchner and Lowe use palaeographic criteria to date the Itala in the first half of the fifth century. The style of the miniatures in the two manuscripts is also different. Nevertheless both emanate from somewhere in central Italy at about the same date.

Degering, Hermann: *Katalog...*, p. 3.
Degering, Hermann and Albert Boeckler: *Die Quedlinburger Itala-Fragmente.*
Kirchner, Joachim: *Scriptura latina...*, p. 14, pl. 6a.
Lowe, E. A.: *Codices latini antiquiores...* Pt. 8, p. 15.
Lülfing, Hans: *Die Handschriftenabteilung...* pp. 349, 379, pl. 4.
Schöne Handschriften... pp. 13–5.
Schulze, Victor: *Die Quedlinburger Itala-Miniaturen...*
Wit, J. de: *Die Miniaturen des Virgilius Vaticanus...*

Plate 2

Gotha, Landesbibliothek. Ms. I. 75. Foll. 106v–122v. Canones apostolorum. North-east Frankish, c. 725. Parchment. 17 leaves. 24 cm. × 16 cm. Fol. 106v.: Initial 'Q(uam)'.

According to an entry by Peter of Andlau on fol. 70, this manuscript was in the Benedictine monastery at Murbach in Alsace in the fifteenth century. It was bought by Duke Ernest II of

Gotha from J.B.Maugérard, a former Benedic‑
tine monk and expert on manuscripts and in‑
cunabula. He forsook his vows in 1802 and
became *commissaire du gouvernement pour objets de
sciences et arts.* In this capacity he was responsible
for transferring the libraries of monasteries and
churches to the Bibliothèque Nationale in Paris,
but he also bought and sold on his own account;
Duke Ernest was one of his best customers.

Jacobs, Friedrich and F.A.Uckert: *Beiträge...*,
   vol.2, pp.123–40.
Lowe, E.A.: *Codices latini antiquiores...*, part 8,
   p.52.
Zimmermann, E.Heinrich: *Vorkarolingische Mi‑
   niaturen...*, pp.79f., 214f., pl.129d, e; 130d,e.

Plate 3

*Merseburg, Domstiftsbibliothek. Ms. I. 83. Bible
fragment: Isaiah and Jeremiah. Region of Chur? Late
eighth century. Parchment. 213 leaves. 26 cm. × 17·5 cm.
Fol.61 v.: Christ as the Suffering Servant.*

All that is known of the history of this manuscript
is that it came to Merseburg by the fifteenth cen‑
tury at the latest, proved by an entry on fol.1 r.

Lowe, E.A.: *Codices latini antiquiores...* Pt.9, p.2.

Plate 4

*Berlin, Deutsche Staatsbibliothek. Hamilton 553. Psal‑
terium Salabergae. Northumberland, mid‑eighth century.
Parchment. 64 leaves. 34·3 cm. × 24·4 cm. Fol.2 r.:
Illuminated page with initial 'B(eatus vir)'.*

The text is written in Anglo‑Saxon majuscules by
various hands. When the manuscript left the con‑

234

vent of Saint‑Jean in Laon and when it came into
the possession of the Dukes of Hamilton is not
known. It was bought by the government of
Prussia for the royal library Berlin in 1882, as
part of the Hamilton collection.

Degering, Hermann: *Katalog...*, p.4
Karl der Grosse, Werk und Wirkung..., p.238, no.394.
Lowe, E.A.: *Codices Latini antiquiores...*, Pt.8,
   p.8.

Lülfing, Hans: *Die Handschriftenabteilung...*, p.342,
   pl.2.
Seidlitz, W. von: *Die illustrierten Handschriften...*,
   p.256f.
Zimmermann, E. Heinrich: *Vorkarolingische Mi‑
   niaturen...*, pp.119f., 272f., pls.249, 250.

Plate 5

*Berlin, Deutsche Staatsbibliothek. Phill. 1676. Ser‑
mones legendi in festivitatibus ecclesiae, homilarium
Alani. So‑called Egino Codex. Verona, 796–9.
Parchment. 309 leaves. 39·3 cm. × 30·6 cm. Fol.24 r.:
St Ambrose.*

The manuscript is written in Carolingian minus‑
cule. An entry on fol.23 b states that it was written
under Bishop Egino between 796 and 799 for the
cathedral library in Verona. It was still there under
Bishop Ratherius (d. 974) but was then sent,
probably by Bishop Deodericus (d. 984), to the
monastery of St Vincent in Metz, from whence it
came to the Jesuit college at Clermont. After the
dissolution of the Jesuit order in France in 1763,
the Dutch lawyer and statesman Gerard Meerman
bought the manuscript collection at Clermont.
The Meerman collection was put up for auction
in 1824 and bought by Sir Thomas Phillipps,

from whom it was acquired by the Prussian Ministry of Culture for the royal library in Berlin in 1889.

Degering, Hermann: *Katalog...*, p. 5
Karl der Grosse, Werk und Wirkung..., p. 282, no. 459
Kirchner, Joachim: *Die Heimat des Eginocodex.*
Kirchner, Joachim: *Beschreibendes Verzeichnis...*, pp. 6–9.
Lowe, E. A.: *Codices latini antiquiores... Pt. 8. p. 11.*
Lülfing, Hans: *Die Handschriftenabteilung...*, pp. 344–8.
Rose, Valentin: *Verzeichnis der lateinischen Handschriften...*, 1 (1893), pp. 77–95.
Vom Advent zum Advent, 1963–4. 1–7 December.

Plate 6

Gotha, Landesbibliothek. Ms. I. 18. Quatuor evangelia. Anglo-Saxon, eighth century. Parchment. 232 leaves. 31·5 cm. × 26 cm. Fol. 126 r.: Beginning of the argument to St Luke's Gospel, 'Quoniam quidem'.

The manuscript evidently comes from an Anglo-Saxon scriptorium of the very highest standards. It was bought at some date between 1795 and 1802 by Duke Ernest II from the Parisian dealer Maugérard.

Jacobs, Friedrich, and F. A. Uckert: *Beiträge...*, vol. 2, p. 34 f.
Lowe, E. A.: *Codices latini antiquiores...*, Pt. 8, p. 51.

Plate 7

Merseburg, Domstiftsbibliothek. Ms. I. 9. Gospel book with praefatio and argumentum. Anglo-Frankish school, first half of ninth century. Parchment. 166 leaves. 33 cm. × 26 cm. Fol. 63 v.: Argument to St Luke's Gospel with initial 'L(ucas)'.

The text is written in Carolingian minuscule. Nothing is known of the provenance or history of the manuscript, which is published here for the first time.

Plate 8

Halberstadt, Dommuseum. Ms. 46. Gospel book. Anglo-Frankish school, ninth century. Parchment. 163 leaves. 29 cm. × 21 cm. Fol. 58 r.: Beginning of St Mark's Gospel with initial 'I(nitium)'.

The manuscript yields no evidence whatever as to the time and place of origin.

Hinz, Paulus: *Gegenwärtige Vergangenheit...*, p. 223.
Schmidt, Gustav: *Die Handschriften...*, 1, p. 22 f.

Plate 9

Weimar, Thüringische Landesbibliothek. Fol. 1. Gospel fragment, with the gospels of Matthew and Mark. School of Sankt Gallen (Mainz?), late ninth century. Parchment. 52 leaves. 35·8 cm. × 27·5 cm. Fol. 9 r.: First canon.

The manuscript is written in Carolingian uncials. It is believed to have entered the possession of the monastery at Tegernsee before 980. Half of it, with the gospels of Luke and John, is in the Bayerische Staatsbibliothek in Munich (Cod. lat. 11019). It is not known how this half reached Weimar.

Ars sacra..., p. 28, no. 60.
Bange, E. F.: *Eine bayerische Malerschule...*, p. 5.
Dobschütz, Ernst von: *Studien...*, pp. 120–2.

Hartmann, Albert: *Deutsche Buchmalerei...*, p.12, no.8.

Merton, Adolf: *Die Buchmalerei...*, pp.90–2, pl.99,1; 100,1; 100a; 100b.

Rothe, Edith: *Das Kirchenjahr...*, pp.117, 154.

Wirtgen, Bernhard: *Die Handschriften...*, p.114f.

Plate 10

Halberstadt, Dommuseum. Ms.59. Priscianus: Latin Grammar. Sankt Gallen, after 900. Parchment. 207 leaves. 32 cm. × 25 cm. Fol.106v. Initial 'T(ermina)'.

There is a similar initial 'T' in a sacramentary still at Sankt Gallen, where it was written about 920 (Cod.342). Comparison of the two manuscripts reveals such a degree of stylistic similarity that the Halberstadt manuscript can certainly be ascribed to Sankt Gallen.

Hinz, Paulus: *Gegenwärtige Vergangenheit...*, p.224.

Merton, Adolf: *Die Buchmalerei...*, pl.47,3, p.281.

Schmidt, Gustav: *Die Handschriften...*, 1, p.25f.

Plate 11

Dresden, Sächsische Landesbibliothek. Ms. A. 63. Quattuor evangelia latine. Carolingian, late ninth century. Parchment. 137 leaves. 27.5 cm. × 20.5 cm. Fol.37v.: St Mark the Evangelist.

This manuscript was severely damaged during the Second World War, and it has proved impossible to restore the colours to their original brilliance.

Bruck, Robert: *Die Malereien...*, pp.6–8, figs.7–8

Falkenstein, Karl: *Beschreibung...*, p.179f.

Katalog der Handschriften..., 1 (1882), p.22.

Rothe, Edith: *Das Kirchenjahr...*, pp.113, 135, 154–6.

Plate 12

Halle, Universitätsbibliothek. 1 Ca/1. (Formerly Quedlinburg, Domgymnasium. Cod.79). Severus Sulpitius: Vita S.Martini. Tours, before 834. Written by Presbyter Adalbaldus. Parchment. 188 leaves. 22.8 cm. × 16.5 cm. Fol.8v: First page of text.

This page is written in capitals and uncials. At the end of the manuscript are the words '*Ego indignus Presbyter Adalbaldus hunc libellum ex iussone Domino meo Fredegiso manu propria scripsi*'.

Eckhard, Tobias: *Codices...*, pp.13–5, no.10.

Köhler, Wilhelm: *Die karolingischen Miniaturen...*, vol.1, pp.45, 91f., 96, 162f., 379, pl.31a–c.

Plate 13

Halle, Universitätsbibliothek. 1 B b/3. (Formerly Quedlinburg, Domgymnasium. Cod.83) Gospel book. Region of Cologne, early tenth century. Parchment. 191 leaves. 32.5 cm. × 23 cm. Fol.145r. Beginning of St John's Gospel with initial 'I(n principio)'.

It is not known how the manuscript came to Quedlinburg.

Eckhard, Tobias: *Codices...*, p.6, no.7.

Ehl, Heinrich: *Die ottonische Kölner Buchmalerei...*, fig.106.

Ehl, Heinrich: *Älteste deutsche Malerei...*, pp.7, 11, pl.9.

Goldschmidt, Adolph: *Die deutsche Buchmalerei...*, 1, p.48, pl.49.

Plate 14

Leipzig, former Stadtbibliothek, now Universitäts-bibliothek. Rep. I. 4°. 57 (Cod.190). Sacramentary fragment. Anglo-Frankish, early tenth century. Parchment. 5 leaves. 30.5 cm. × 22.5 cm. Fol.1v.: Crucifixion.

The inscription in uncials on the background and frame runs as follows: *In cruce Christe tua confige nocentia cuncta. Annuat hoc agnus, munde pro peste peremptus. Fulgida stella maris pro cunctis posca misellis. Et tu iunge preces cum virgine virgo Iohannes.*

Bruck, Robert: *Die Malereien...,* pp.12–4, fig.13, 14.

Gernentz, Hans Joachim: *Religiöse deutsche Dichtung...,* pl.1, p.443f.

Goldschmidt, Adolph: *Die deutsche Buchmalerei...,* I, p.63, pl.84.

Karl der Grosse, Werk und Wirkung..., p.293, no.475.

Merton, Adolf: *Die Buchmalerei...,* pp.83, 88, pl.97, 97a, 97b, 98, no.1.

Naumann, Robert: *Catalogus...,* p.57f.

Naumann, Robert: *Die Malereien...,* pp.2–4.

Porcher, Jean: *L'enluminure française...,* pl.3.

Schmidt, Adolf: *Das Reichenauer Evangelistar...,* pp.33–40.

Vom Advent zum Advent, 1963–4. March 1964.

Plate 15

Berlin, Deutsche Staatsbibliothek. Ms. theol., lat. fol.1. Gospel book from Enger, near Herford, the so-called Codex Wittekindeus. Fulda school, c.975. Parchment. 129 leaves. 39.5 cm. × 29.5 cm. Fol.14v.: St Matthew the Evangelist.

After the treaty of partition between Brandenburg and the principality of Neuburg in 1647 the manuscript was presented by the town of Herford to the electoral library in Berlin. Of the magnificent binding with gold and jewels made in Magdeburg in the mid-eleventh century, only four pieces of ivory remain, carved in Milan in *c.975*. We decided not to reproduce this miniature in colour, since there is an excellent colour reproduction of it in Boeckler's fundamental work on the codex.

Boeckler, Albert: *Der Codex Wittekindeus.*

Goldschmidt, Adolph: *Deutsche Buchmalerei,* vol.1, pp.20, 52f., pl.60.

Reimann, Georg and Horst Büttner: *Mittelalterliche Buchmalerei...,* p.35, pl.7.

Rose, Valentin: *Verzeichnis...,* vol.2, pt.1 (1901), p.42f.

Schöne Handschriften..., pp.35–7.

Vom Advent zum Advent, 1961–2. 16–22 September.

Zimmermann, E.Heinrich: *Die Fuldaer Buchmalerei...,* pp.58–65, figs.24–6, pls.6, 7.

Plate 16

Leipzig, Universitätsbibliothek. Ms.76. Quattuor evangelia latine. North Saxony, early tenth century. Parchment. 224 leaves. 27.8 cm. × 22 cm. Fol.12v: Beginning of St Matthew's Gospel.

The manuscript appears to have been exposed to damp at some time, which has made the purple ground patchy. Nothing is known of its history.

Boeckler, Albert: *Abendländische Miniaturen...,* pp.51, 130.

Bruck, Robert: *Die Malereien...,* pp.1–4, fig.1–3.

Helssig, Rudolf: *Katalog...,* p.77f.

Rothe, Edith: *Das Kirchenjahr...,* pp.11, 71, 145, 150.

Plate 17

Leipzig, former Stadtbibliothek, now Universitäts-bibliothek. Rep. I. 4°. 57a. Single leaf from a gospel book. West Saxony, early tenth century. Parchment. 29·5 cm. × 23·7 cm.: St Luke the Evangelist.

Robert Naumann mentions this leaf in his work on the illuminated manuscripts in the Leipzig Stadtbibliothek of 1855, and it is doubtless thanks to him that it has been preserved. He must have found it in a pile of uncatalogued manuscripts and recognized its value immediately.

Bruck, Robert: *Die Malereien...*, p.5.
Goldschmidt, Adolph: *Die deutsche Buchmalerei...*, I, p.49, pl.52.
Naumann, Robert: *Die Malereien...*, p.1f.

Plate 18

Dessau, Anhaltische Landesbibliothek. Hs. Georg 4. 2°. Gospel book fragment. Bavarian, mid-eleventh century. Parchment. 102 leaves. 36·5 cm. × 27 cm. Fol.18r.: Beginning of St Matthew's Gospel with initial 'L(iber)'.

This manuscript found its way into the private library of the princes of Anhalt by the agency of Provost Georg III of Magdeburg cathedral (1507-53), a friend of Luther and Melanchthon. When the Benedictine monastery at Nienburg, near Bernburg on the Saale, was secularized, he appropriated the library. The manuscript lacks part of St Matthew's Gospel, the end of St Luke's and the beginning of St John's. I am indebted to the late Dr Prokert of Halle for pointing out the resemblance to the Freising Gospels.

Bange, E.F.: *Eine bayerische Malerschule...*, pp.39-44, pl.16, no.38.

Boeckler, Albert: *Abendländische Miniaturen...*, pp.50, 113, pl.42.
Swarzenski, Hanns: *The Anhalt Morgan Gospels...*, p.81.

Plate 19

Merseburg, Domstiftsbibliothek. Ms. I. 129. Calendar and Sacramentary. Sankt Gallen, early eleventh century. Parchment. 221 leaves. 22·5 cm. × 20 cm. Fol.38r.: Illuminated page with Initial 'T(e igitur)' and autograph of Bishop Thietmar.

There is another entry in the hand of Bishop Thietmar in the calendar among necrological entries, so there can be no doubt that the manuscript belonged to him. The manuscript was probably given to the monastery by Emperor Henry II; a contemporary chronicle reports that he gave the church three valuable *plenaria*, one of which would have been this manuscript, since the word *plenarium* means in this context a service-book of any kind. The style indicates that it originated in Sankt Gallen. The article by Rademacher is accompanied by coloured illustrations.

Dümmler, Ernst: *Das alte Merseburger Todten-buch...*, pp.223-64.
Rademacher, Otto: *Über die Merseburger Kalendarien...*, pp.174-8.

Plate 20

Leipzig, former Stadtbibliothek, now Universitäts-bibliothek. Rep. I. 4°. 57 (Cod. 190). Evangelistary. Reichenau, c.970. Parchment. 206 leaves. 30·5 cm. × 22·5 cm. Fol.97r.: Initial 'M(aria)'.

The manuscript is written in Carolingian minuscules and richly bound. The front cover has a Byzantine carved ivory Virgin and Child. The manuscript probably came into the possession of the city of Leipzig after the secularization of the convent of Benedictine nuns on the island of Reichenau in 1757. For a time the library remained where it was, but was removed to Karlsruhe in 1804. The Leipzig Evangelistary belongs, like its sister manuscript the Gero Codex in Darmstadt, to the Eburnant group, which receive their name from the scribe of the Hornbach Sacramentary in Soleure. We owe the grouping of the Reichenau manuscripts by styles to that leading scholar in the field of Western manuscripts, Albert Boeckler.

Boeckler, Albert: *Die Reichenauer Buchmalerei...*, p. 16.
Bruck, Robert: *Die Malereien...*, pp. 10–2, fig. 11.
Naumann, Robert: *Catalogus...*, p. 57 f.
Naumann, Robert: *Die Malereien...*, pp. 2–4.
Reimann, Georg, and Horst Büttner: *Mittelalterliche Buchmalerei...*, pp. 13 f., 34, pl. 1–5.
Rothe, Edith: *Das Kirchenjahr...*, pp. 17, 73, 77, 145, 150.
Schmidt, Adolf: *Das Reichenauer Evangelistar...*, pp. 22–3.

Plate 21

Berlin, Deutsche Staatsbibliothek. Ms. theol. lat. fol. 2. Sacramentary from the treasury of Minden cathedral. Minden, first half of eleventh century. Parchment. 325 leaves. 29 cm. × 21·5 cm. Fol. 132 v.: The women at the sepulchre.

The Treaty of Westphalia (1648), made the diocese of Minden part of Prussia. Elector Frederick William, anxious to add to his library, was by no means averse to accepting gifts from his new

territories. In 1683 a number of manuscripts were presented by Minden cathedral chapter to the royal library in Berlin, among them this sacramentary. It is rewarding to compare it with Reichenau manuscripts, particularly Henry II's Evangelistary in the Bayerische Staatsbibliothek in Munich (Cod. lat. 4452). The Ottonian emperors, who commissioned some splendid manuscripts from Reichenau, made sure that monasteries in Saxony received good models.

Degering, Hermann: *Katalog...*, p. 8.
Gernentz, Hans Joachim: *Religiöse deutsche Dichtung...*, pl. 3–5, pp. 444–6.
Leidinger, Georg: *Das Perikopenbuch Kaiser Heinrichs II.*
Lülfing, Hans: *Die Handschriftenabteilung...*, p. 321, pl. 1.
Rose, Valentin: *Verzeichnis...*, vol. 2, pt. 2 (1903), pp. 676–9.
Schöne Handschriften..., pp. 44–6.
Vöge, Wilhelm: *Die Mindener Bilderhandschriftengruppe*, pp. 198–213.
Vom Advent zum Advent, 1961–2, 22–4 April.

Plate 22

Leipzig, former Stadtbibliothek, now Universitätsbibliothek. Rep. I. 4°. 58a (Cod. 165). Bedae Venerabilis historiae ecclesiasticae gentis Anglorum libri 5. Cologne, before 1149. Parchment. 170 leaves. 26 cm. × 18 cm. Fol. 1 v.: Christ in majesty, surrounded by the symbols of the evangelists. 19·3 × 14 cm.

There is the following entry on fol. 1 v: *liber sanctorum martini et eliphi in colonia.* Archbishop Bruno of Cologne, the brother of Emperor Otto I, had the remains of Eliphius, who was beheaded in 350, placed in the abbey of Sankt Martin in

Cologne. Moreover a dedicatory picture on fol. 11 depicts the church of Gross-Sankt-Martin, so the Cologne origin is beyond doubt. This church was rebuilt between 1149 and 1172; the picture is of the older building, which enables us to date the manuscript before 1149.

Bruck, Robert: *Die Malereien...*, pp. 43–5, figs. 36, 37.
Gernentz, Hans Joachim: *Religiöse deutsche Dichtung...*, pl. 6, p. 446f.
Naumann, Robert: *Catalogus...*, p. 49f.
Naumann, Robert: *Die Malereien...*, pp. 4–6.
Vom Advent zum Advent, Nov.–Dec. 1955.

Plate 23

Jena, Universitätsbibliothek. Ms. Bos. q. 6. Otto von Freising's universal chronicle and annals of Marbach. Schäftlarn, 115777. Parchment. 151 leaves. 24·5 cm. × 16·5 cm. Fol. 10 r.: Adam and Eve; Noah.

The manuscript must have been made shortly before 1177 in the diocese of Freising, probably in the monastery at Schäftlarn, and by the thirteenth century it was in Alsace. The eighth book and the Marbach annals were added later. The captions on this page read: (for the creation of Eve) *Ecce patres primi producti plasmate limi;* (for the expulsion) *Post epulas mortis pelluntur dulcibus ortis;* (for the flood) *Sors fuitat rerum, cadet orbis in orbe dierum. Primo furem unda necat igne ruina secunda.*

Goethe, Johann Wolfgang von: *Chronik...*, pp. 301–5.
Kappner, Hermann: *Die Geschichtswissenschaft...*, p. 92.
Lehfeld, P.: *Bau- und Kunstdenkmäler...*, p. 140.
Otto, Bischof von Freising: *Chronik...*, (1960), p. lxix f., pl. 1–14.

Scheidig, Walter: *Der Miniaturenzyklus...*, pp. 6–9, pl. 1.

Plate 24

Leipzig, Universitätsbibliothek. Ms. 774. Psalterium. Soignies, Hainault, second half of eleventh century. Parchment. 132 leaves. 27 cm. × 19 cm. Fol. 31 v.: Initial 'B(eatus vir)'.

The manuscript comes from the Cistercian monastery of Altzella, near Nossen in Saxony, which was founded in 1162 and occupied in 1175 by monks from Schulpforta and Walkenried. Altzella was the first Cistercian monastery in the territory of Meissen. After secularization in 1540, Duke Maurice of Saxony ordered a major part of the library to be transferred to the library of Leipzig university. The Cistercians appear to have had no scriptoria of their own in the twelfth century. Only in 1301 did the General Chapter of the order decree that the monks should devote themselves to learning, which included writing. Cistercian monks took degrees at Erfurt and Leipzig universities in the fifteenth century. We know that there was an important scriptorium at Altzella itself in the fifteenth and sixteenth centuries.

Beyer, Eduard: *Das Cistercienser-Stift...*
Bruck, Robert: *Die Malereien...*, pp. 19–32, figs. 20–28.
Kloster Altzella..., pp. 44–52.
Schott, Max: *Zwei Lütticher Sacramentare...*, pp. 52–4.
Springer, Anton: *Die Psalterillustration...*, p. 208f.

Plate 25

Gotha, Landesbibliothek. Ms. I. 70. Leaves 98v–149r.

Liber florum epytaphii sacrorum [by Abbot Theofrid of Echternach]. Echternach, c.1100. Parchment. 149 leaves. 27·5 cm. × 18·5 cm. Fol.58v.: Abbot Theofrid with a bowl of flowers in his hand, standing before his 'Flora'. 20 cm × 13·3 cm.

The abbey at Echternach, in the Habsburg lands, was not dissolved until 1794, after it fell into the hands of the French. Most of the manuscripts made their way to Paris and some were sold privately by Maugérard to, among others, Duke Ernest II of Gotha. In its time the Echternach scriptorium produced some very fine manuscripts, which are to be found today in the Escorial, in Brussels, Bremen, Nuremberg and elsewhere. The inscription in the book in this miniature runs: *Extruo pyramides. Cyboria coligo flores.*

Jacobs, Friedrich, and F.A.Uckert: *Beiträge...*, vol.2, pp.345–9.
Swarzenski, Hanns: *Vorgotische Miniaturen...*, pp.23, 94.
Vöge, Wilhelm: *Eine deutsche Malerschule...*, p.382.

Plate 26

Leipzig, Universitätsbibliothek. Ms.319. Gregorius: Homilia in Ezechielem, liber 1, 2. Thuringia-Meissen, late twelfth century. Parchment. 181 leaves. 34 cm. × 24 cm. Fol.2v.: Pope Gregory dictating to a priest.

On fol. 3r and 3v is the inscription: *Liber celle s(an)c(t)e Marie*, and on foll.93v, 94r and 181r: *Liber veteris celle sancte Marie*. The manuscript is entered in the *Index bibliothecae* of the monastery of Altzella under G 16.

Bruck, Robert: *Die Malereien...*, p.56, fig.44.
Helssig, Rudolf: *Katalog...*, p.454.

Plate 27

Halberstadt, Dommuseum. Ms.1. Bible from the Augustinian monastery in Hamersleben. Halberstadt, c.1170. Parchment. 281 leaves. 52·5 cm. × 36 cm. Fol.1r.: St Pancras.

At the bottom of the picture is the inscription *Liber monasterii b(ea)ti pancratii m(ar)t(yr)is in hamersleve Halberstad(ensi)s dyoces(is)*. It is doubtful whether the Hamersleben monastery had its own scriptorium in the twelfth century. The manuscript was probably executed in one of the Halberstadt scriptoria.

Hinz, Paulus: *Gegenwärtige Vergangenheit...*, p.225.
Jacobus de Voragine: *Legenda aurea...*, p.423f.
Meyer, Erich: *Das Dommuseum...*, p.29.
Schmidt, Gustav.: *Die Handschriften...*, I, p.8f.

Plate 28

Leipzig, Universitätsbibliothek. Ms.198. Origenes: Homiliae in the Latin translation of Rufinus. Pegau, late twelfth century. 239 leaves. Parchment. 41 cm. × 28·5 cm. Fol.1v.: Illuminated page with the seven days of Creation.

At the foot of fol.2r is the entry: *Liber monasterii sancti Jacobi apostoli in Pegaw*. It can safely be assumed that this Benedictine monastery had its own scriptorium. After secularization the entire library was transferred to the university of Leipzig.

Bruck, Robert: *Die Malereien...*, p.74.
Helssig, Rudolf: *Katalog...*, pp.277–9.
Schlesinger, Walter: *Kirchengeschichte Sachsens...*, vol.2, pp.184–9.
Schmidt, Ludwig: *Beiträge...*, pp.13–24.

Plate 29

Halberstadt, Dommuseum. Ms.132. Lectionary of Canon Marcwardus (d. 1148). Halberstadt, second quarter of twelfth century. Parchment. 231 leaves. 29 cm. × 18·5 cm. Fol.8v.: Christ in a mandorla with Peter, Paul and the symbols of the evangelists.

The manuscript was formerly the property of the cathedral school at Halberstadt, where all manuscripts which were not needed for services were transferred after the Reformation. It was thanks to the superintendent of the school that they survived the heavy air raid of 1945.

Hinz, Paulus: *Gegenwärtige Vergangenheit...*, p.224f.
Schmidt, Gustav: *Die Handschriften...*, 2, p.7f.
Vom Advent zum Advent, 1960–1. 27 Nov.–3 Dec.

Plate 30

Leipzig, Universitätsbibliothek. Ms.92. Pauline Epistles with collectanea of Petrus Lombardus. Posa, near Zeitz? c.1200. Parchment. 224 leaves. 32 cm. × 21 cm. Fol.1v.: Initial 'P(rincipia) verum requirenda sunt'.

The manuscript was given to the monastery of Altzella by Hermann, dean of Meissen. The inscription reads: *Liber Celle sancte Marie quem contulit ei Hermannus Decanus Misnensis.* The codex is in the Altzella *Index* under D 16.

Beyer, Eduard: *Das Cistercienser-Stift...*, p.118, note 11, p.121.
Bruck, Robert: *Die Malereien...*, p.84f., figs 69, 70.
Helssig, Rudolf: *Katalog...*, pp.96–8.
Schmidt, Ludwig: *Beiträge...*, p.210.

Plate 31

Jena, Universitätsbibliothek. Ms. El. fol.12. Bible from the Premonstratensian monastery at Mildenfurt. Posa, c.1210. Parchment. 214 leaves. 45·5 cm. × 32 cm. Fol. 28r.: Beginning of Exodus with initial 'H(ec sunt nomina)'.

The Premonstratensian monastery at Mildenfurt near Weida in Thuringia was founded in 1193 and belonged, like Posa, to the diocese of Naumburg. It is not likely that it already had a scriptorium of its own within twenty years of its foundation. It is, however, probable that monasteries circulated their work to others in the same diocese. The bible's ownership is confirmed by the following inscription on fol.1r: *Liber s(an)c(t)e Marie virgine in mildēforde. hic continet Pentateuch...* The second part of the bible (Elect. fol.14) contains a copy of a letter from Pope Innocent III *ad Archiepiscopes et episcopes prope Magdeburgum constitutos datae... 1213.* The manuscript must therefore have been written earlier, about 1210.

Dobschütz, Ernst von: *Studien...*, p.132.
Mylius: *Memorabilia...*, pp.311–3.

Plate 32

Schulpforta, Heimoberschule. Ms. A. 10. Augustinus de civitate Dei. Benedictine monastery of Posa, near Zeitz, c.1180. Parchment. 289 leaves. 36 cm. × 24 cm. Fol.3r.: Cities of the world.

Some lines in the leonine metre on the flyleaf tell us about the scribe of this manuscript: *Hec Erkenbertus spe firmus et hoc ope certus | Stella Maria maris tibi uouit, que tuearis | Qui tibi tollit ea, fur raptor hic est anathema | Et ni reddat ea, dampnetur sorte suprema | Et pater Azzo bonus in uota fauendo patronus |*

Dignus mercede requiescat perpete sede. Amen. Erken/bert is mentioned in records between 1168 and 1185, first as *frater*, then as *sacerdos*, in 1182 as *Buzavgiensis abbas*, and in 1185 as *presbyter*. Why he retired after such a short time as abbot, we do not know. He may have found he could better pursue learning and work in the scriptorium as a presbyter. Abbots changed frequently at this time, which suggests that the monastery was going through a period of crisis. At all events Erken/bertus seems to have been the leading spirit in the scriptorium, which continued to flourish after 1200, supplying books to religious establishments near and far.

Bergner, Heinrich: *Beschreibende Darstellung...*, pp. 170–80.
Böhme, Paul: *Nachrichten...*, pp. 170–8.
Laborde, A.: *Les manuscrits...*, vol. I, pp. 218–25.
Pahnke, Robert: *Schulpforta*, 1956.
Rosenfeld, Felix: *Urkundenbuch...*, pp. 198, 248, 287, 294.
Schlesinger, Walter: *Kirchengeschichte Sachsens...*, vol. 2, pp. 197–200.
Vom Advent zum Advent, 1963–4. 28 June–4 July.

Plate 33

Leipzig, Universitätsbibliothek. Ms. 374. Bernhardus Clarevallensis: Sermones super cantica canticorum. Pegau, late twelfth century. Parchment. 166 leaves. 32 cm. × 22 cm. Fol. 2 r.: Christ in a mandorla; Youth, bride and Solomon.

The following inscription appears on fol. 2v: *P(er)tinet mo(naster)y(um) pegauen.* The manu/script bears a stylistic resemblance to the manu/script A 94 of the Dresden Landesbibliothek, which is now unfortunately lost. (Cf. Bruck, fig. 34, p. 41.) Haseloff ascribed this manuscript to Halberstadt, but it is more likely that it originated in the Benedictine monastery in Pegau.

Bruck, Robert: *Die Malereien...*, pp. 47–53, figs 38–41.
Helssig, Rudolf: *Katalog...*, p. 564.
Schmidt, Ludwig: *Beiträge...*, pp. 13–24.
Vom Advent zum Advent, 1962–3. Oct.–Nov.

Plate 34

Brandenburg, Domarchiv. No shelf mark. Lectionary fragment. Magdeburg region c. 1245. Parchment. 107 leaves. 31 cm. × 22·5 cm. Fol. 5 v.: Illuminated page with Initials 'H(ec)', 'P(ropter)', 'P(aulus servus)'.

In the *Kunstdenkmälern von Stadt und Dom Branden/burg* this manuscript is referred to as an epistolary. However, as the text includes excerpts from the Song of Solomon, the beginning of St John's Gospel and passages from the writings of St Je/rome, it is better to call it a lectionary. The manuscript retains its original magnificent bind/ing, which portrays Christ with the symbols of the evangelists. The scribe was Rutger, bishop from 1241 to 1249.

800 Jahre Dom zu Brandenburg..., pp. 42, 75.
Die Kunstdenkmäler..., p. 318, pl. 69.

Plate 35

Halberstadt, Dommuseum. Ms. 3. The Halberstadt Bible. Halberstadt, early thirteenth century. Parchment. 254 leaves. 47 cm. × 33 cm. Fol. 6 v.: Initial 'I(n prin/cipio)', with God the Father portrayed as Christ. 14 cm × 12 cm.

The miniator and scribe have drawn deliberate attention to the fact that Genesis opens with the same words, 'In principio', as St John's Gospel. The 'Word' of St John relates to Christ's pre-existence as the creative Logos. The Council of Nicea (325) declared God the Father and Christ to be consubstantial, refuting the Arian heresy.

Hinz, Paulus: *Gegenwärtige Vergangenheit...*, p.225f.
Meyer, Erich: *Das Dommuseum...*, p.29.
Schmidt, Gustav: *Die Handschriften...*, 1, p.9.
Vom Advent zum Advent, 1960–1. 29 Jan.–1 Feb.

Plate 36

Brandenburg, Domarchiv. No shelf mark. The Brandenburg Evangelistary. Region of Magdeburg, early thirteenth century. Parchment. 109 leaves. 33·8 cm. × 24 cm. Fol.34r.: Entry into Jerusalem.

Up to 1945 the codex had a binding whose splendour is now recorded only in a photograph. It portrayed the Crucifixion, in a bejewelled frame.

800 Jahre Dom zu Brandenburg..., pp.41f., 74f., pl.40–2.
Das Brandenburger Evangelistar..., p.39f., pl.16.
Gernentz, Hans Joachim: *Religiöse deutsche Dichtung...*, pl.7, p.447.
Habicht, Curt: *Das Brandenburger Evangelistar...*, pp.424–35.
Die Kunstdenkmäler..., pp.351–4, pl.70–3.
Vom Advent zum Advent, 1957–8. 30 March–2 April.
Weitzmann, Kurt: *Aus den Bibliotheken des Athos...*, pp.81–3.

Plate 37

Jena, Universitätsbibliothek. Ms. El. fol. 3. Single leaf from a martyrology inside the cover of a gospel book. South German, early thirteenth century. Parchment. 26·5 cm. × 22·5 cm. Back cover: Martyrdom of St Lawrence.

The manuscript was the property of Elector Frederick the Wise of Saxony who founded the university of Wittenberg in 1502 and began the formation of a library for the use of the professors and students in 1512. Georg Spalatin was the first librarian. When Elector John Frederick the Magnanimous abdicated in 1547 he took his library with him to his estates in Thuringia, but later gave it to the university of Jena, which he founded in 1558.

Dobschütz, Ernst von: *Studien...*, pp.122–9.
Jacobus de Voragine: *Legenda aurea...*, pp.609–25.
Lehfeld, P.: *Bau- und Kunstdenkmäler...*, p.139.
Mylius, Johann Christoph: *Memorabilia...*, p.306f.
Willkomm, Bernhard: *Die Jenaer Universitätsbibliothek...*, p.3f.

Plate 38

Halberstadt, Dommuseum. Ms. 119. Lectionary. Halberstadt, mid-thirteenth century. Parchment. 205 leaves. 31 cm. × 22 cm. Fol.3r.: Illuminated page with initial 'F(ratres)' showing St Paul. 21 cm. × 10 cm.

The manuscript contains no clues as to the identity of the scribe or the scriptorium.

Hinz, Paulus: *Gegenwärtige Vergangenheit...*, p.228.
Mrusek, Hans-Joachim: *Drei deutsche Dome...*, pp.76, 228.
Schmidt, Gustav: *Die Handschriften...*, 2, p.4.

Plate 39

Leipzig, Universitätsbibliothek. Ms. 305. Gregorius: Moralia, Sermones, Definitiones viciorum et virtutum. Thuringia-Meissen, mid-thirteenth century. Parchment. 154 leaves. 34 cm. × 23.5 cm. Fol. 151 v.: Tree of Virtues.

The entries *Liber celle sancte Marie* and *liber veteris celle sancte Marie* appear on different pages. In this example the scroll held by Christ bears the inscription *Ex me flos floris, ex me decus omne decoris*, while that held by Humility reads *Hac specie florum vernant facta prata polorum*. The branches on the left-hand side of the tree are labelled *fides, temperantia* and *prudentia* and those on the right *spes, fortitudo, justicia*, while the trunk represents *caritas*. These are the seven Cardinal virtues. Each of the heart-shaped flowers bears the name of a virtue also.

Bruck, Robert: *Die Malereien...*, pp. 87–90, figs. 72, 73.
Helssig, Rudolf: *Katalog...*, pp. 434–7.

Plate 40

Sankt Marienstern, convent library. Oct. 6. Psalterium. Northern Thuringia, first half of thirteenth century. Parchment. 208 leaves. 14·5 cm. × 10·5 cm. Fol. 8 v.: Initial 'B(eatus vir)', with King David.

The convent of Sankt Marienstern was founded in 1248 and was a daughter-house of Altzella. Lying between Bautzen and Kamenz, it survived the Reformation since at the time it was in Bohemian territory, under a Catholic ruler. In the Thirty Years War the district was ceded to Saxony, but the convent still enjoyed the protec-

tion of the Austrian emperors, and even survived the upheavals of the Napoleonic wars. Today it is one of the two remaining convents in Saxony. The manuscript contains a *calendarium, psalterium, lectiones, collecta, canticum, Te Deum*, and *Magnificat*. It is published here for the first time.

Schmidt, Eva: *Die Zisterzienserinnenabtei...*

Plate 41

Dresden, Sächsische Landesbibliothek. Ms. A. 126. Calendarium perpetuum. Northern Thuringia, first half of thirteenth century. Parchment. 16 leaves. 23 cm. × 15·5 cm. Fol. 13 v.: Resurrection.

On fol. 10 r there appear in a later hand prayers and mottos which mention the names Nedernbeza, Obernbeza and Gunsrade. Bruck suggests that these may refer to villages in northern Thuringia: Obernbosa and Niedernbosa, to the south-east of Sondershausen, and Günzerode, south-west of Frankenhausen on the Wipper. It is not possible to ascribe the manuscript to a specific scriptorium.

Bruck, Robert: *Die Malereien...*, pp. 61–70, figs 48–54.
Falkenstein, Karl: *Beschreibung...*, p. 195.
Gernentz, Hans Joachim: *Religiöse deutsche Dichtung...*, p. 447f., pls 8, 9.
Katalog der Handschriften..., I (1882), p. 58f.

Plate 42

Halberstadt, Dommuseum. Ms. 114. Missal of Provost Semeko (d. 1245). Halberstadt, 1238–45. Parchment, 429 pp. 32·5 cm. × 22·5 cm. P. 64: Initial 'P(uer)' with Nativity.

Another proof of the Halberstadt origin of the manuscript is that the day on which Bishop Konrad brought numerous relics to Halberstadt *(adventus reliquiarium)* is marked in the calendar as a feast day. On p.6 is the following inscription: *Hunc librum comparavit Magister Johannes Semeko Maior Praepositus ecclesie Halberstadensis.*

Hinz, Paulus: *Gegenwärtige Vergangenheit...*, pp.226–8.
Meyer, Erich: *Das Dommuseum...*, p.29.
Mrusek, Hans-Joachim: *Drei deutsche Dome...*, pp.76, 227.
Schmidt, Gustav: *Die Handschriften...*, 2, p.3.

Plate 43

Sankt Marienthal, convent library. Ms. F.5.: 31. Psalterium. Halberstadt? first half of thirteenth century. Parchment. 190 leaves. 21·5 cm. × 14·8 cm. Fol.10r. Moses and the Burning Bush. 15·6 cm. × 10·7 cm.

The manuscript was previously in Altzella, and was perhaps taken by a monk to a safe place when the monastery was dissolved in 1540. It was not written in Altzella, which did not have its own scriptorium until Cistercians were sent to the Bernardine College in the university of Leipzig in 1411.

Bruck, Robert: *Die Malereien...*, pp.75–84, figs 59–68.
Günther, Fritz: *Ein Besuch...*
Schmidt, Ludwig: *Beiträge...*, pp.201–72.

Plate 44

Sankt Marienthal, convent library. Ms. 15. Martyrologium et regula Sancti Benedicti. Posa, mid-thirteenth

century. *Parchment. 158 leaves. 28·5 cm. × 20 cm. Fol.113r.: Initial 'A(usculta)' with St Benedict.*

Sankt Marienthal was founded in about 1230 and escaped dissolution for the same reasons as Sankt Marienstern, being under imperial protection. The manuscript may have come to Sankt Marienthal via Altzella, though there is no positive evidence of this. Altzella seems to have received many manuscripts from Posa.

Bruck, Robert: *Die Malereien...*, p.86f., fig.71.

Plate 45

Merseburg, Domstiftsbibliothek. Ms. I. 1–3. Merseburg Bible, 3 vols. Benedictine monastery of Posa, near Zeitz, c.1240. Parchment. Vol.1: 239 leaves. 51·5 cm. × 35 cm. Fol.8r.: story of Joseph.

The manuscript may be ascribed to Posa for stylistic reasons.

Burckhardt, Johannes, and Otto Kustermann: *Beschreibende Darstellung...*, p.125.
Deckert, Hermann: *Dom und Schloss...*, pp.65–7.
Doering, Oskar: *Aus Merseburger Handschriften...*
Stange, Alfred: *Beiträge...*, p.328f.
Vom Advent zum Advent, 1961–2. April.

Plate 46

Sankt Marienstern, convent library. Oct. 3. Psalterium. Thuringia-Meissen school, second half of thirteenth century. Parchment. 332 leaves. 12·5 cm. × 8·5 cm. Fol.8v.: Visitation. 9·3 cm. × 6·5 cm.

The manuscript contains no indication of where or when it was written. It came to Sankt Marienstern from Altzella, and is first published here.

Schmidt, Ludwig: *Beiträge...*, 18 (1897), pp. 201–72.

Plate 47

Leipzig, former Stadtbibliothek, now Universitätsbibliothek. Rep. II. 4°. 144a (Cod. 189). Psalterium. Italy? 1330–40. Parchment. 195 leaves. 19 cm. × 13·5 cm. Fol. 1 v.: Annunciation; Visitation; Nativity.

The small initials, decorated in red, also occur in legal manuscripts of the fourteenth century from Bologna. Robert Bruck therefore places this manuscript in Italy. Alfred Stange prefers the idea of a Rhineland origin.

Bruck, Robert: *Die Malereien...*, pp. 101–6, figs 86, 87.
Naumann, Robert: *Catalogus...*, p. 57.
Naumann, Robert: *Die Malereien...*, pp. 6–9.
Stange, Alfred: *Deutsche Malerei der Gotik*, I, p. 67.
Vom Advent zum Advent, 1963–4. Wrapper and Week 19.

Plate 48

Sankt Marienstern, convent library. Fol. 2. Missal. ThuringiaMeissen, c. 1300. Parchment. 191 leaves. 47 cm. × 34 cm. Fol. 13 v.: Initial 'P(uer)' with Nativity.

The actual script is the only evidence the manuscript contains as to its date of origin. The individual letters are already placed very close together. Capital 'I's still lack cross strokes. The 'd' is usually rounded. At the beginning and in the middle of words the long 's' is used; final 's' is short. The shapes of the vowels 'a' and 'e' also

suggest the period around 1300. So far as we know, nothing has hitherto been published about this manuscript, which is reproduced here for the first time.

Plate 49

Sankt Marienstern, convent library. Qu. 1. Breviary without psalter and hymnal. ThuringiaMeissen, c. 1300. Parchment. 133 leaves. 33 cm. × 24 cm. Fol. 41 r.: Resurrection.

Like the psalter and missal *(pls 46, 48)*, this manuscript came to Sankt Marienstern from the senior foundation of Altzella. We know of no published work about it, and it is reproduced here for the first time.

Plate 50

Erfurt, Stadtbibliothek. Cod. Ampl. 2°. 31. Aristoteles: Opera. Northern Italy, second half of thirteenth century. Parchment. 201 leaves. 28 cm. × 19 cm. Fol. 168 v.: Initial 'P(ostquam)' with Aristotle teaching.

The manuscript contains a number of works, the majority of them being Aristotle's. On fol. 101 v is the entry *Huius libri 4 transtulit Magister Girardus Cremonensis de Arabico in Latinum*, which allows the conclusion that the manuscript is Italian in origin. It belongs to the Bibliotheca Amploniana, presented in 1412 by Magister Amplonius Ratinck de Berka (Rheinsberg on the lower Rhine) to the Collegium Amplonianum which he founded. As Karl Christ writes in Milkau's *Handbuch*, 'Amplonius, physician and theologian, was the most important bibliophile of the Middle Ages'. The nucleus of his library consisted of at least 635 manuscripts, augmented during his life-time (1364–1435) by a further 400 volumes. When the university of Erfurt was disbanded in 1816, the Bibliotheca Amploniana fell into oblivion. Only after offers had been made by the town of Rheinsberg and the library of Bonn university did Erfurt city library acquire the valuable collection of manuscripts; by this time forty-five of the codices had decayed beyond hope of repair.

Handbuch der Bibliothekswissenschaft, 3 (1940), pp. 232, 652.
Schum, Wilhelm: *Beschreibendes Verzeichnis...*, p. 25 f.

Plate 51

Zwickau, Ratsschulbibliothek. Ms. I. IV, Bd. 3. Vulgate Fragment in 3 vols. Saxon provincial school, c. 1260–5. Parchment. 148 leaves. 45·8 cm. × 33 cm. Vol. 3, fol. 103 v.: Beginning of the Epistle to the Hebrews with initials 'E(pistola)' and 'M(ultifariam)'.

Comparison with manuscripts from Posa now in Schulpforta reveals a definite stylistic affinity with the Posa school.

Bruck, Robert: *Die Malereien...*, pp. 93–5, figs 76–8.
Kloss, Ernst: *Die schlesische Buchmalerei...*, pp. 4–30.

Plate 52

Dresden, Sächsische Landesbibliothek. Ms. Oc. 50. Revelation in Lorraine dialect. Metz? mid-fourteenth century. Parchment. 59 leaves. 24·5 cm. × 17·5 cm. Fol. 50 r.: Illustrations to Revelation 13: 1–2; 20: 9.

Apart from initials the manuscript contains 72

miniatures of various sizes. It was previously in the library of the Gotha family of Bachov von Echt.

Bruck, Robert: *Die Malereien...*, pp. 144–62, figs 109–115.
Ebert, Friedrich Adolf: *Geschichte...*, p. 310.
Falkenstein, Karl: *Beschreibung...*, p. 419.
Katalog der Handschriften..., 3 (1906), p. 116.
Olschki, Leonardo: *Manuscrits français...*, p. 17, pl. 15.
Stange, Alfred: *Deutsche Malerei der Gotik...*, 1, p. 66.

Plate 53

Weimar, Thüringische Landesbibliothek. Qu. 56. Breviary. Erfurt? fourteenth century. Parchment. 183 leaves. 28·2 cm. × 20·7 cm. Fol. 19 v.: Initials 'H(odie)' and 'V(irgo)', border with the Stem of Jesse.

An inscription on fol. 1 v states that the manuscript came from the Benedictine monastery of Sankt Peter in Erfurt. It is likely that it was also written there. The interpretation of the border is aided by scrolls: *Yesse su(m) ego, David sum ego.*

Theele, Joseph: *Die Handschriften...*, p. 189.

Plate 54

Bautzen, Stadt- und Kreisbibliothek. Ms. fol. 56. Thomas of Stitni: Conversation of a father with his sons, in Czech. Bohemian, late fourteenth century. Parchment and paper. 511 pp. 28 cm. × 19 cm. Fol. 1 r.: Illustration of the title.

The codex is part of the library of the Von Gersdorff-Weichasches Gestift, which was transferred in its entirety to the city library at Bautzen.

248

Günther, K.: *Slawische Handschriften...*, p.333.
Katalog der Ausstellung..., p.107.

octavi. We know of no published work on the manuscript, which is reproduced here for the first time.

Plate 55

Jena, Universitätsbibliothek. Ms. Bos. q.3. Marytrology in the dialect of Thuringia and Upper Saxony. Central Germany, before 1300. Parchment. 113 leaves. 24·5 cm. × 19 cm. Fol.17v.: Voyage of the bishops Germanus and Lupus to Britain.

There is more than one school of thought as to the place of origin of this manuscript. It used to be thought to have been written in the Premonstratensian monastery at Mildenfurt near Neustadt on the Orla. Nowadays it is generally held to have been made in one of the Benedictine monasteries of Thuringia or Upper Saxony. The illustrations are pen and ink drawings, which were coloured later.

Hannemann, Kurt: *Unterweisung...*, coll. 639–50.
Kappner, Hermann: *Die Geschichtswissenschaft...*, p.92.
Neumeister, Ingeborg: *Die Miniaturen...*
Wilhelm, Friedrich: *Das Jenaer Martyrologium...*, pp.68, 103–5.

Plate 56

Erfurt, Domarchiv. Ms. Jus. 2. Liber sextus corpus juris canonici. Bologna, early fourteenth century. Parchment. 110 leaves. 43 cm. × 29 cm. Fol.1r.: Presentation to Pope Boniface VIII.

The manuscript appears to have been written in Bologna for study purposes. It is not known how it got to Erfurt. The heading in red letters reads: *Incipit liber sextus decretalium domini Bonifacii pape*

Plate 57

Berlin, Deutsche Staatsbibliothek. Hamilton 407. Codex of scientific works. Paris? c.1310. Parchment. 283 leaves. 26·5 cm. × 20 cm. Fol.267r.: Deer, cuttlefish and medicinal plants.

Foll.229r–282v of the manuscript contain 428 figures of plants, minerals, animals etc., with their names in French or Latin. This section is based on the first Western treatise on medicines, the *Liber de simplici medicina* of Joannes Platearius (d. 1161). This work remained an authority as late as the early days of printing; Peter Schöffer of Mainz drew on it for his *Herbarius* (1484) and *Gart der Gesundheit* (1485).

Catalogue..., p.67.
Lemm, Siegfried: *Kurzes Verzeichnis...*, p.30f.
Schuster, Julius: *Secreta Salernitana...*, pp.203–37.

Plate 58

Mühlhausen, Stadtarchiv. Ms.60/43. Monaldus: Summa juris canonici. Mühlhausen? second half of fourteenth century. Parchment. Unpaginated. 20·2 cm. × 14·5 cm. First page: Initials 'Q(uoniam)' and 'A(bbas)'.

The manuscript may have been written in the convent of Barefoot Friars in Mühlhausen. The Fransiscans had a college in nearby Erfurt, where the university was founded in 1392, giving the order a firm cultural foothold in Thuringia. The manuscript is reproduced here for the first time.

Lexikon für Theologie..., vol.7, col.266.

Wetzer and Welte: *Kirchenlexikon...*, vol. 8, col. 1767.

Plate 59

Zwickau, Ratsarchiv. No shelf mark. Codex statutorum Zwiccaviensium. Zwickau, 1348. Parchment. 107 leaves. 36·3 cm. × 26·8 cm. Fol. 72v.: Punishment of criminals.

The manuscript was probably written in the Franciscan friary in Zwickau; the order took a keen interest in the study of jurisprudence.

Bruck, Robert: *Die Malereien...*, pp. 169–171, figs 118–21.
Homeyer, G.: *Die deutschen Rechtsbücher...*, pt. 2, p. 280, no. 1245.
Stange, Alfred: *Deutsche Malerei der Gotik*, 1, p. 110.

Plate 60

Weimar, Thüringische Landesbibliothek. Fol. max. 4. Biblia pauperum. Central Germany, c. 1340. Parchment. 10 leaves. 48 cm. × 33 cm. Fol. 7v.: Entombment; Descent into Hell.

The manuscript was previously in the Benedictine monastery of Sankt Peter in Erfurt; linguistically too, it seems to be of Thuringian origin. Each section of the text consists of a caption, usually in leonine hexameters, verses from the prophets, and one passage from each of the Old and New Testaments. This copy has 35 sections; the final picture is of the Last Judgment.

Cornell, Henrik: *Biblia Pauperum...*, p. 89f.
Gabelentz, Hans von der: *Die Biblia pauperum...*
Gernentz, Hans Joachim: *Religiöse deutsche Dichtung...*, p. 448f., pl. 10.

Schmidt, Gerhard: *Die Armenbibeln...*, pp. 39, 70f.
Stange, Alfred: *Deutsche Malerei der Gotik* 1, pp. 83, 85, 90.
Theele, Joseph: *Die Handschriften...*, p. 182.

Plate 61

Weimar, Thüringische Landesbibliothek. Fol. max. 4. Revelation. Central Germany, v. 1340. Parchment. Foll. 11r–22v. 48 cm. × 33 cm. Fol. 17v.: St Michael and the dragon.

Cf. the note on *pl. 60*. This plate illustrates Revelation 12 : 7–9. It is a pen and ink drawing coloured with wash.

Gabelentz, Hans von der: *Die Biblia pauperum...*
Gernentz, Hans Joachim: *Religiöse deutsche Dichtung...*, p. 449, pl. 11.
Vom Advent zum Advent, 1960–1. September.

Plate 62

Leipzig, former Stadtbibliothek, now Universitätsbibliothek. Rep. II. 4°. 143 (Cod. 417.) Historia Alexandri Magni, Macedoniae regis. (Liber de proeliis.) Italian, mid-fourteenth century. Parchment. 115 leaves. 22 cm. × 15 cm. Fol. 59v.: Alexander's battle with Porus.

The manuscript's Italian origins are attested by the style of the miniatures, by characteristics of the script, and by some Italian verses at the end.

Bruck, Robert: *Die Malereien...*, pp. 176–200, figs 126–8.
Curtius Rufus, Quintus: *Von den Thaten Alexanders...*, Bk 8, chap. 47–9.
Naumann, Robert: *Catalogus...*, p. 132.
Naumann, Robert: *Die Malereien...*, pp. 33–66.

Plate 63

Leipzig, former Stadtbibliothek, now Universitäts-bibliothek. Rep. V. fol. 20 (Cod. 128). Fragment of a German translation of the Old Testament. German, second half of fourteenth century. Parchment. 215 leaves. 41·5 cm. × 31·5 cm. Fol. 43 v.: Moses gives the Commandments to the Children of Israel.

The fragment goes from Leviticus 6 : 30 to 2 Kings 25 : 27. This leaf is the beginning of the book of Numbers. Although the text is German the open book in front of Moses has a Latin in-scription: *Audi israhel praecepta domini et ea in corde quasi in libro.*

Bruck, Robert: *Die Malereien...*, p. 226 f., fig. 142.
Naumann, Robert: *Catalogus...*, p. 40.
Naumann, Robert: *Die Malereien...*, pp. 9–11.

Plate 64

Berlin, Deutsche Staatsbibliothek. Phill. 1906. Des-moulin, Guyart: Bible historiale. Paris, written by Colin Nouvel 1368. Parchment. 505 leaves. 45 cm. × 31 cm. Fol. 10 v.: The Creation.

The following entry occurs on fol. 501 r: *Colin Nouvel a escript cette bible et fu parfaite an l'a(n) 1368.* Entry no. 832 in the catalogue of Meerman manu-scripts in the Phillipps collection states that the manuscript came from the Collegium Parisiensis Societatis Jesu. Its final leaves consist of documents relating to the Pompadour family between 1490 and 1582, so it must have been in the family's possession during that period. At the end of Revelation are the words: *s'a l'argent* – the work was paid for.

Berger, Samuel: *La bible française...*, pp. 214, 284, 418 f.
Kirchner, Joachim: *Beschreibendes Verzeichnis...*, pp. 77–86.
Lemm, Siegfried: *Kurzes Verzeichnis...*, p. 14.
Olschki, Leonardo: *Manuscrits français...*, p. 35 f., pl. 40.
Schöne Handschriften..., pp. 73–5.

Plate 65

Schwerin, Mecklenburgisches Landeshauptarchiv. Ur-kundenbestand – Fürstenhaus. Ernst von Kirchberg: Mecklenburgische Reimchronik. Mecklenburg, after 1378. Parchment. 224 leaves. 42 cm. × 30·5 cm. Fol. 1 v.: Duke Albert II of Mecklenburg and his son, Albert III, king of Sweden.

On the death of Duke Albert II in 1379, Ernst von Kirchberg had translated 110 chapters of the *Chronica slavorum* of the Holstein priest Helmold into High German verse. He also added 85 further chapters to bring the account of the history of Mecklenburg up to 1337. The chronicle starts in the reign of Charlemagne and is 25,000 lines long. As well as Helmold, the author drew on the Saxon history of the world by Eike von Repkow and chronicles by Arnold von Lübeck, Albert von Stade and Detmar. The Schwerin manu-script is the original, intended for Albert II.

Lisch, G. C. F.: *Ernst von Kirchberg...* (Both articles).
Schirrmacher, Friedrich: *Ernst von Kirchberg...*, (Both articles).
Schröder, Carl: *Mecklenburg...*, p. 2 f.
Stange, Alfred: *Deutsche Malerei der Gotik*, 2, pp. 25 f., 75, 153 f., fig. 192.

Thoms, Heinrich: *Die Mecklenburgische Reim-chronik...*

Plate 66

Leipzig, former Stadtbibliothek, now Universitäts-bibliothek. Rep. I. fol.1 (Cod.70). Livy: Annals, Bks 1–10, 21–40. Northern Italy, c.1350. Parch-ment. 203 leaves. 41·5 cm. × 28·5 cm. Fol.2r.: Building a castle.

Underneath the miniature the pink initial 'F (ac-turusne sim operae pretium)' on a gold ground contains the figure of a man in a green robe with a red, ermine-trimmed collar and cap, with a sheet of paper and pens in front of him. This is probably a self-portrait of the miniator. The arms at the foot of the page are those of the family of Sansimone, which settled in Italy in the thirteenth century. Beside them are the arms of the Gonzaga de Vescovato family with the letters G and V.

Bruck, Robert: *Die Malereien...*, pp.163–8, fig.116.
Naumann, Robert: *Catalogus...*, p.22.
Naumann, Robert: *Die Malereien...*, pp.27–33.

Plate 67

Jena, Universitätsbibliothek. Ms. El. fol. 51c. Decretum Gratiani. Bologna, second half of fourteenth century. Miniator: Niccolò di Giacomo di Nascimbene. Parch-ment. 335 leaves. 47·5 cm. × 30 cm. Fol.101r.: Trial of a bishop. 20 cm. × 19·5 cm.

The manuscript used to belong to the Cistercian monastery of Grünhain in the Erzgebirge, which was founded in 1236 and destroyed by fire during the Reformation. The library was first taken to

Wittenberg and then, on the orders of Elector John Frederick, to Jena. The following entry appears at the beginning: *Hic liber Decreti fuit Magistri Jacobi Molitoris de Grupka, quem testatus est monasterio beate Marie sanctique Nicolai in Grünhayn.*

Ancona, Paolo d': *Dictionnaire...*, p.158f.
Bruck, Robert: *Miniature...*, pp.285–98.
Lehfeld, P.: *Bau- und Kunstdenkmäler...*, p.140.
Mylius, Johann C.: *Memorabilia...*, p. 328f.

Plate 68

Dresden, Sächsische Landesbibliothek. Ms.Oc. 77. Henry Romain: Gestes et faits des anciens. French, late fourteenth century. Parchment. 200 leaves, 35·5 cm. × 27 cm. Fol. 3v.: Foundation of Rome.

The coats of arms in the border are those of the Montmorencys, an old and noble family with lands to the north of Paris, and those of the biblio-phile Jean de Malestroit, Seigneur de Derval et Combourg, whose wife, Hélène de Laval, was a Montmorency. The manuscript later came into the possession of Anne Henriette de Condé and when her library was auctioned in 1725 was bought by Count Brühl, whose library was incorporated in that of the Elector of Saxony in 1768.

Bruck, Robert: *Die Malereien...*, p.297.
Ebert, Friedrich Adolf: *Geschichte...*, pp.325–7.
Falkenstein, Karl: *Beschreibung...*, p.434.
Katalog der Handschriften..., 3 (1906), p.136f.
Olschki, Leonardo: *Manuscrits français...*, p.20, pl.20.

Plate 69

Jena, Universitätsbibliothek. Ms. El. fol.80. Bartholo-maeus Anglicus: De proprietatibus rerum, in the French

translation by Jehan Corbechon. French, c.1400. Parchment. 380 leaves. 42·5 cm. × 31 cm. Fol.9r.: Creation; presentation of the book to Charles V of France.

The manuscript must at one time have belonged to the families of Borselle and Bucham, whose arms appear on the binding. The text on fol.9r is prefaced by the words: *Cy commence le livre des proprietez des choses translates de latin en françois du commendement Charles le quint de son nom par la grace de Dieu roy de france par maistre Jehan corbechon de lordre saint augustin lan de grace MCCCLXXII.* The scribe's name is given on fol.380v: *Escript par Fremin de Reuelle.* He also wrote a psalter for Jean de Berry.

Dexel, Walter: *Untersuchungen...*, pp.24–32.
Lehfeld, P.: *Bau- und Kunstdenkmäler...*, p.144.
Mylius, Johann Christoph: *Memorabilia...*, pp.348–51.
Olschki, Leonardo: *Manuscrits français...*, p.25f., pl.28.

Plate 70

Leipzig, Universitätsbibliothek. Ms.665. Speculum virginum. Thuringia-Meissen, late fourteenth century. Parchment. 165 leaves. 35·5 cm. × 26 cm. Fol.39v.: Tree of wickedness.

Comparison shows the miniator of the *Speculum* to have been influenced a great deal by the miniator of the Landgrave's psalter in Stuttgart (Landesbibliothek, H.B.II.24). The heads and the treatment of the garments show this particularly clearly. After careful consideration of all possible alternatives Karl Löffler was convinced that the psalter originated in the Benedictine monastery of Reinhardsbrunn. Could it be that two important

miniators worked in the same place, 150 years apart?

Bruck, Robert: *Die Malereien...*, pp.233–8, figs 147–151.
Löffler, Karl: *Der Landgrafenpsalter...*

Plate 71

Gotha, Landesbibliothek. Chart. A.594. Hans Vintler: Die Blumen der Tugend. Tyrol, 1411. Paper. 230 leaves. 40 cm. × 28·5 cm. Fol.172v.: Witchcraft.

Only five manuscript copies and one printed edition (Augsburg, 1486) of this work are known. The author gives his name in three separate places, pp.4, 449 and 450. He is mentioned a number of times in contemporary records of between 1407 and 1419. On p.452 the date of authorship is given as 1411. The book is a free version, in rhyme, of the Latin prose work *Flores virtutum* which is cited at the beginning.

Ehrismann, Gustav: *Geschichte...*, vol.2, 2ii, p.638f.
Jacobs, Friedrich, and F.A.Uckert: *Beiträge...*, 2 (1836), pp.327–30.

Plate 72

Weimar, Thüringische Landesbibliothek. Fol.35. Psalter in Latin and Low German. Diocese of Hildesheim? early fifteenth century. Parchment. 191 leaves. 29. cm. × 19.5 cm. Fol.7v.: Initial 'B(eatus vir)' with King David.

The heading, in red ink, is written in German: *Dissen salmē saltu wetē dat ene David dichtede...* ('Know that these psalms were written by one

David'). It seems most likely that the manuscript was written in or near Hildesheim, but there is no definite proof. We know of no work published on it, and it is here reproduced for the first time.

Plate 73

Zittau, Christian-Weise-Bibliothek. Ms. A. I. Vesperal and Matutinal. Bohemian, c.1420. Parchment. 451 leaves. 64·5 cm. × 44·5 cm. Fol.1r.: Initial 'G(aude)' with Annunciation.

The manuscript came to Zittau in 1421, when the chapter of Prague cathedral fled there. The text begins with the Vespers for the first Sunday in Advent.

Beer, Ellen J.: *Initial und Miniatur*..., p.50.
Bruck, Robert: *Die Malereien*..., pp.246–54, figs 155–64.
Stange, Alfred: *Deutsche Malerei der Gotik*, 9, p.127, fig.255.

Plate 74

Leipzig, former Stadtbibliothek, now Universitätsbibliothek. Rep. II. fol. 61 (Cod.129). Psalter in German. German, written by Heinrich Vorster, 1386. Parchment. 96 leaves. 33·5 cm. × 24 cm. Fol.3v.: Initial 'B(eatus vir)'.

At the end of the text are the words: *Sub anno incarnationis domini Mo CC Co octuagesimo sexto in vigilia Assumptionis marie hora vesperarum Completus est istic liber Per manus henrici vorster tytulum etcetera.*

Bruck, Robert: *Die Malereien*..., p.229f.
Naumann, Robert: *Catalogus*..., p.40.
Naumann, Robert: *Die Malereien*..., pp.6–9.

Plate 75

Greifswald, Universitätsbibliothek. Ms.1068. Prayerbook. Dutch, late fourteenth century. Parchment. 212 leaves. 13 cm. × 9·5 cm. Fol.118r.: Illuminated page with initial 'H(ere du salte)'.

The manuscript was previously in a convent in the diocese of Utrecht.

Deutsch, Josef: *Die Handschriften*..., pp.3–6.
Müller, H.: *Verzeichnis*..., p.19.

Plate 76

Gotha, Landesbibliothek. Ms. I. 98. Moralitates Thomae de Anglia super libros metamorphoseos Ovidii. Northern Italy, late fourteenth century. Parchment. 67 leaves. 36·5 cm. × 25·5 cm. Fol.9r.: First page of Ovid's text, with two miniatures and border.

According to Cyprian' *Catalogus* (1714) the manuscript came from the library of a cardinal in Rome. The coat of arms indicates that he was a member of the Fiesco family, which furnished the Church with thirty cardinals and two popes, as well as supplying numerous generals and admirals to the cities of Genoa, Milan and Florence. The actual text of the *Metamorphoses* begins on fol. 9r with the words: *Incipit liber primus metamorphoseos Ovidii fabula prima*, while foll. 1r–8v contain the commentary. This was so popular that it appeared in print in Paris in 1511, published by Jehan Petit.

Cyprian, E.G.: *Catalogus*..., p.18.
Jacobs, Friedrich, and F.A.Uckert: *Beiträge*..., 1 (1835), p.252f.
Roob, Helmut: *Unvollendete Miniaturen*..., pp.174–7.

Stechow, Wolfgang: *Apollo...*, pp.16–18, figs 10 and 11.

Plate 77

Jena, Universitätsbibliothek. Ms. El. fol.86 (formerly 88). Jacobus de Voragine: Legenda aurea, in a French translation by Jean Golein. Paris, early fifteenth century. Parchment. 367 leaves. 38 cm. × 28·5 cm. Fol. 5v.: Frontispiece: the Assumption of Virgin.

The following entry appears on fol.307r: *Festes nouvelles selon l'usage de Paris translates de latin en françois par le maistre en theologie de l'ordre de notre dame du carme.* This refers to Jean Golein, a Carmelite monk, who is frequently mentioned from 1369 on as King Charles V's translator, and who died in 1403. The binding bears the arms of the Bucham and Borselle families.

Dexel, Walter: *Untersuchungen...*, pp.33–9.
Jacobus de Voragine: *Legenda aurea...*, pp.630–58.
Mylius, Johann Christoph: *Memorabilia...*, p.357f.
Olschki, Leonardo: *Manuscrits français...*, p.27f., pl.30.

Plate 78

Gotha, Landesbibliothek. Cod. Chart. A. 777. Speculum humanae salvationis. German, c.1400. Paper. 51 leaves. 31 cm.× 21·5 cm. Fol.35v.: Illustrations to chapter 33: Ascension; Jacob's Ladder.

The text and illustrations of this manuscript correspond to those of the first editions printed by Zainer and Sorg. The prologue is followed by the table of contents, 42 chapters of text and the Sorrows and Joys of Mary, each accompanied by a prayer.

Breitenbach, Edgar: *Speculum...*
Hesse, Ludwig Friedrich: *Über das Speculum...*, pp.199f., 212–9, 255f.
Jacobs, Friedrich, and F.A.Uckert: *Beiträge...*, vol.1, p.159f.
Lutz, J, and P.Perdrizet: *Speculum...*, p.x.

Plate 79

Berlin, Deutsche Staatsbibliothek. Hamilton 675. Thomasin von Zirclaria: Der welsche Gast. Southwest Germany, c.1400. Parchment. 120 leaves. 31·5 cm.× 23 cm. Fol.6r.: Three allegories of the knightly virtues.

The manuscript is written in the Alemannic dialect of Swabia, its place of origin. It is the latest in date of the surviving manuscripts of *Der welsche Gast*, and was at one time in the possession of Maximilian I; his arms, quartered with those of his second wife Bianca Maria Sforza, were inserted at the front of the book.

Catalogue..., p.111.
Ehrismann, Gustav: *Geschichte...*, vol.2, 2ii, pp.308–12.
Oechelhaeuser, Adolf von: *Der Bilderkreis...*, pp.9–11.
Seidlitz, W. von: *Die illustrierten Handschriften...*, 7 (1884), p.305.

Plate 80

Dessau, Anhaltische Landesbibliothek. Hs. Georg 230. 2°. Otto von Passau: Die vierundzwanzig Alten oder der güldene Thron der liebhabenden Seele. Written by Nikolaus von Pirna in Saxon dialect in 1446.

Paper. 213 leaves. 40 cm. × 27.5 cm. Fol. 97v.: The fourteenth elder and the loving soul.

The first bibliophile of the princely house of Anhalt was George I (d. 1474). Unfortunately we do not know what it was that first attracted him to book collecting. He was surpassed by Prince George III, the Blessed (1507–53), the friend of Luther and Melanchthon, who founded the royal library which is now preserved in Dessau as the Georgbibliothek. The name of the scribe and the date are to be found on fol. 212. The manuscript may have been written in the Franciscan convent in Leipzig.

Boeckler, Albert: *Deutsche Buchmalerei der Gotik...*, pl. 40, p. 78.
Haebler, Konrad: *Deutsche Bibliophilen...*
Hosäus, Wilhelm: *Deutsche mittelalterliche Handschriften...*, pp. 211–3.
Matthaei, Kurt: *Altdeutsche Handschriften...*, p. 529.
Schmidt, Wieland: *Das Berliner Exemplar...*, pp. 108–14, figs 10–14.

Plate 81

Dessau, Anhaltische Landesbibliothek. Hs. Georg 2. 2°. Psalter in central German dialect. Saxony, c. 1480. Parchment. 107 leaves. 34 cm. × 22.5 cm. Fol. 1v.: Crucifixion.

At the end the following entry occurs: *Finitus est liber iste per andreā howeman de crossenn.* There are three places called Crossen from which the scribe Andreas Howeman could have come: on the Elster, the Mulde and the Oder. The style of the miniatures is typical of central Germany.

Hosäus, Wilhelm: *Deutsche mittelalterliche Handschriften...*, pp. 215–7.
Matthaei, Kurt: *Altdeutsche Handschriften...*, p. 530.

Plate 82

Zittau, Christian-Weise-Bibliothek, formerly Stadtbibliothek. Ms. A. V. Gradual. Zittau, 1435. Parchment. 321 leaves. 58 cm. × 39 cm. Fol. 15v.: Initial 'P(uer cor mundi)' with Adoration of the Child. 16.5 cm. × 16.3 cm.

The following entry occurs on fol. 177v: *Anno domini MoCCCCoXXXVo completus est liber iste gradualis pro ecclesia prochiali Civitatis Zittauiensis. Et est compa(ra)tus p(er) honorabilem f(rat)rem dominu(m) johan Gotfridi de goltb(er)g tunc temp(or)ibus ibidem Cō me̅ndatore̅ et plebanum Et ideo orate pro eo et pr(o) (o)mn(i)b(us) b(e)n(e)ff(a)c(t)orib(u)s ad d(o)m(i)n(um) ihnn xpm̅...* The parish church of Zittau, for which the gradual was copied, is the Johanniskirche. Johann Gottfried von Goldberg, the priest referred to, was *plebanus* or parish priest from 1418 to 1439 and Commander of the knightly fraternity of St John the Baptist, a branch of the Order of St John of Jerusalem.

Bruck, Robert: *Die Malereien...*, pp. 283–6, figs 185, 186.
Schlesinger, Walter: *Kirchengeschichte...*, vol. 2, p. 348.

Plate 83

Dessau, Anhaltische Landesbibliothek. Ms. Georg 7. 8°. Ex vita Domini de passione eiusdem. Region of Halberstadt? c. 1450. Parchment. Unpaginated. 15 cm. × 11 cm. Deposition.

As well as the Passion, the manuscript contains a life of St Katherine. In style the miniatures bear a certain resemblance to a Halberstadt lectionary (Ms. 115) which Gottschalk Weghener made in 1434 for Johannes von Hoym, bishop of Halber-

stadt. There is no published work on the manuscript and it is reproduced here for the first time.

Plate 84

*Rostock, Universitätsbibliothek. Ms. theol. 25. Bre-
viary. Low Countries, fifteenth century. Parchment.
209 pp. 19 cm.×12·5 cm. P. 142: Resurrection of the
dead.*

Apart from this miniature the manuscript contains an illuminated page with the heading:
Incipiunt septem psalmi poenales. The breviary probably came from the library of Duke Christian
Ludwig of Mecklenburg. Nothing is known to
have been published about it, and it is reproduced
here for the first time.

Plate 85

*Gotha, Landesbibliothek. Ms. II. 137. Breviary.
Flemish, Master of the Privileges of Ghent and Flanders, 1440–60. Parchment. 72 leaves. 18·5 cm.
×12·5 cm. Fol. 10 v.: Raising of Lazarus.
10·3 cm.×6·1 cm.*

We have Friedrich Winkler's important book to
thank for the attribution of this manuscript to a
specific miniator. It contains seven whole-page
miniatures and the same number of decorated
pages. It lacks the customary calendar of feasts and
begins with prayers to the Trinity. The headings
are written in French.

Jacobs, Friedrich and F. A. Uckert: *Beiträge…,*
  2 (1836), p. 364f.
Winkler, Friedrich: *Die flämische Buchmalerei…,*
  pp. 31, 171.

Plate 86

*Leipzig, former Stadtbibliothek, now Universitäts-
bibliothek. Rep. II. 144 c (Cod. 208). Livre d'heures.
French, mid-fifteenth century. Parchment. 78 leaves.
20 cm.×13 cm. Fol. 29 v.: Adoration of the Child.*

The manuscript contains thirteen whole-page
miniatures. The calendar of French saints shows
it to be French, although there is a strong Italian
flavour in the style.

Bruck, Robert: *Die Malereien…,* pp. 309–11,
  fig. 200.
Naumann, Robert: *Catalogus…,* p. 66.
Naumann, Robert: *Die Malereien…,* pp. 12–5.

Plate 87

*Rostock, Universitätsbibliothek. Ms. theol. 22. Bre-
viary. French, second half of fifteenth century.
Parchment. 162 leaves. 20 cm.×11·5 cm. P. 87: Visitation.*

To judge by the habits of the monks depicted in
the manuscript, it was made in a Cistercian monastery. The calendar is written in French and the
choice of saints points to the Loire valley. The
manuscript was previously in the library of Duke
Christian Ludwig of Mecklenburg (1623–92),
who was converted to Catholicism in Paris in
1663 and married, as his second wife, Isabelle-
Angélique de Montmorency-Bouteville. The
consequent connections with the French court and
aristocracy were of profit to his bibliophile interests.
After his death his library went to Mecklenburg
and finally was presented to the university of
Rostock.

Lindner, F.: *Ein französisches Breviarium…,*
  pp. 41–6.

Lindner, F.: *Ein französisches Calendarium...*, pp. 352–71.
Lindner, F.: *Lobgedicht...*, p. 4.

Plate 88

Leipzig, former Stadtbibliothek, now Universitäts-bibliothek. Rep. II. 4°. 144d. Livre d'heures. French, second half of fifteenth century. Parchment. 182 leaves. 17·5 cm.×12·5 cm. Fol. 96v.: King David at prayer.

As the calendar is written in French, it seems certain that the manuscript is French in origin. It is mentioned by neither Naumann nor Bruck, so must have been acquired by the Stadtbibliothek at some date after 1906. Nothing has been published about it and it is reproduced here for the first time.

Plate 89

Dresden, Sächsische Landesbibliothek. Ms. Oc. 54. Petrarch: Des remèdes de l'autre fortune (De Remedis utriusque fortunae), in a French translation by Jehan d'Augin. Paris, mid-fifteenth century. Parchment. 202 leaves. 39 cm.×27·5 cm. Fol. 5r.: Dedication of the book to Charles VII of France.

The miniatures have been attributed to the young Jacques de Besançon, but further study would be necessary to prove the attribution beyond doubt. The text of the dedication runs: *A tres hault et tres puissant pri(n)ce aourne du don a salmon octroye du pere de toute lumiere. Charles par la grace de dieu roy de France... F. daugin indigne chanoine de la sainte chapelle royal a Paris et moins souffisant bachell'z en theologie.* After the *explicit* there is the owner's mark of Jacques d'Armagnac, duc de Nemours (*obit.* 1477); the coat of arms on fol. 15 indicate that the

manuscript then passed to Antoine, Bastard of Burgundy (d. 1504). It is believed, though not by Ebert, to have belonged finally to Anne Henriette de Condé (d. 1723). It was acquired by Goetze for Dresden in 1700.

Bruck, Robert: *Die Malereien...*, pp. 306–8, fig. 198.
Ebert, Friedrich Adolf: *Geschichte...*, p. 311 f.
Falkenstein, Karl: *Beschreibung...*, p. 425 f.
Katalog der Handschriften... 3 (1906), p. 117 f.
Olschki, Leonardo: *Manuscrits français...*, p. 20 f., pl. 21.

Plate 90

Schwerin, Mecklenburgische Landesbibliothek. Ms. 10. Antiphonarium Suerinense. Schwerin, fifteenth century. Parchment. 184 leaves. 45·5 cm.×31 cm. Fol. 1v.: Illuminated page with initial 'E(cce dies)'.

So far as we know this has not previously been mentioned in any work and is published here for the first time.

Plate 91

Weimar, Thüringische Landesbibliothek. Fol. max. 10. Decretalium Libri 6. Italian, late fourteenth century. Parchment. 143 leaves. 46·2 cm.×28 cm. Fol. 4v.: Tree of consanguinity.

The exact title is: *Decretalium Libri 6 cum apparatu Joh. Andreae et Domini Dyni... et glossis minoribus Jo. Rymeni.* A further entry runs: *hunc librum elegantissimum in materia et forma ego Johannes Ryman audivi, studui et correxi ac postillavi pro parte cum ea qua potui diligencia.* The manuscript was formerly in the Kartause (Charterhouse) in Erfurt, which was founded in 1372 and dissolved in 1803.

Lehmann, Paul: *Mittelalterliche Bibliothekskataloge...*, 2 (1928), pp. 231, 237, 249.

Plate 92

Bautzen, Domarchiv. Ms. I. Loc. 20. Antiphonarium. German, c.1450. Parchment. Unpaginated. 53 cm. × 39 cm. Initial 'A(d te)' and border.

Nothing is known of the origin or history of this manuscript.

Katalog der Ausstellung Alt-Lausitzer Kunst..., p.108.

Plate 93

Dessau, Anhaltische Landesbibliothek. Hs. 18a. Breviarium Magdeburgense. Magdeburg, second half of fifteenth century. Parchment. 530 Leaves. 21 cm. × 14·5 cm. Fol. 8v.: The Miracle of Pentecost.

The calendar and the presence of the patron saints Maurice and Katherine on this miniature make it certain that the manuscript originated in Magdeburg. The coat of arms of a one-time owner was added at a later date. It is not known when the breviary came to Dessau. There is no published study on it and it is reproduced here for the first time.

Plate 94

Zittau, Christian-Weise-Bibliothek, formerly Stadtbibliothek. Ms. A. VII. Missale Pragense. Bohemia, c.1415. Parchment. 233 leaves. 47·5 cm.× 32 cm. Fol.7v.: Initial 'A(d te levavi)' with Christ blessing.

A Crucifixion, unfortunately in a poor state of preservation, on fol.202v exemplifies the type of humanized Christ figure which occurs in art and sculpture of the early fifteenth century. The Christ of fol.7v is in the same style—gentle Jesus, rather than a stern judge. The folds of his garments are

rather limp, but none the less rhythmic and mobile.

Bruck, Robert: *Die Malereien...,* p.282, fig.183.
Stange, Alfred: *Deutsche Malerei der Gotik,* 2, p.77.
Vom Advent zum Advent, 1963–4. October.

Plate 95

Leipzig, former Stadtbibliothek, now Universitätsbibliothek. Rep. IV. fol. 1 (Cod. 304). Weichbildum Saxonicum cum glossa germanica. Diocese of Regensburg, 1453. Written by Erhard Heykel of Penighausen. Paper. 278 leaves. 31·5 cm. × 21·5 cm. Fol. 3r.: Initials 'G(ot)' and 'V(on)' with Eike von Repkow.

That the figure in the initial 'V' is indeed meant to be Eike is confirmed by the beginning of the text: *Got gebe syner selen rath der dis buch getichtet hat Ecke von rephan* ('God counsel the soul of Ecke von Rephan who wrote this book'). On fol.260v are the words: *Scriptum per me Erhardum heykel de peniczhawsen Ratisponens(is) dioc. Anno dni LIII° feria 5ta Braxedis virginis. cet.*

Bruck, Robert: *Die Malereien...,* p.308f.
Homeyer, G.: *Die deutschen Rechtsbücher...,* p.150, no.669.
Naumann, Robert: *Catalogus...,* p.94.

Plate 96

Zeitz, Stiftsbibliothek. Hs. fol. 2. Cicero: Epistolae. Italy? second half of fifteenth century. Paper. 202 leaves. 30 cm.× 20·5 cm. Fol.3r.: Initial 'E(go)' with border.

It is hard to ascertain the place of origin of the manuscript. While the initials and ornamentation are in a style typical of central Germany, the water-mark makes it probable that the paper is Italian. I am grateful to Dr Weiss, director of the Papier-museum in Leipzig, for this information.

Bech, Fedor: *Verzeichnis…*
Wegener, P.: *Verzeichnis…*, p.7.

Plate 97

Gotha, Landesbibliothek. Ms. I. 117. Vouquelin, Jean: Histoire du roy Alixandre. French, second half of fifteenth century. Parchment. 254 leaves. 31 cm. × 21·5 cm. Fol. 1 r.: Birth of Alexander and initial 'P(our ce que)'.

In the preface the author states that he wrote the work '*au commendement de… Monsgr Jehan de bour-gogne*'. This copy was probably written in eastern France, since an entry at the end shows it to have belonged to Philip of Cleves. The coat of arms in the border combines the arms of Cleves and Burgundy, as a sign of intermarriage. According to an old catalogue the manuscript was bought for Gotha in Schweinfurt in 1654.

Jacobs, Friedrich, and F. A. Uckert: *Beiträge…*, vol. 1, pp. 379–415.
Olschki, Leonardo: *Manuscrits…*, p. 53 f., pl. 65.

Plate 98

Leipzig, former Stadtbibliothek, now Universitäts-bibliothek. Rep. II. fol. 21 (Cod. 111). Hugo von Trimberg: Der Renner. Alsace, 1419. Paper. 183 leaves. 40·5 cm. × 28·5 cm. Fol. 2 r.: The Racer.

Der Renner was one of the most popular and in-fluential works of the late Middle Ages. No fewer than 60 surviving manuscript copies testify to that,

and it was also printed in Frankfurt in 1549. Gottsched, Gellert and Lessing all read it. The Leipzig manuscript can be dated exactly from the concluding words: *Dis buch wart vs geschriben also die glocke VII slug vor mittage am nehsten sanntage vor sant paules des bekererstag in dem Jore do man zalte von christus geburte Tusint vier hundert vnd nuntzehē Jor* ('The writing of this book was completed as the clock struck seven in the morning on the Sunday next before the feast of St Paul the Apostle in the year accounted one thousand four hundred and nineteen from the birth of Christ').

Bruck, Robert: *Die Malereien…*, pp. 272–9, fig. 180.
Ehrismann, Gustav: *Geschichte…*, vol. 2, 2ii, pp. 337–42.
Naumann, Robert: *Catalogus…*, p. 34.
Naumann, Robert: *Die Malereien…*, pp. 66–75.
Stange, Alfred: *Deutsche Malerei der Gotik* 4, p. 52.

Plate 99

Dresden, Sächsische Landesbibliothek. Ms. M. 66. Wolfram von Eschenbach: Parzival. Atelier of Diebold Lauber, Alsace, mid-fifteenth century. Paper. 548 leaves. 28 cm. × 20 cm. Fol. 63 r.: Knights leaving the castle.

Unfortunately the manuscript is not complete; 15 of the 60 illustrations are missing. The watermark in the paper is an ox-head with stave and star.

Benziger, Karl: *Parzival…*, pp. 33–7, 54–7, pl. 32–4.
Bruck, Robert: *Die Malereien…*, pp. 302–5, figs 196, 197.
Ehrismann, Gustav: *Geschichte…*, vol. 2, 2i, pp. 225–70.
Falkenstein, Karl: *Beschreibung…*, p. 394.
Katalog der Handschriften…, 2 (1883), p. 466 f.

Plate 100

Gotha, Landesbibliothek. Ms. I. 99. Marcus Junianus Justinus: Historicae Philippicae. Italian, 1494. Parchment. 190 leaves. 30·5 cm.×21 cm. Fol.1 r.: Illuminated page with initial 'C(um multi)' and the author at work. 27·8×18·5 cm.

At the end of the manuscript there is a nineteenth-century note that it belonged to Pope Pius III (1439–1503) and the date 1494. Pius III was the nephew of Pius II and was pope for only three weeks. His mother, the sister of Pius II, bore the name of Piccolomini-Todeschini and during his forty-three years as a cardinal her son used the Piccolomini arms. Justinus based his history on a lost work of Pompeius Trogus, a history of the world from Ninus of Assyria to Augustus.

Jacobs, Friedrich, and F.A.Uckert: *Beiträge...,* 1 (1835), p.242.
Salmi, Mario: *La miniatura italiana...,* fig.88, pl. 54, 56.

Plate 101

Gotha, Landesbibliothek. Mon. typ. 1477, fol.12. Decretum Gratiani cum glossa Bartolomaei Brixiensis. Early printed edition. Nicolas Jensen, Venice, 1477. Parchment. Unpaginated. 42·5 cm.×28 cm. Fol.2 r.: Dedicatory picture and painted border with initials 'H(umanum)' and 'O(mnes)'.

Two mottoes are written in gold letters on black grounds, above: *Bonis premium, malis odium,* and in the centre: *Perfice principio florens celeberima Petre.* It is not known for whom this copy was painted. Salmi ascribes the illumination to Franco de Russi.

Jacobs, Friedrich, and F.A.Uckert: *Beiträge...,* 3 (1838), p.254.
Salmi, Mario: *La miniatura...,* p.58.

Plate 102

Zittau, former Stadtbibliothek, now Christian-Weise-Bibliothek, Ms. A. IV. Missal. Zittau? fifteenth century. Parchment. 83 leaves. 63·5 cm.×44·5 cm. Fol.1 r.: Initial 'V(enite)' enclosing three singing monks, 10·5×11·5 cm., and border.

A comparison with the Gradual *(pl.82)* shows that the script as well as the initials and the heads of the figures are all very similar. We may conclude that both manuscripts are from the same scriptorium. The manuscript is published here for the first time.

Plate 103

Berlin, Deutsche Staatsbibliothek. Ms. lat. fol. 942. Missal. Silesia? mid-fifteenth century. Parchment. 53, 10, 109 leaves. 33·5 cm.×23·5 cm. Crucifixion.

The manuscript was bought by the Deutsche Staatsbibliothek in 1950 from Gerd Rosen of Berlin. In addition to the Crucifixion it contains a small miniature (the face of Christ) and eight large initials. Some features of the style are Silesian: the rather squat figures of Mary and John, the heads, the treatment of the garments, the black background with gold tendrils like a tapestry. In the library's catalogue it is described as a Saxon missal. It was recently discovered to have been made for the archdiocese of Gnesen.

Gernentz, Hans Joachim: *Religiöse deutsche Dichtung...,* p.450, pl.12.

Kloss, Ernst: *Die schlesische Buchmalerei*...
Rosen, Gerd: *Versteigerung*..., p. 53 f., pl. 3.

Plate 104

Leipzig, former Stadtbibliothek, now Universitäts-bibliothek. Rep. II. fol. 15 (Cod. 298). Eike von Rep-kow: Sachsenspiegel. Leipzig? 1461. Parchment and paper. 301 leaves. 40 cm. × 29 cm. Fol. 160 r.: Initial 'U(mme)' with soldiers on the march.

At the end, on fol. 291 r, there is the following entry: *Finitum Anno Domini MoCCCCoLXIo in die Margarete Virginis hora quasi prima.* The copy was probably made in a university town: Wieland Schmidt suggests Leipzig, where there was a Franciscan convent. *(Cf. pl. 80.)*

Bruck, Robert: *Die Malereien*..., p. 323 f., fig. 207
Homeyer, G.: *Die deutschen Rechtsbücher*..., p. 148, no. 662.
Karl der Grosse... p. 513, np. 698.
Naumann, Robert: *Catalogus*..., p. 92.
Naumann, Robert: *Die Malereien*..., p. 100 f.
Schmidt, Wieland: *Das Berliner Exemplar*..., p. 114 f., fig. 16.

Plate 105

Jena, Universitätsbibliothek. Ms. Sag. fol. 13. Johannes von Saaz: Der Ackermann und der Tod. Central Germany, c. 1475, Paper. 22 leaves. 29 cm. × 20 cm. Fol. 8 r.: The harvest of Death.

We know of 16 manuscript copies of *Der Acker-mann aus Böhmen* as well as 17 printed editions. The acrostic in the final prayer gives the author's name: Johannes de Tepla. He was also known by his father's name, Henslinus de Sitbor, or Johannes Henslinus de Sitbor. He studied in Prague, and

went to Saaz in 1378 where he was successively town clerk, headmaster and imperial notary. He later returned to Prague where he died in 1414.

Bernt, Alois: *Forschungen*..., pp. 326–37.
Bernt, Alois, and Konrad Burdach: *Der Acker-mann*..., pp. xv–xviii.
Johannes von Saaz: *Der Ackermann*...
Johannes von Tepl: *Der ackerman*...
Schramm, Albert: *Der Bilderschmuck*..., I (1922), p. 1, pl. 2, fig. 4.

Plate 106

Dresden, Sächsische Landesbibliothek. Ms. A. 311. Horarium latine. Master of the Dresden Prayerbook, Bruges, 1470–90. Parchment. 150 leaves. 14 cm. × 9·5 cm. Fol. 7 v.: July, harvest scene. 12 cm × 8·5 cm.

The manuscript contains 12 pictures illustrating the months and 16 miniatures. Friedrich Winkler identified the artist, whose style he also established in a number of other manuscripts, by this prayer-book. He was active in Bruges between 1470 and 1500, and the bulk of his work consists of prayerbooks. One can trace in them the transition from courtly patronage to popular demand.

Bruck, Robert: *Die Malereien*..., pp. 337–45, figs. 216–32.
Kästner, Erhard: *Bekränzter Jahreslauf*..., p. 30 f.
Katalog der Handschriften..., I (1882), p. 104.
Winkler, Friedrich: *Die flämische Buchmalerei*..., pp. 95, 98, 170.

Plate 107

Weimar, Thüringische Landesbibliothek. Oct. 83. Bre-viarium Romanum. Liège, 1470–80. Parchment. 179 leaves. 14 cm. × 9·4 cm. Fol. 104 v.: Entombment.

The manuscript contains ten miniatures. Nothing is known of its provenance.

Gernentz, Hans Joachim: *Religiöse deutsche Dichtung...*, pl. 15, p. 451 f.

Plate 108

Jena, Universitätsbibliothek. Ms. El. fol. 82. Xenophon: Cyropaedia, in a French translation by Vasco Gomez de Lucena (Vasque de Lucène). Illuminated by Loyset Liedet, Flemish, c. 1470. Parchment. 246 leaves. 40·5 cm. × 28·5 cm. Fol. 167 r.: Army on the move.

The translator Vasco Gomez de Lucena (1435 to 1512) spent most of his life at the Burgundian court. The following entry occurs on fol. 21: *... translatee de grec en latin par Pogge de Florence et de latin en françois par Vasque de Lucène, l'an mil CCCC soixante et dix.* There is a similar note on fol. 247 v. The manuscript was owned at one time by Henry, count of Nassau-Dillenburg and Vianden (1483 to 1538), whose arms appear on fol. 1 v. The miniator Loyset Liedet is mentioned in records of the Bruges painters' guild between 1469 and 1478 and probably died in or soon after the latter year.

Guerre, Danielle: *Le traitè des faiz...*, pp. 236–46.
Lehfeld, P.: *Bau- und Kunstdenkmäler...*, p. 145.
Mylius, Johann Christoph: *Memorabilia...*, pp. 351–3.
Winkler, Friedrich: *Die flämische Buchmalerei...*, pp. 75, 173.

Plate 109

Leipzig, former Stadtbibliothek, now Universitäts-

bibliothek. Rep. I. fol. 11 b (Cod. 71/72). Valerius Maximus: Factorum et dictorum memorabilium libri novem, with a French translation by Simon Hesdin and Nicolas de Gonnesse. Master of the Dresden Prayerbook, Bruges, before 1480. Parchment. Vol. 1: 404 leaves, vol. 2: 386 leaves. 41 cm. × 30·5 cm. Frontispiece to Bk 6: Death of Lucretia.

The manuscript was made for Jean de Gros of Bruges (d. 1484), the treasurer of the Order of the Golden Fleece. The French paraphrase accompanying the Latin original text is that begun by the theologian Simon de Hesdin on the orders of Charles V of France. After Charles' death (1380) his brother, the duke of Berry, commissioned the completion of the translation from Nicolas de Gonnesse, who finished it in 1420. This history is given at the end of the preface and at the end of the whole work.

Bruck, Robert: *Die Malereien...*, pp. 261–72, pl. 172–79.
Naumann, Robert: *Catalogus...*, p. 22 f.
Naumann, Robert: *Die Malereien...*, pp. 75–86.
Olschki, Leonardo: *Manuscrits français...*, p. 23 f., pl. 25, 26.
Winkler, Friedrich: *Der Leipziger Valerius Maximus...*
Winkler, Friedrich: *Die flämische Buchmalerei...*, pp. 95–8, 175, pl. 52, 53.

Plate 110

Halle, Archiv der Frankeschen Stiftung. J. 5. Prayerbook. German, 1471. Parchment. 149 leaves. 10·8 cm. × 7·5 cm. Fol. 127 r. Illuminated page with Initial 'A(ve domina sancta)'.

The date 1471 occurs on fol. 112 v.

Weiske, Karl: *Mitteilungen...*, p.10, no.2.

Plate 111

Zeitz, Stiftsbibliothek. Hs. quart. 79. Albertus Magnus: Quattuor libri Methavrorum. Written by Michael Forestus, completed on 27 June 1484 in Czabernia in Alsace. Paper. 222 leaves. 21 cm.×14 cm. Fol.172r.: Initial 'T(empus autem)', with scenes illustrating the manufacture of steel.

The text ends on fol.219r with the words: *Expliciunt libri mineralium Alberti Magni Christo propitio per me Michaelem Foresii anno 1484, 27.Juni. In Czabernia Alsacie Germanor(um) illustrisimo ac reverendissimo D.Alberto duci Bavarie et Argen(torati) E(pisco)po elsacie a lantgravio sexto pontificatus sui a(n)no favente cum gr(ati)a.* The scribe names himself again on fol.171v: *Explicit liber secundus... Magni Alberti M.Forestio transcribe(n)te.* At that time Alsace was part of the Habsburg lands.

Wegener, P.: *Verzeichnis...*, p.8.

Plate 112

Berlin, Deutsche Staatsbibliothek. Ms. lat. oct. 439. Book of Hours. Northern France, second half of fifteenth century. Parchment. 154 leaves. 19·2 cm. ×11 cm. Fol.66v.: Flight into Egypt and initial 'D(eus)'.

The manuscript was presented to the Deutsche Staatsbibliothek in 1953 by Dr Bruno Kaiser. According to the accessions register it came from the former Ministry of Finance.

Johannsen, Christa: *In der Stille gehütete Schätze...*, p.94, plate facing p.96.

Plate 113

Gotha, Landesbibliothek. Ms. II. 68. Livre d'heures. French, School of Troyes? third quarter of fifteenth century. Parchment. 156 leaves. 18·8 cm.×13·3 cm. Fol.108r.: Death of a rich woman, 17×13 cm.; Initial 'D(ilexi)'.

The manuscript contains a French calendar of feasts and thirteen whole-page minatures.

Jacobs, Friedrich, and F.A.Uckert: *Beiträge...*, 2 (1836), p.356.

Plate 114

Jena, Universitätsbibliothek. Ms. El. fol. 85 (formerly 87). Boethius: De consolatione philosophiae, translated into French by Jean de Meun. Written in Ghent by David d'Aubert for Margaret of England. Master of Mary of Burgundy, Flemish, 1476. Parchment. 148 leaves. 37·5 cm.×26·5 cm. Fol.13v.: Dedicatory picture.

On the last page of the manuscript the scribe wrote: *David aubert manu propria ... a l'ordre de Margarite d'Angleterre, Duchesse de Bourgogne, de lothrik, de brabant, lembour luxembourg ... Milquatrecens LXX et seze.*

Lehfeld, P.: *Bau- und Kunstdenkmäler...*, p.144.
Mylius, Johann Christoph: *Memorabilia...*, pp.355–7.
Olschki, Leonardo: *Manuscrits français...*, p.31f., pl.35.
Winkler, Friedrich: *Die flämische Buchmalerei...*, pp.103, 104, 113, 173, pl.67.

Plate 115

Gotha, Landesbibliothek. Ms. I. 118. Jean Charlier-Gerson: De mendicitate spirituali. Flemish, c.1480.

Parchment. 136 leaves. 31 cm. × 23 cm. Fol. 1 r.:
Conversation of the soul with mankind.

The coat of arms in the lower border and the
signature, *Phē de clavis*, at the end show the manuscript to have been made for Duke Philip of Cleves.
After the heading, in red ink, *Le prologue de ce
present livre*, the text begins with the initial 'C(y)'
and the words *Cy commence le secret parlement de
l'homme contemplatif a son ame*... It is a matter of
conjecture how the manuscript found its way to
Gotha.

Jacobs, Friedrich, and F. A. Uckert: *Beiträge*...,
2 (1836), pp. 168–72.

Plate 116

*Weimar, Thüringische Landesbibliothek. Qu. 57. Bre-
viary. Duchy of Bar, Meuse, second half of fifteenth
century. Parchment. 151 leaves. 19·8 cm. × 14 cm.
Fol. 38v.: Pietà. 17·4 × 12·2 cm.*

The arms of the duchy on fol. 45 v show the manuscript to have been made for a duke of Bar. It is
not known now it came to Weimar.

Gernentz, Hans Joachim: *Religiöse deutsche Dichtung*..., p. 450 f., pl. 13, 14.
Vom Advent zum Advent, 1960–1. Week thirteen.

Plate 117

*Weimar, Thüringische Landesbibliothek. Qu. 59. Prayer-
book of Margarete of Rodemachern. Western Germany,
last quarter of fifteenth century. Parchment. Text:
297 leaves. 17 cm. × 14 cm. Illustrations in wooden
case: 34 leaves. 16 cm. × 13 cm. Fol. 31 r.: The Lady
of Rodemachern with her guardian angel.*

Margarete von Nassau-Saarbrücken, Lady of
Rodemachern, came from a very cultured family.
Her mother, Elisabeth von Nassau-Saarbrücken
(1397–1456) was the first German woman writer of
romances, whose translation of four of the French
chansons de geste made the prose romance a popular
literary genre. Her works were frequently printed
in the sixteenth century and became chapbooks.
Margarete's prayerbook was inherited by her grand-
daughter Countess Margarete of Wittgenstein, and
later came to Weimar.

Ehrismann, Gustav: *Geschichte*..., vol. 2, 2ii,
pp. 510–2.
Gernentz, Hans Joachim: *Religiöse deutsche Dich-
tung*..., p. 451, pl. 16.
Schenk zu Schweinsberg, Eberhard: *Margarete von
Rodemachern*..., pp. 117–52.

Plate 118

*Jena, Universitätsbibliothek. Ms. El. fol. 96 (formerly
98). Desmoulin, Guyart: Bible historiale, vol. 2. Flemish, c. 1460–80. Master of Girart de Roussillon and
Master of the Vienna Chronicle of England? Parchment. 446 leaves. 50 cm. × 38 cm. Fol. 291 v.: St John
on Patmos.*

The manuscript's origin is given in the following
note: *C'est le premier volume de la bible, dont il y en
a deux. Lequel est à Mons. Charles de Croy, Conte de
Chimay* (d. 1527). The Belgian family of the dukes
of Croy acquired the county of Chimay in Hainault
in 1397. The Master of *Girart de Roussillon* appears
to have been one of the earliest miniaturists at the
court of Duke Philip the Good of Burgundy
(1396–1467). In the fifteenth century the Burgundian court moved its principal seat to Flanders,
which was of fundamental importance for the

artistic development of that province. The Master of *Girart de Roussillon* came strongly under the influence of Rogier van der Weyden. The identification with Jean de Dreux has not been proved.

Berger, Samuel: *La bible française…*, pp. 163, 298, 428 f.

Lehfeld, P.: *Bau- und Kunstdenkmäler…*, p. 144.

Mylius, Johann Christoph: *Memorabilia…*, pp. 367–73.

Winkler, Friedrich: *Die flämische Buchmalerei…*, pp. 8 f., 41, 44, 173.

Plate 119

Jena, Universitätsbibliothek. Ms. El. fol. 89. Quintus Curtius Rufus: De rebus gestis Alexandri Magni, in a French translation by Vasco Gomez de Lucena. Pupil of Philippe de Mazerolles. Flemish, c. 1480. Parchment. 189 leaves. 36 cm. × 26 cm. Fol. 91 r.: The wives of Darius before Alexander.

The stylistic resemblance to the work of Philippe de Mazerolles, court painter to Charles the Bold of Burgundy (1467–77), led Friedrich Winkler to ascribe the miniatures to a pupil.

Curtius Rufus: *Von den Thaten…*, Bk. 3, ch. 31 f.

Mylius, Johann Christoph: *Memorabilia…*, p. 360 f.

Olschki, Leonardo: *Manuscrits français…*, p. 30 f., pl. 34.

Winkler, Friedrich: *Die flämische Buchmalerei…*, p. 173.

Plate 120

Halle, Universitätsbibliothek. 1 Da/6 (formerly Cod. 89). St Athanasius: Life of St Antony (incomplete) in French. France, late fifteenth century.

35 leaves. 26·5 cm. × 19·5 cm. Fol. 1 a (1 r.): St Antony and St Athanasius; initial 'C(i comence)'.

The text begins: *Ci comence la vie saint Antoyne.* The manuscript was formerly the property of the historian Johann Christoph von Dreyhaupt. It is published here for the first time and no earlier work on it is known.

Plate 121

Gotha, Landesbibliothek. Ms. II. 24. Breviary made for Ferdinand and Isabella of Spain. Spanish, late fifteenth century. Parchment. 551 leaves. 21·5 cm. × 15 cm. Fol. 199 r.: Illuminated page with initial 'B(eatus vir)'.

Even without the arms of Ferdinand and Isabella, which occur three times in the manuscript, its Spanish origin would be proven by the calendar. Inside the front cover is the inscription: *Albertus Dux Saxoniae et Flandris attulit.* Albert, fifth son of Ernest I, the Pious, travelled in the Netherlands in 1662 with his brothers and probably brought the manuscript to Gotha from there.

Bordona, J. Dominguez: *Die spanische Buchmalerei…*

Glück, Heinrich, and Ernst Dietz: *Die Kunst des Islams…*, figs 202, 211.

Jacobs, Friedrich, and F. A. Uckert: *Beiträge…*, 2 (1836), pp. 352–5.

Rathgeber: *Bibliotheca Gothana…*, pp. 1–12.

Plate 122

Halle, Archiv der Frankeschen Stiftungen. A. 82. Breviary with notes in Bavarian dialect. Bavarian, fifteenth century. 389 leaves. 18 cm. × 13 cm. Fol. 123 r.: Illu-

minated page with initial 'P(rimo)' enclosing Christ Child.

Nothing is known of the history of the manuscript.

Weiske, Karl: *Mitteilungen...*, p.10f., no.3.

Plate 123

Weimar, Thüringische Landesbibliothek. Oct. 82. Breviarium Romanum, Low Countries, fifteenth century. Parchment. 164 leaves. 15·7 cm.× 11·2 cm. Fol.103r.: Illuminated page with initial 'H(eir in dyn)' and border with King David, 13cm.× 10·5 cm.

The heading in Dutch runs: *Hier begint die seven psalm in duitsch.* The scroll reads: *Waer warachtige penitencie is d. is gods bermh(er)tichz* ('True penitence comes from the mercy of God'). The manuscript is reproduced here for the first time.

Plate 124

Dresden, Sächsische Landesbibliothek. Ms. Oc. 58. Regnier d'Anjou: Sur les tournois. French, after 1467. Parchment. 78 leaves. 42 cm.× 29·5 cm. Fol.8v.: Judges entering the city.

The manuscript is composed of several parts. Foll. 1–42 contain the work on tournaments, followed by a book of ceremonies. The last two leaves bear a French chronicle of the years 1400–67. The text begins: *Ici est la forme et maniere, comment les juges...* The tournament book is dedicated to the author's brother, Charles of Anjou, Count of Maine. The manuscript came to Dresden in 1721 from the library of Duke Maurice William of Saxe-Zeitz.

Bruck, Robert: *Die Malereien...*, pp.387–91, figs 250–3.
Ebert, Friedrich Adolf: *Geschichte...*, p.314–6.
Falkenstein, Karl: *Beschreibung...*, pp.427–9.
Katalog der Handschriften..., 3 (1906), pp.120–2.
Olschki, Leonardo: *Manuscrits français...*, p.21, pl.22.

Plate 125

Gotha, Landesbibliothek. Chart. A. 688. Histoire d'Ysaie le Triste (incomplete). Central France, late fifteenth century. Paper. 491 leaves. 32 cm.× 21 cm. Fol.296v.: Reception of two knights.

The prose romance *Ysaie le Triste* is a continuation of the Arthurian cycle. Other models are the *chansons de geste, Aucassin et Nicolette* and others. The author is unknown. Every chapter begins: *On dit le conte.* According to Zeidler it dates from the fourteenth century.

Jacobs, Friedrich, and F. A. Uckert: *Beiträge...*, 3 (1838), pp.69–85.
Zeidler, J.: *Der Prosaroman...*

Plate 126

Dessau, Anhaltische Landesbibliothek. Hs. Georg 7. 2°. Old Testament in German. Thuringia, late fifteenth century. Paper. 350 leaves. 37·5 cm.× 26 cm. Fol.40r.: Jacob sends beasts to Esau and wrestles with the angel (Genesis 32).

The captions beneath the pictures simply describe the event depicted. I thank Dr W. Fleischer of the Germanisches Institut of Leipzig university for establishing the text as Thuringian. The manuscript is reproduced here for the first time.

Plate 127

Leipzig, former Stadtbibliothek, now Universitäts-bibliothek. Rep. II. fol. 60a (Cod. 203). Missal. Italian, before 1494. Parchment. 147 leaves. 41·5 cm. × 29 cm. Fol. 3 r.: Annunciation.

On fol. 100r there is a prayer *'pro rege Ferdinando'* by Henricus Panhormitanus, archbishop of Ace-renza and Matera, two dioceses in southern Italy, between 1471 and 1483. The dioceses formed part of the kingdom of Naples at that time, under King Ferdinand I (d. 1494). The arms at the bottom of the page are those of Filippo Strozzi the younger (1489–1538), a patron of the arts, who must have owned the manuscript. There is a note on the first page that in 1583 it belonged to Archbishop Fran-ciscus Antonius Sanctorius of Santa Severina in Calabria. It is not known how it eventually reached the Leipzig Stadtbibliothek.

Bruck, Robert: *Die Malereien...*, pp. 357–65, figs 233–5.
Naumann, Robert: *Catalogus...*, p. 65.
Naumann, Robert: *Die Malereien...*, pp. 15–27.

Plate 128

Halberstadt, Dommuseum. Ms. 113. Missal. Saxony, second half of fifteenth century. Parchment. 155 leaves. 35 cm. × 25 cm. Fol. 66 v.: Crucifixion. 26·2 cm. × 18 cm.

The missal was presented to the Dominican priory in Halberstadt by Berthold, a member of the order. He died in 1492 and was active in Erfurt and Göttingen. The reason for the Maltese cross in the border is unknown.

Hinz, Paulus: *Gegenwärtige Vergangenheit...*, p. 228f.

Meyer, Erich: *Das Dommuseum Halberstadt...*, p. 29.
Schmidt, Gustav: *Die Handschriften...*, 2, p. 3.

Plate 129

Stralsund, Stadtarchiv. Ms. IV. 290. Baldi opera. Italy, late fifteenth century. Parchment. 435 leaves. 42·5 cm. × 28·5 cm. Fol. 1 r.: Illuminated page with initial 'Q(uoniam)'.

There is unfortunately nothing in the Stralsund archives which records how the manuscript came there, or where from. It is reproduced here for the first time.

Plate 130

Sankt Marienstern, convent library. Fol. 3. Antiphon-ary. Altzella, early sixteenth century. Parchment. 121 leaves. 53·5 cm. × 35·5 cm. Fol. 1 v.: Initial 'A(ngelus)' with Resurrection.

All the manuscripts in the library of Sankt Marienstern came from the mother-foundation of Altzella. The style shows that this one was written and illuminated there also. It is reproduced here for the first time.

Plate 131

Jena, Universitätsbibliothek. Ms. El. fol. 1. Evangelist-ary presented by Pope Leo X to Elector Frederick the Wise. Miniatures by Jakob Elsner, Nuremberg, 1507. Parchment. 35 leaves, fol. 27 ff. blank. 35 cm. × 25 cm. Fol. 6 v.: Illuminated page with initials 'I(n)' and 'C(um)'.

The date 1507 is given on the page which displays the elector's coat of arms.

Bruck, Robert: *Friedrich der Weise...*, pp. 192–9.

Mylius, Johann Christoph: *Memorabilia...*, pp. 301–5.

Stange, Alfred: *Deutsche Malerei der Gotik*, 9, p. 83 f.

Willkomm, Bernhard: *Die Jenaer Universitäts-bibliothek...*, p. 2 f., pl. 3, 4.

Plate 132

Weimar, Thüringische Landesbibliothek. Fol. max. 6. Missal. Low Countries, early sixteenth century. Parchment. 90 leaves. 43·5 cm.×32 cm. Fol. 12 r.: Illuminated page with Nativity and Annunciation to the Shepherds.

There is apparently no published work on this manuscript, which is reproduced here for the first time.

Plate 133

Dresden, Sächsische Landesbibliothek. Ms. Oc. 75. Boccaccio: Des cas des nobles hommes et femmes, livres 2–5 traduits par Laurens de Premierfait, clerc du diocèse de Troyes. French, c. 1520. Parchment. 92 leaves. 50 cm.×36 cm. Fol. 44 r.: Beginning of Bk 3, pilgrims resting and initial 'P(elerins)'.

The manuscript has an unusual history. It consists of 9 books, of which 1 and 6–9 are in the Bibliothèque Nationale in Paris (Ms. franç. 128 and 20086). From the coat of arms on fol. 1 of Bk 6 the first owner must have been Robert Du Mas, Seigneur de l'Isle. On fol. 1 v of the second book (in Dresden) is the inscription: *ce present livre a esté donné au roy François premier par Charles de Bourbon, Conestable de France.* Francis I reigned 1515–47. Bks 1–5 later came into the Bibliothèque

Béthune, as is shown by the arms on the morocco binding. Finally Bks 2–5 were presented by Prince Radziwill, Chancellor of Lithuania, to Augustus the Strong and have been in Dresden ever since.

Bruck, Robert: *Die Malereien...*, pp. 380–2, fig. 247.

Falkenstein, Karl: *Beschreibung...*, p. 422 f.

Katalog der Handschriften..., 3 (1906), p. 135 f.

Plate 134

Schwerin, Mecklenburgische Landesbibliothek. Ms. 376. Reimchronik des Nikolaus Marschalk, gen. Thurius. Mecklenburg, before 1513. Parchment. 139 leaves. 24·8 cm.×17·5 cm. Fol. 57 r.: The Miracle of the Holy Blood at Doberan. 10·8×11·8 cm.

The manuscript can be dated before 1513, because the marriage of Duke Henry V to Helen of the Palatinate in that year is not mentioned. The leather binding bears the impression of the letters U H Z M and the date 1556, which indicates that it belonged to Duke Ulrich of Mecklenburg, who had it bound in that year. He was the son of Albert VII, the Handsome, and ruled in Güstrow from 1555 to 1603. The manuscript came to Schwerin in 1951, when the Landesbibliothek in Neustrelitz was dispersed.

Karbe, W.: *Herzog Heinrich V...*, pp. 164–6.

Lisch, G. C. F.: *Buchdruckerei...*, 4 (1839), pp. 92 to 133.

Müffelmann, L.: *Die Reim-Chronik...*

Schröder, Carl: *Mecklenburg...*, p. 3.

Wegele: *Nicolaus Marschalk...*, p. 431 f.

Westphalen, Ernst Joachim von: *Monumenta inedita...*, col. 598.

Plate 135

*Sankt Marienstern, convent library. Fol.6. Anti-
phonal. Altzella, 1516. Parchment. 162 leaves. 54 cm.
× 37·5 cm. Fol.3r.: Initial 'D(um perambulet)'
with St Andrew.*

On fol. 1v is the inscription: *Carmen panegiricum
fratris Michaelis Cantoris Cellensis in laudem ceno-
biorum ordinis Cysterciensis Celle et Stelle beate Marie
virginis.* This poem mentions the names of all who
were concerned with the manuscript: the two
scribes Johannes de Fribergk and Johannes Helbig,
the miniator Roswinus Andreae and the abbess of
Sankt Marienstern, Elisabeth von Temritz (1515–
23). The lower border on fol.120r includes portraits of Abbot Martin of Altzella and Abbess
Elisabeth, with their coats of arms, and the caption:
*Martinus veteris Celle dum culmina rexit 1516 et Stelle
Maria Elisabet scriptus liber iste est.* It illustrates the
close relationship that existed between the mother
and daughter foundations.

Katalog der Ausstellung..., p.109.

Plate 136

*Naumburg, Domkapitel. Antiphonary in 8 vols.
(No shelf mark.) Written for the chapter of Meissen
cathedral between 1500 and 1504. Parchment. 78 cm.
× 54 cm. Vol.4, fol.49r.: Initial 'E(cce)' with
St John on Patmos. 16×15 cm.*

The following entry appears on fol. 1 of the first
volume: *Anno domini incarnationis quingentesimo
super milesimum Presul Prepositus Decanus... eccl.
Misn. ordinavit... huc librum.* Vol.7 also bears the
date 1500, whereas vol.6 is dated 1504. The entire
eight volume work was produced between these

dates. In content, vols 2 and 3, vols 4, 5 and 8 and
vols 6 and 7 are the same. The work was commissioned by Bishop Johannes de Salhusen and the
chapter of Meissen cathedral. In the early years
of the sixteenth century, Altzella was the leading
scriptorium in the region of Meissen, so it is probable that the antiphonary was written and illuminated there. Bergner distinguished the hands of
four separate artists. So large a work would always
have employed several miniators and scribes.
Bergner, Heinrich: *Beschreibende Darstellung...,*
    pp.193–8.

Plate 137

*Greifswald, Universitätsbibliothek. Ms. 977. Missale
Romanum. Made for the ecclesiastical province of
Bremen, completed 1503. Parchment. 340 leaves.
44·5 cm.×32 cm. Fol.173v.: Crucifixion.*

On fol. 158r a note gives 1503 as the date of
completion. For a time the manuscript was in the
possession of the Cistercian monastery at Eldena, but
it cannot have been written there; the absence of
any local saints in the calendar allows us to conclude that it originated in a nunnery. From the
Propium it appears that it was written in the province of Bremen or the neighbouring dioceses of
Cammin and Verden.

Hansel, Hans: *Zur Herkunft..., p.58–75.*

Plate 138

*Weimar, Landeshauptarchiv. Reg. O. 20/21. Spalatin,
Georg: Sächsische Chronik. German, 1513. Parchment. 268 leaves. 46 cm.×31 cm. Fol.193r.: Coronation of Otto I. 25×17 cm.*

The full title of the work may be translated as

follows: 'Epitome of famous men and women, lords spiritual and temporal of the noble house of the dukes of Thuringia and the margraves of Meissen, collected by Georgius Spalatinus 1513'. The manuscript opens with a chronological table, followed by the origins of the Saxons, their history and their laws. At the end there are recounted some contemporary miracles. Bruck's attribution of the miniatures to Hans Burgkmair the elder is not convincing. Burgkmair does not include the *Sächsische Chronik* in his own catalogue of his oeuvre.

Bruck, Robert: *Friedrich der Weise...*, p.128f., pl.32–6.
Burkhard, Arthur: *Hans Burgkmair d.Ä.*

Plate 139

Schwerin, Mecklenburgisches Landeshauptarchiv. Urkundenbestand—Fürstenhaus. Die annkunfft der hertzogen vonn Megkelberg aus dem Koniglichenn Stammenn der Obetrittenn gebornn. Mecklenburg, 1526. Parchment. 56 leaves. 38 cm.×26 cm. Fol.52r.: Duke Albert VII, the Handsome, and his wife Anna of Brandenburg. 25 cm×23·8 cm.

Albert the Handsome (1488–1547) was the son of Duke Magnus II and reigned in Mecklenburg-Güstrow from 1534 to 1547. The manuscript is reproduced here for the first time.

Plate 140

Sankt Marienstern, convent library. Fol.5. Missal, vol.2. Altzella, 1529. Parchment. 159 leaves. 57·5 cm. ×38·5 cm. Fol.143v.: Initial 'R(equiem)' with Death on a bier.

The following entry appears on fol.1v: *Liber stelle sancte Marie scriptus per fratrem Johannem helbigium Cellensem olim confessorem monialium dicti monsterii Accedente ad hoc favore et commissione reverendi patris Dni pauli abbas Cellensis Anno salutis christiane Millesimo quingentesimo vicessimo nono sub regimine dicti reverendi patris Pauli Abbatis Cellensis et venerabile dne Abbatisse Margarethe de Metzecraden in Marienstern...* Abbot Paul Bachmann succeeded Martin von Lochau in 1522. Margarete von Metzecraden was Abbess of Sankt Marienstern from 1524 to 1542.

Katalog der Ausstellung..., p.109.

Plate 141

Erfurt, Stadtarchiv. 5/801–M1. Register of the inheritance of Herebord von der Margariten und Lewenburg. Erfurt, 1525. Parchment. 72 leaves. 29·7 cm. ×20·7 cm. Fol.1v.: Herebord von der Margariten und Lewenburg and his wife, with their arms.

The preface on fol.2 states the book to be a 'register and inventory of the rents and properties of Herebord von der Margariten und Lewenburg, which he inherited from his beloved father, the late Gerlach von der Margariten'. The preface concludes with the statement that the book was compiled, and the writing of it ordered, by Gerlach von der Margariten and Lewenburg, Herebord's brother, in the year 1520. Herebord was born in Erfurt in 1496. He was Syndic in 1514, rector of the university in 1515–16, and subsequently in the service of Albrecht, Archbishop of Mainz, and of the emperors Maximilian I and Charles V. He was thus clearly a man of substance and experience, whose advice would be of value to both spiritual and secular princes. The manuscript is published here for the first time.

Plate 142

Halle, Archiv der Franckeschen Stiftungen. G. 69. Armorial of the Burgraves of Nuremberg. Nuremberg, after 1527. Paper. 94 pp. 31·5 cm.× 20·5 cm. Fol. 1 r.: Count Godefridus zu Lambogen.

The title of the work runs: 'The origins of the ancient burgraves of the imperial city of Nuremberg, first instituted, according to the chroniclers, by King Conrad, duke in Franconia'. Conrad I reigned from 911 to 918.

Weiske, Karl: *Mitteilungen...*, p. 20, no. 30.

Plate 143

Weimar, Thüringische Landesbibliothek. Fol. 328. Ingenieurkunst- und Wunderbuch. Nuremberg region, completed c. 1520. Parchment. 325 leaves. 33·5 cm. × 25·5 cm. Fol. 104 r.: Conjuring tricks.

The long history associated with the manuscript is for the most part implausible. On the back cover there is a portrait of Maximilian I, who is hardly likely to have had anything to do with it. It is supposed to have belonged to Ferdinand of Aragon and Naples (1452–1516) who became king of Sicily in 1468. The same year saw the death of the Albanian prince and national hero George Castriota, known as Skanderbeg, who was in Naples in 1461–2, commanding mercenaries in the pay of Aragon. Ferdinand is supposed to have given the manuscript to him. The story then jumps to 1590, when the manuscript is said to have been bought in Warsaw by a Franconian nobleman,

Christoffel von Waldenroth, for the sum of 100 Reichsthaler. He offered it to Duke John Ernest of Saxe-Weimar on 16 February 1621, but received only 5 gulden for it. In this way this unique manuscript came to Thuringia.

Feldhaus, Franz Maria: *Die Technik...*, col. 22, figs 447, 555.

Jähns, Max: *Geschichte...*, p. 274 f.

Marx, E.: *Bericht...*, pp. 317–21.

Vulpius, Christian August: *Sogenanntes Scanderbegisches ... Wunderbuch...*, pp. 289–308.

Plate 144

Jena, Universitätsbibliothek. Ms. El. fol. 2. Epistolary presented by Pope Leo X to Elector Frederick the Wise, with minatures by Jakob Elsner. Nuremberg, 1507. Parchment. 37 leaves, fol. 26 ff. blank. 35 cm.× 25 cm. Fol. 4 v.: Deposition, after Dürer's Great Passion. B. 13, I. P. 13 a.

The Deposition is the earliest of the woodcuts in Dürer's series, the *Great Passion*, and is generally dated 1507, although it did not appear in print until 1511.

Bruck, Robert: *Friedrich der Weise...*, pp. 192–9.

Lehfeld, P.: *Bau- und Kunstdenkmäler...*, p. 142 f.

Mylius, Johann Christoph: *Memorabilia...*, p. 305 f.

Stange, Alfred: *Deutsche Malerei der Gotik*, 9, p. 83 f.

Willkomm, Bernhard: *Die Jenaer Universitätsbibliothek...*, p. 3.

Plate 145

Dresden, Sächsische Landesbibliothek. Biogr. art. 70 = S. B 80. Dürer, Albrecht: Marienleben. Printed, Nuremberg, 1511. Paper. Unpaginated. 45·6 cm.

×31·5 cm. Fol.10: Adoration of the Shepherds, with a border added later.

The book was in the Dresden library by 1595. An old library catalogue of that date describes it as 'beautifully illuminated and decorated with foliage round the edges'. Each leaf has one of the 20 woodcuts on the recto, and, in some copies, a portion of the Latin life of the Virgin by Benedictus Chelidonius on the verso. Fol. 2 is a kind of title-page: *Epitome in divae parthenices Mariae historiam ab Alberto Durero Norico per figuras digestam cum versibus annexis Chelidonii. Nurnberge per Albertum Dürer pictorem Anno christiano Millesimo quingentesimo undecimo*. The Dresden copy lacks the text.

Dürer, Albrecht: *Das Marienleben*...
Falkenstein, Karl: *Beschreibung*..., p.803.
Heidrich, Ernst: *Zur Chronologie*..., p.232.
Meder, Joseph: *Dürer-Katalog*..., pp.165–80.
Schunke, Ilse: *Das europäische Buch*..., p.4.

Plate 146

Sankt Marienstern, convent library. Fol.4. Missal, vol.1. Altzella, 1522–3. Parchment. 126 leaves. 57.2 cm.×38.5 cm. Fol.1r.: Initial 'A(d te levavi)' with King David.

Between foll. 8r and 47r the names of sisters and prioresses and twice the name Johannes Helbig and the date 1522 are written in black initial letters. These entries are of great value for the history of the convent.

Katalog der Ausstellung..., p.109.

Plate 147

Jena, Universitätsbibliothek. Chorbuch 3. Eight masses. Low Countries, c.1520. Parchment. 115 leaves.

56·5 cm.×37 cm. Fol.30r.: Elector Frederick the Wise of Saxony at prayer, with his guardian angel; initial 'B(assus)'.

Above the miniature is the elector's motto: *Tant que je pius*. With the Reformation the choirbook lost its liturgical function and was relegated to the electoral library in Wittenberg. It passed to the university library in Jena in 1558.

Bruck, Robert: *Friedrich der Weise*..., p.205, pl.27.
Lehfeld, P.: *Bau- und Kunstdenkmäler*..., p.141f.
Roediger, Karl Erich: *Die geistlichen Musikhandschriften*..., p.40f.
Willkomm, Bernhard: *Die Jenaer Universitätsbibliothek*..., p.3, pl.3.

Plate 148

Weimar, Thüringische Landesbibliothek. Fol.10. German translation of the Vulgate, vol.2, New Testament. Western Thuringia, early sixteenth century. Paper. 241 leaves, 34·8 cm.×25 cm. Fol.15v.: Salome with the head of John the Baptist. 21 cm.×19·5 cm.

According to entries in the manuscript, it belonged at one time to David Godofred Schoeber and, in 1653, to Johannes Andreas Piccart, professor of theology at Schweinfurt. As in the case of the German Old Testament in Dessau *(pl.126)*, my thanks are due to Dr W. Fleischer for placing the text linguistically. The manuscript is reproduced here for the first time.

Plate 149

Weimar, Thüringische Landesbibliothek. Oct. 81. Breviarium Romanum. Lower Saxony, early sixteenth century. *Parchment. 101 leaves. 16·5 cm.×11·5 cm. Fol. 29 r.: Christ and St Veronica. 13·4×9·2 cm.*

The manuscript is reproduced here for the first time. So far as we know, it has not been mentioned in print before.

Plate 150

Halle, Universitätsbibliothek. Yo. Matricula of the university of Wittenberg, vol. 1. Wittenberg, 1502–52. Parchment. 223 leaves. 30·5 cm.×22 cm. Fol. 107 v.: Arms of Rector Ulrich Schilling of Cannstatt with medallions of Luther, Melanchthon, Jonas and Bugenhagen.

Schilling's successor in 1533 was Caspar Cruciger, whose arms, comprising the Good Shepherd and the Holy Dove, appear on fol. 113 v of the same volume. Cruciger, too, expressed his esteem for his distinguished colleagues by surrounding his arms with theirs. The second volume displays the arms of Nassau painted by Lucas Cranach the younger.

Album..., 1 (1841), pp. 143–5, 2 (1894), p. xvi.

Plate 151

Rostock, Universitätsbibliothek. Ms. philol. 91. Pfinzing, Melchior: Theuerdank. German, c. 1520. Parchment. 290 leaves. 38 cm.×25 cm. Fol. 73 r.: Pl. 32. Theuerdank's shipwreck.

The manuscript was presented to Rostock university library in 1795 by the Schwerin Regierungsbibliothek (government library). The leaves were numbered according to the second edition printed by Schönsperger in Augsburg in 1519. Only 51 of the 118 plates were completed, thereafter spaces were left blank. The title refers to 'The dangers and other adventures of the praiseworthy, valiant and famous hero and knight, Lord Tewrdannck'. The Benedictine Leonhard Wagner is now believed to have been the inventor of the Theuerdank type. The manuscript is here reproduced for the first time.

Worringer, Wilhelm: *Die altdeutsche Buchillustration...*, pp. 132–4.

Plate 152

Rostock, Universitätsbibliothek. Ms. Meckl. B. 114/1. Marschalk, Nicolaus, alias Thurius: Reimchronik. Mecklenburg, 1573. Paper. 135 leaves. 25 cm. × 20·2 cm. Fol. 0 v., facing 1 r.: Dedicatory picture, author presenting the work to Duke Henry V.

The arms of Mecklenburg with the name of Duke Ulrich (1527–1603) and the date 1573 appear on the page before this picture, so we may assume that the copy was made by order of Duke Ulrich. Quite a lot is known of the author's life. Marschalk was born in 1465 in Rossla in Thuringia, hence the surname Thurius. He studied at Erfurt and Wittenberg and became an emissary of the elector of Saxony. In 1505 he entered the service of Duke Henry V of Mecklenburg (1479–1552) as counsellor. In 1510 he became professor of Roman and canon law at Rostock university. With a fellow-Thuringian, Günther Winter, he set up Rostock's third printing press in his own home, principally for the publication of his own works. He died in 1525 and is buried in Doberan.

Karbe, W.: *Herzog Heinrich V...*, pp. 164–6.
Lisch, G. C. F.: *Buchdruckerei...*, 4 (1839), pp. 92–133.
Müffelmann, L.: *Die Reim-Chronik...*
Schröder, Carl: *Mecklenburg...*, p. 3 f.
Wegele: *Nicolaus Marschalk...*, p. 431 f.

Westphalen, Ernst Joachim von: *Monumenta inedita...*, coll. 561–652.

Plate 153

Berlin, Deutsche Staatsbibliothek. Phill. 1926. Eighteen miniatures illustrating Petrarch. French, midsixteenth century. Parchment. 27 leaves. 19·5 cm. × 13·2 cm. Fol. 6 r.: Triumph of Death.

Below the picture are the words: *Mors vincit castitatem.* Petrarch met Laura in Avignon in 1327. She was then 20 and died as early as 1348. She has much the same significance for Petrarch as Beatrice for Dante.

Degering, Hermann: *Katalog...*, p. 21.
Kirchner, Joachim: *Beschreibendes Verzeichnis...*, pp. 120–2.

Plate 154

Greifswald, Universitätsbibliothek. Nd. Hs. 36. Collection of various works in one codex. Foll. 1 r.–11 r. Statutes of Wesel in Latin and Low German. Wesel, c. 1530. Parchment. 114 leaves. 28 cm. × 19 cm. Fol. 5 v.: Illuminated page with initial 'W(ant)'.

The manuscript was acquired by Greifswald in 1927, and therefore does not appear in Josef Deutsch's catalogue of 1926. The heading in red letters begins with the words: *Sint dat dat heyll der stadt in den rechten is gelegen...* ('Since the wellbeing of the city lies in its laws...'), a quotation from Aristotle. The manuscript is reproduced here for the first time.

Plate 155

Dresden, Sächsische Landesbibliothek. Ms. A. 319.

Prayerbook. German, 1556. Parchment. v, 71 leaves. 15 cm. × 11 cm. Fol. 45 r.: Adoration of the Shepherds.

The title-page bears the following description of the book: *Viel schoner andechtiger gebett durch einen Gelerten aus gottlicherr heiliger Schrifft tzusammengetragenn. Scriptum et picturis ornatum a Luca Cranachio 15 die mensis Julii Anno 1556.* While the prayers may well, as this description says, have been culled from Holy Scripture by a scholar, its attribution of the illustrations to Cranach is clearly false. The pen and ink drawing is a copy, with a few alterations, of the woodcut in Dürer's Little Passion.

Bruck, Robert: *Die Malereien...*, p. 407, fig. 267.
Dürer, Albrecht: *Die kleine Passion...*, p. 4.
Katalog der Handschriften..., I (1882), p. 106.

Plate 156

Erfurt, Stadtarchiv. 1–1/X, B XIII–46, vol. 2. Matricula of Erfurt university, 1498–1599. Parchment. 334 leaves. 27·7 cm. × 20·5 cm. Fol. 186 r.: St Jerome, signed H(ans) B(rosamer) 1549. 13·5 × 15·5 cm.

Above the picture is the rector's name: Magister Joannes Elingerott Gottingen. The accompanying text runs: *Sicut in apibus ut divus Iheronimus et canon testantur, princeps unus et grues unam sequuntur liberato ordine et in armentis rector unus, in naturalibus etiam omnibus iste accedens consensus ad hoc ipsum, quod optimum in toto universo, ut mundi unus gubernator, qui universa administret, singula ratione dispenset verbo iubeat et virtute omnia consumat.*

The painter Hans Brosamer was born in Fulda in 1500 and died in Erfurt in 1554.

Fiedler, Alfred: *Vom Stammbuch...*

Jacobus de Voragine: *Legenda aurea...*, pp. 817–23.
Thieme, Ulrich, and Felix Becker: *Allgemeines Lexikon der bildenden Künstler...*, 5 (1911), p. 66f.
Weissenborn, J. C.: *Acten...*, vol. 2, pp. 372–5.
Wiegand, Fritz: *Die Erfurter Studentenmatrikel...*, p. 47, pl. 3.

Plate 157

Jena, Universitätsbibliothek. No shelf mark. Bible of Elector John Frederick. Printed by Hans Lufft, Wittenberg, 1541, with coloured woodcuts by Lucas Cranach the younger. Parchment. Unpaginated. 39 cm. × 26 cm. Miniature on the front cover of vol. 1 by Cranach, 1543: Illustration of Protestant dogma. 28·5 cm. × 21 cm., not including the frame.

Bible quotations: Above left: Romans 1:18. Below left, Romans 3:23; 1 Corinthians 15:56; Romans 4:15; Romans 3:20; Matthew 11:13. Above right, Isaiah 7:14. Below right, Romans 1:17; Romans 3:25; John 1:29; Peter 1:2; 1 Corinthians 15:55–7.

Lehfeld, P.: *Bau- und Kunstdenkmäler...*, p. 143.
Mylius, Johann Christoph: *Memorabilia...*, p. 272f.
Thulin, Oskar: *Cranach-Altäre...*, p. 139.
Troschke, Asmus von: *Miniaturbildnisse...*, pp. 15, 20f.
Willkomm, Bernhard: *Die Jenaer Universitätsbibliothek...*, p. 4.

Plate 158

Dresden, Sächsische Landesbibliothek. Ms. C. 62. Kriegsbuch von mancherley Stratagematibus... German, 1572. Paper. 27 leaves. 37·5 cm. × 24 cm. Fol. 10 v.: Warship in full sail.

The title runs: 'War book of various stratagems... Weapons brought to light, the like of which were never seen before, far less heard of...' On foll. 14 r and 15 v is the signature H. W. 1572.

Bruck, Robert: *Die Malereien...*, p. 408 f., figs 268, 269.
Katalog der Handschriften..., 1 (1882), p. 189.

Plate 159

Dresden, Sächsische Landesbibliothek. Ms. B. 104. Bretschneider, Daniel: Inventionen zu Schlittenfahrten. Dresden, second half of sixteenth century. Parchment. 51 leaves. 15 cm. × 38 cm. Transverse octavo. Fol. 7 v.: St George and the dragon.

There is no text. The title-page runs: 'A book of all kinds of inventions for sledge parties, how they may be built and easily driven ... designed by Daniel Bretschneider, citizen and painter of Dresden.'

Bruck, Robert: *Die Malereien...*, pp. 410–3.
Katalog der Handschriften..., 1 (1882), p. 122.

Plate 160

Dresden, Sächsische Landesbibliothek. Ms. F. 169. Appointment of Nicola Marcelo as mayor of Bergamo. Venice, 1557. Parchment. 138 leaves. 22·5 cm. × 17 cm. 2nd frontispiece: St Mark.

The full title runs: *Nos Laurentius Priolus dei gratia Dux Venetiarum etc. committimus tibi Nicolao Marcelo quod vadas et sis Potestas Civitatis Bergomi. 1557.* The motto on the scrolls is *Victoria et pace – nunc et semper.* The manuscript is in a magnificent Venetian binding.

Bruck, Robert: *Die Malereien...*, p. 403 f., figs 263, 264.
Falkenstein, Karl: *Beschreibung...*, p. 292.
Katalog der Handschriften..., 1 (1882), p. 415.

LOCATION OF MANUSCRIPTS

The manuscripts are listed here under the libraries where they are now housed. The references take the form of the library shelf mark, when there is one, and the relevant plate number in the present volume; further details will be found in the Notes on the Plates. Also included are brief descriptions of other illuminated manuscripts in some of the libraries concerned, which have not been reproduced in this volume.

BAUTZEN

Domarchiv

Ms. I. Loc. 20. *(pl.92)*.

Stadt- und Kreisbibliothek

Ms. fol. 56. *(pl.54)*.
Ms. fol. 51. Hus, Johannes: Works. Bohemian,
   1412.

BERLIN

Deutsche Staatsbibliothek

Hamilton 407. *(pl.57)*.
Hamilton 553. *(pl.4)*.
Hamilton 675. *(pl.79)*.
Ms. lat. fol. 942. *(pl.103)*.
Ms. lat. oct. 439. *(pl.112)*.
Phill. 1676. *(pl.5)*.
Phill. 1906. *(pl.64)*.
Phill. 1926. *(pl.153)*.
Ms. theol. lat. fol. 1. *(pl.15)*.
Ms. theol. lat. fol. 2. *(pl.21)*.
Ms. theol. lat. fol.485 *(pl.1)*.
Hamilton 248. Gospel book. Carolingian. Metz,
   mid-ninth century.
Hamilton 250. The four Gospels. Italy, late ninth
   century.
Hamilton 292. Italian Herbarium. Seventeenth
   century.

BRANDENBURG

Domstift

No shelf mark. Evangelistary. *(pl.36)*.
No shelf mark. Lectionary fragment. *(pl.34)*.
No shelf mark. Lectionary. Saxony, early thirteenth
   century.

DESSAU

Anhaltische Landesbibliothek

Hs. Georg. 2. 2°. *(pl.81)*.
Hs. Georg 4. 2°. *(pl.18)*.
Hs. Georg 7. 2°. *(pl.126)*.
Hs. Georg 7. 8°. *(pl.83)*.
Hs. Georg 230. 2°. *(pl.80)*.
Hs. 18a. *(pl.93)*.
Hs. Georg 17. Breviary. German (Magdeburg?),
   fifteenth century.

DRESDEN

Sächsische Landesbibliothek

Ms. A. 63. *(pl.11)*.
Ms. A. 126. *(pl.41)*.
Ms. A. 311. *(pl.106)*.
Ms. A. 319. *(pl.155)*.
Ms. B. 104. *(pl.159)*.
Ms. C. 62. *(pl.158)*.
Ms. F. 169. *(pl.160)*.

Ms. M. 66. *(pl.99)*.

Ms. Oc. 50. *(pl.52)*.

Ms. Oc. 54. *(pl.89)*.

Ms. Oc. 58. *(pl.124)*.

Ms. Oc. 75. *(pl.133)*.

Ms. Oc. 77. *(pl.68)*.

Biogr. art. 70. *(pl.145)*.

Ms. A. 50. *Bible historiale*. German, first half of fifteenth century.

Ms. A. 147. *Horarium*. French, mid-fifteenth century.

Ms. A. 196. Bible history. German, late sixteenth century.

Ms. A. 324. Wehse, Johann: Prayerbook. Saxony, 1654.

Ms. Db. 93. Galen: *Opera*. French? mid-fifteenth century.

Ms. J. 1. Portraits of the dukes of Saxony. Saxony, mid-seventeenth century.

Ms. J. 404. *Vademecum*. German, 1586.

Ms. Oc. 51. Rousselet: *Prières de la messe*. Paris, early eighteenth century.

Ms. Oc. 52. Pagés: *Prières*. French, early eighteenth century.

ERFURT

Domkapitel

Ms. Jus. 2. *(pl.56)*.

Ms. Liturg. 6. Antiphonary. Made for Erfurt cathedral, *c*. 1500.

Stadtarchiv

1–1/X, B XIII–46, vol. 2. *(pl.156)*.

5/801–M 1. *(pl.141)*.

1–1/X B XIII–40, vol 1. Rector's account book. Erfurt, 1511.

280

Wissenschaftliche Bibliothek

Cod. Ampl. 2°. 31. *(pl.50)*.

GOTHA

Landesbibliothek

Ms. I. 18. *(pl.6)*.

Ms. I. 70. *(pl.25)*.

Ms. I. 75. *(pl.2)*.

Ms. I. 98. *(pl.76)*.

Ms. I. 99. *(pl.100)*.

Ms. I. 117. *(pl.97)*.

Ms. I. 118. *(pl.115)*.

Ms. II. 24. *(pl.121)*.

Ms. II. 68. *(pl.113)*.

Ms. II. 137. *(pl.85)*.

Chart. A. 594. *(pl.71)*.

Chart. A. 688. *(pl.125)*.

Chart. A. 777. *(pl.78)*.

Mon. typ. 1477, fol. 12. *(pl.101)*.

Ms. I. 54. *Biblia pauperum*. German text. 1464.

Ms. I. 71. *Sancti Wilbrordi epternacensis liber aureus 2*. Written by Theodoricus, Echternach, 1191.

Cod. I. 92. Frutolf: *Chronicon sive historia universalis*. Thuringia, mid-twelfth century.

Ms. I. 120. Thomasin von Zerclaere: *Der welsche Gast*. German, 1340.

Ms. II. 78. Prayerbook. French, late fifteenth century.

GREIFSWALD

Universitätsbibliothek

Ms. 977. *(pl.137)*.

Ms. 1068. *(pl.75)*.

Nd. Hs. 36. *(pl.154)*.

HALBERSTADT

Ms. 1. *(pl.27)*.

Ms. 3. *(pl.35)*.

Ms. 46. *(pl.8)*.

Ms. 59. *(pl.10)*.

Ms. 113. *(pl.128)*.

Ms. 114. *(pl.42)*.

Ms. 119. *(pl.38)*.

Ms. 132. *(pl.29)*.

Ms. 115. Lectionary, written by Gottschalk Weghener for Bishop Johannes von Hoym, 1434.

Ms. 153. Missal. Shows Lower Saxon influence. 950–75.

HALLE

Franckesche Stiftungen, Hauptbibliothek

A. 82. *(pl.122)*.

G. 69. *(pl. 142)*.

J. 5. *(pl.110)*.

J. 6. Prayerbook. German? second half of fifteenth century.

P. 6. Miscellaneous texts. Low Countries, 1502.

P. 13. *Magna Charta.* English laws in Latin and French. France? fifteenth century.

Universitätsbibliothek

1 B b/3. *(pl.13)*.

1 C a/1. *(pl.12)*.

1 D a/6. *(pl.120)*.

Yo. *(pl.150)*.

Yg. St. Nr.1. Album. Halle, 1754.

Za. 67. Missal. Rhineland, before 1418.

JENA

Universitätsbibliothek

Ms. Bos. q. 3. *(pl.55)*.

Ms. Bos. q. 6. *(pl.23)*.

Chorbuch 3. *(pl.147)*.

Ms. El. fol.1. *(pl.131)*.

Ms. El. fol.2. *(pl.144)*.

Ms. El. fol.3. *(pl.37)*.

Ms. El. fol.12. *(pl.31)*.

Ms. El. fol.51c. *(pl.67)*.

Ms. El. fol.80. *(pl.69)*.

Ms. El. fol.82. *(pl.108)*.

Ms. El. fol.85. *(pl.114)*.

Ms. El. fol.86. *(pl.77)*.

Ms. El. fol.89. *(pl.119)*.

Ms. El. fol.96. *(pl.118)*.

No shelf mark: Elector John Frederick's bible, vol.1. *(pl.157)*.

Ms. Sag. fol.13. *(pl.105)*.

Ms. Bos. q. 2. Gospel book. Tenth century.

Ms. El. fol.13. Bible fragment. German, late twelfth century.

Ms. El. fol.15. Vulgate fragment. Saxon–Thuringian school. Early thirteenth century.

Ms. El. fol.51b. *Biblia pauperum.* Lower Bavaria, 1462.

Stammbuch 7. Album of Andreas Segner. 1618–65.

Stammbuch 90. Album of J.B.W.Sternberger. 1773–7.

LEIPZIG

Universitätsbibliothek

Ms. 76. *(pl.16)*.

Ms. 92. *(pl.30)*.

Ms. 198. *(pl.28)*.

Ms. 305. *(pl.39)*.

Ms. 319. *(pl. 26)*.

Ms. 374. *(pl. 33)*.

Ms. 665. *(pl. 70)*.

Ms. 774. *(pl. 24)*.

Ms. 290. *Gregorii moralia*. German, late twelfth century.

Ms. 965. *Arbor consanguinitatis*. Italy, early, fourteenth century.

Ms. 967. *Arbor consanguinitatis*. Italy, early fourteenth century.

(Former Stadtbibliothek)

Rep. I. fol. 1 (70). *(pl. 66)*.

Rep. I. fol. 11 b (71/72). *(pl. 109)*.

Rep. I. 4°. 57 (190). *(pl. 14, 20)*.

Rep. I. 4°. 57a. *(pl. 17)*.

Rep. I. 4°. 58a (165). *(pl. 22)*.

Rep. II. fol. 15 (298). *(pl. 104)*.

Rep. II. fol. 21 (111). *(pl. 98)*.

Rep. II. fol. 60a (203). *(pl. 127)*.

Rep. II. fol. 61 (129). *(pl. 74)*.

Rep. II. 4°. 143 (417). *(pl. 62)*.

Rep. II. 4°. 144a (189). *(pl. 47)*.

Rep. II. 144c (208). *(pl. 86)*.

Rep. II. 144d. *(pl. 88)*.

Rep. IV. fol. 1 (304). *(pl. 95)*.

Rep. V. fol. 20 (128). *(pl. 63)*.

Rep. II. fol. 9b (243). *Decretum Gratiani*. Bologna, mid-fourteenth century.

Rep. II. fol. 13 (374). Guilielmo Durantis: *Speculum judiciale*. Bologna, mid-fourteenth century.

Rep. IV. 88d. Album of Magister Frentzel. Leipzig, 1646–1707.

MERSEBURG

Bibliothek des Domkapitels

Ms. I. 1–3. *(pl. 45)*.

Ms. I. 9. *(pl. 7)*.

Ms. I. 83. *(pl. 3)*.

Ms. I. 129. *(pl. 19)*.

Ms. 18. Augustine: Commentary on the Psalms. Thuringia-Meissen, c. 1200.

Ms. I. 23. Philipus de Pergamo: *Speculum sententiarum*. German? fifteenth century.

Ms. I. 43. Honorius: *Super canticam canticorum*. German? fifteenth century.

Ms. I. 54. Evangelistary. Tenth century.

MÜHLHAUSEN

Stadtarchiv

Ms. 60/43. *(pl. 58)*.

Ms. 61/24. *Badersche Chronik*. 1791.

NAUMBURG

Bibliothek des Domkapitels

No shelf mark. Antiphonary, 8 vols. *(pl. 136)*.

ROSTOCK

Universitätsbibliothek

Ms. Meckl. B. 114/1. *(pl. 152)*.

Ms. philol. 91. *(pl. 151)*.

Ms. theol. 22. *(pl. 87)*.

Ms. theol. 25. *(pl. 84)*.

Ms. theol. 23. Prayerbook. French, fifteenth century.

SANKT MARIENSTERN

Klosterbibliothek

Oct. 3. *(pl. 46)*.

Oct. 6. *(pl. 40)*.

Qu. 1. *(pl. 49)*.
Fol. 2. *(pl. 48)*.
Fol. 3. *(pl. 130)*.
Fol. 4. *(pl. 146)*.
Fol. 5. *(pl. 140)*.
Fol. 6. *(pl. 135)*.
Oct. 2. Processional. Altzella, 1524.
Oct. 5. Psalter. Thuringia-Meissen, thirteenth century.
Fol. 1. Choirbook. Neuzelle, 1717.

SANKT MARIENTHAL

Klosterbibliothek

Ms. F. 5/31. *(pl. 43)*.
Ms. 15. *(pl. 44)*.
Ms. F. 1/3. Gradual. Bohemia? *c.* 1500.

SCHULPFORTA

Bibliothek der Heimoberschule

Ms. A. 10. *(pl. 32)*.
Ms. A. 1–3. Bible, vols 1–3. Posa, near Zeitz, late twelfth century.
Ms. A. 5. Psalter. Posa, late twelfth century.
Ms. A. 26. Antiphonary. Schulpforta, *c.* 1500.

SCHWERIN

Mecklenburgische Landesbibliothek

Ms. 10. *(pl. 90)*.
Ms. 376. *(pl. 134)*.

Landeshauptarchiv

Urkundenbestand – Fürstenhaus *(pl. 65, 139)*.

No shelf mark. Rixner, Georg: *Origines et insignia…* Schwerin, 1530.

STRALSUND

Stadtarchiv

Ms. IV. 290. *(pl. 129)*.
No shelf mark. Bible. German, thirteenth century.

WEIMAR

Thüringische Landesbibliothek

Oct. 81. *(pl. 149)*.
Oct. 82. *(pl. 123)*.
Oct. 83. *(pl. 107)*.
Qu. 56. *(pl. 53)*.
Qu. 57. *(pl. 116)*.
Qu. 59. *(pl. 117)*.
Fol. 1. *(pl. 9)*.
Fol. 10. *(pl. 148)*.
Fol. 35. *(pl. 72)*.
Fol. 328. *(pl. 143)*.
Fol. max. 4. *(pls 60–1)*.
Fol. max. 6. *(pl. 132)*.
Fol. max. 10. *(pl. 91)*.
Qu. 57b. *Breviarium Romanum*. Cologne, 1453.
Fol. 9. German bible. Thuringia, early sixteenth century.
Fol. 224b. Kötzler heraldry book. Nuremberg, eighteenth century.
Fol. 322. Lorbeer, Johann Christoph: *Ost-indische Reise*. 1681.
Fol. 329. Book of warfare. German, 1661.
Fol. 351c. Weischner, Carl Friedrich: *Anweisung zum Fechten*. German, 1731.
Fol. max. 13. Tables of world history. Seventeenth century.

Landeshauptarchiv

Reg. o. 20/21. *(pl.138)*.

ZEITZ

Stiftsbibliothek

Hs. 2°. 2. *(pl.96)*.
Hs. quart. 79. *(pl.111)*.

ZITTAU

Christian-Weise-Bibliothek

Ms. A. I. *(pl.73)*.
Ms. A. IV. *(pl.102)*.
Ms. A. V. *(pl.82)*.

Ms. A. VII. *(pl.94)*.
Ms. A. II. Vesperal and Matutinal. German, *c.* 1500.
Ms. A. III. Gradual. German, 1512.
Ms. A. VI. Vesperal and Matutinal. Bohemian, *c.* 1420.

ZWICKAU

Ratsarchiv

No shelf mark. *Codex statutorum Zwiccavien-sium. (pl.59)*.

Ratsschulbibliothek

Ms. I. IV, vols 1–3. *(pl.51)*.
Ms. I. XIII, 1. Vulgate. Probably France, four-teenth century.

BIBLIOGRAPHY

Album Academiae Vitebergensis ab a.Chr. 1502 usque ad a. 1602. 3 vols. Leipzig, Tauchnitz, 1843; Halle, Niemeyer, 1894, 1905.

Altzella. *Kloster Altzella*. Text by Heinrich Magirius and Alfred and Gudrun Berger. Berlin, Union Verlag, 1962. 64 pp. *(Das Christliche Denkmal, 60–1).*

Ancona; Paolo d' and Erhard Aeschlimann: *Dictionnaire des miniaturistes du Moyen Âge et de la Renaissance dans les différentes contrées de l'Europe...*, 2nd ed. Milan, Hoepli, 1949. 239 pp., 148 pl. 4°.

Ars sacra. (Catalogue of an exhibition of early mediaeval art held at the Bayerische Staatsbibliothek, Munich, June–October 1950.) Munich, Gesellschaft für wissenschaftliches Lichtbild, 1950. xvi, 154 pp.

Bange, Ernst Friedrich: *Eine bayerische Malerschule des XI. und XII. Jahrhunderts.* Munich, Schmidt, 1923. 168 pp. 186 ills on 67 pl.

Bech, Fedor: *Verzeichnis der alten Handschriften und Drucke in der Domherren-Bibliothek zu Zeitz.* Berlin, Weidmann, 1881. xi, 58 pp. 4°.

Beer, Ellen Judith: *Initial und Miniatur. Buchmalerei aus neun Jahrhunderten in Handschriften der Badischen Landesbibliothek.* 2nd ed. Basle, Feuermann-Verlag, 1965. 92 pp., 15 col. pl., 18 figs. (Jubilee exhibition, 1965.)

Benziger, Karl J.: *Parzival in der deutschen Handschriftenillustration des Mittelalters. Eine vergleichende Darstellung...* Strassburg, Heitz, 1914. 60 pp., 46 ills. on 41 pl. (*Studien zur deutschen Kunstgeschichte*, 175.)

Berger, Samuel: *La bible française au moyen âge. Étude...* Paris, Imprimerie nationale, 1884. xvi, 450 pp.

Bergner, Heinrich: *Beschreibende Darstellung der älteren Bau- und Kunstdenkmäler der Stadt Naumburg.* Halle an der Saale, Hendel, 1903. viii, 322 pp. *(Beschreibende Darstellung der älteren Bau- und Kunstdenkmäler der Provinz Sachsen, 24.)*

Bergner, Heinrich: *Beschreibende Darstellung der älteren Bau- und Kunstdenkmäler des Kreises Naumburg (Land).* Halle an der Saale, Hendel, 1908. viii, 252 pp., 1 map. *(Beschreibende Darstellung der Bau- und Kunstdenkmäler der Provinz Sachsen, 26.)*

Bernt, Alois: 'Forschungen zum *Ackermann aus Böhmen*'. In: *Zeitschrift für deutsche Philologie*, 55 (1930), pp. 160–208, 301–37.

Bernt, Alois, and Konrad Burdach: *Der Ackermann aus Böhmen.* Berlin, Weidmann, 1917. xxii, 414 pp., 8 pl.

Beyer, Eduard: *Das Cistercienser-Stift und Kloster Alt-Zelle in dem Bistum Meissen. Geschichtliche Darstellung...* Pts. 1–3. Dresden, Heinrich, 1852. 288 pp.

Bodmer, Heinrich: *Dürer.* Leipzig, Goldmann, 1944. xxxi pp., 128 pl., x col. pl. 4°.

Boeckler, Albert: 'Die Buchmalerei'. In: *Handbuch der Bibliothekswissenschaft* 1 (1931), pp. 150–253.

Boeckler, Albert: *Deutsche Buchmalerei der Gotik.* Königstein im Taunus, Langewiesche Nachf. (1959). 79 pp.

Boeckler, Albert: *Deutsche Buchmalerei vorgotischer Zeit.* Königstein im Taunus, Langewiesche Nachf. (1959). 90 pp.

Boeckler, Albert: *Die Reichenauer Buchmalerei.* Munich, Verlag der Münchener Drucke, 1925. 48 pp. 4°. (From: *Die Kultur der Abtei Reichenau.*)

Boeckler, Albert: *Abendländische Miniaturen bis zum Ausgang der romanischen Zeit.* Berlin and Leipzig, De Gruyter, 1930. viii, 133 pp. 106 pl. (*Tabulae in usum scholarum*, 10.)

Boeckler, Albert: *Der Codex Wittekindeus.* Leipzig, Harrassowitz, 1938. 26 pp., 3 pl. 4°.

Böhme, Paul: *Nachrichten über die Bibliothek der kgl. Landesschule Pforta. 2: Handschriften einschliesslich*

Urkunden. Naumburg, Sieling, 1883. 40 pp. (*Schulprogramm 1883*, Nr. 223.)

Bömer, Alois: 'Die Schrift und ihre Entwicklung'. In: *Handbuch der Bibliothekswissenschaft* 1 (1931), pp. 27–149.

Bordona, J. Dominguez: *Die spanische Buchmalerei vom siebenten bis zum siebzehnten Jahrhundert*. 2 vols. Florence, Pantheon; Munich, Wolff, 1930. xxi, 45 pp., 80 pl.; xix, 77 pp., pl. 81–160. 4°.

Brandenburger Evangelistar–See *Evangelistar, Das Brandenburger...*

Breitenbach, Edgar: *Speculum humanae salvationis. Eine typengeschichtliche Untersuchung*. Strassburg, Heitz, 1930. 277 pp., 12 pl. (*Studien zur deutschen Kunstgeschichte, 272*.)

Bruck, Robert: *Friedrich der Weise als Förderer der Kunst*. Strassburg, Heitz, 1903. viii, 336 pp., 41 pl., 5 fig. (*Studien zur deutschen Kunstgeschichte, 45*.)

Bruck, Robert: *Die Malereien in den Handschriften des Königreichs Sachsen*. Dresden, Meinhold, 1906. xii, 469 pp. 4°.

Bruck, Robert: 'Miniature di Niccolò di Giacomo da Bologna nel codice *Decretum Gratiani* della Biblioteca Universitaria di Jena'. In: *La Bibliofilia*, 29 (1927–8), pp. 285–98.

Burckhardt, Johannes, and Otto Küstermann: *Beschreibende Darstellung der älteren Bau- und Kunstdenkmäler des Kreises Merseburg*. Halle an der Saale, Hendel, 1883. vii, 271 pp. 4°. (*Beschreibende Darstellung der älteren Bau- und Kunstdenkmäler der Provinz Sachsen, 8*.)

Burkhard, Arthur: *Hans Burgkmair d. Ä.* Berlin, Klinkhardt & Biermann, 1932. 70 pp., 76 pl. 4°. (*Meister der Graphik, 15*).

Catalogue of the magnificent collection of manuscripts from Hamilton Palace. London, Dryden Press (1882), 114 pp.

Christ, Karl: 'Das Mittelalter' ('Geschichte der Bibliotheken'). In: *Handbuch der Bibliothekswissenschaft*, 3 (1940), pp. 90–285.

Cornell, Henrik: *Biblia pauperum*. Stockholm, published by the author, 1925. xv, 372 pp., 72 pl. 4°.

Curtius Rufus, Quintus: *Von den Thaten Alexanders des Grossen. Verdeutscht von Johannes Siebelis*. 3 vols. Stuttgart, Krais & Hoffmann, 1860. 14, 399 pp.

Cyprian, Ernst Salomo: *Catalogus codicum manuscriptorum Bibliothecae Gothanae*. Leipzig, Gleditsch, 1714. 124 pp.

Deckert, Hermann: *Dom und Schloss zu Merseburg*. Burg, Hopfer, 1935. 76 pp., 206 fig.

Degering, Hermann: *Katalog der Schausammlung der Preussischen Staatsbibliothek*. Berlin, published by the author, 1925. ix, 54 pp.

Degering, Hermann: *Die Schrift. Atlas der Schriftformen des Abendlandes vom Altertum bis zum Ausgang des 18. Jahrhunderts*. Berlin, Wasmuth (1929). xvi pp., 240 pl. 4°. (*Wasmuths Werkkunst, 6*.)

Degering, Hermann, and Albert Boeckler: *Die Quedlinburger Italafragmente*. Berlin, Cassiodor-Gesellschaft, 1932. Text: 208 pp., and 25 pl., 4° and 2°. (*Cassiodor-Gesellschaft, 1*.)

Deutsch, Josef: *Die Handschriften der Abteilung für niederdeutsche Literatur bei der Universitätsbibliothek Greifswald*. Leipzig, Harrassowitz, 1926. 121 pp. (*Beihefte zum Zentralbl. für Bibliothekswesen, 57*).

Dexel, Walther: *Untersuchungen über die französischen illuminierten Handschriften der Jenaer Universitätsbibliothek vom Ende des 14. bis zur Mitte des 15. Jahrhunderts*. Strassburg, Heitz, 1917. v, 48 pp., 10 pl. 4°. (*Zur Kunstgeschichte des Auslandes, 115*.)

Dobschütz, Ernst von: *Studien zur Textkritik der*

Vulgata. Leipzig, Hinrichs, 1894. viii, 139 pp., 2 pl.

Doering, Oskar: *Aus Merseburger Handschriften. Blatt aus einer Bibel des 13. Jahrhunderts.* (Magdeburg, Baensch, 1900.) 6 pp. fol. (*Jahresgabe des Vereins zur Erhaltung der Denkmäler der Provinz Sachsen, 1900.*)

Doering, Oskar: *Christliche Symbole. Leitfaden...* 2nd ed. rev. by Michael Hartig. Freiburg im Breisgau, Herder, 1940. x, 197 pp., 103 figs.

Dom zu Brandenburg, 800 Jahre Ed. for the Cathedral Chapter by Jürgen Henkys. Berlin, Evangelische Verlagsanstalt (1965). 104 pp., 56 figs.

Dümmler, Ernst: 'Das alte Merseburger Todtenbuch'. In: *Neue Mittheilungen aus dem Gebiet historisch-antiquarischer Forschungen*, 11 (1867), pp. 223–64.

Dürer, Albrecht: *Das Marienleben*. Woodcuts, with commentary by E. Waldmann. Leipzig, Insel-Verlag, 1921. 22 pl. (*Insel-Bücherei*, 335.)

Dürer, Albrecht: *Die kleine Passion*. Leipzig, Insel-Verlag, n.d. Unpaginated. (*Insel-Bücherei*, 250.)

Ebert, Friedrich Adolf: *Geschichte und Beschreibung der Königlichen öffentlichen Bibliothek zu Dresden*. Leipzig, Brockhaus, 1822. xviii, 358 pp.

Eckhard, Tobias: *Codices manuscripti Quedlinburgenses*. Quedlinburg, Sievert, 1723. 92 pp.

Ehl, Heinrich: *Die ottonische Kölner Buchmalerei. Ein Beitrag...* Bonn and Leipzig, Schroeder, 1922. 307 pp.

Ehl, H.: *Älteste deutsche Malerei*. Berlin, Wasmuth, n.d. 12 pp., 48 pl. (*Orbis pictus. Weltkunst-Bücherei*, 10.)

Ehrismann, Gustav: *Geschichte der deutschen Literatur bis zum Ausgang des Mittelalters*. Vol. 2, section 2, pts i, ii. Munich, Beck, 1927, 1935. xvii, 350; xviii, 699 pp. (*Handbuch des deutschen Unterrichts*, 6.)

Evangelistar, Das Brandenburger. Ed. Josef Gülden, Edith Rothe, Bernhard Opfermann. Leipzig, St Benno-Verlag, 1961. 80 pp., 60 pl. 4°.

Falkenstein, Karl: *Beschreibung der Königlichen Öffentlichen Bibliothek zu Dresden*. Dresden, Walther, 1839. iv, 887 pp.

Feldhaus, Franz Maria: *Die Technik der Vorzeit, der geschichtlichen Zeit und der Naturvölker. Ein Handbuch...* Leipzig and Berlin, Engelmann, 1914. xv pp., 1400 coll., 873 figs., 4°.

Fiedler, Alfred: *Vom Stammbuch zum Poesiealbum. Eine volkskundliche Studie*. Weimar, Böhlau, 1960. 68 pp., 6 pl. (*Kleine Beiträge zur Volkskunstforschung*, 7.)

Gabelentz, Hans von der: *Die Biblia pauperum und die Apokalypse der grossherzoglichen Bibliothek zu Weimar*. Strassburg, Heitz, 1912. 57 pp., 42 pl. Fol.

Gernentz, Hans Joachim: *Religiöse deutsche Dichtung des Mittelalters*. Berlin, Union Verlag, 1964. 457 pp., 16 pl.

Glück, Heinrich and Ernst Dietz: *Die Kunst des Islams*. Berlin, Propylaen-Verlag, 1925. 618 pp., 39 pl. 4°. (*Propylaen-Kunstgeschichte*, 5.)

Goethe, Johann Wolfgang von: 'Chronik des Otto von Freisingen'. In: *Archiv der Gesellschaft für ältere deutsche Geschichtskunde* 2 (1829), pp. 301–5.

Goldschmidt, Adolph: *Die deutsche Buchmalerei*. 2 vols. Florence, Pantheon; Munich, Wolff (1928). 68, 85 pp., 88, 102 pl. 4°.

Günther, Fritz, and Josef R. Noswitz: *Ein Besuch im Kloster St Marienthal*. Leipzig, St Benno-Verlag, 1964. 35 pp.

Günther, K.: 'Slawische Handschriften in Deutschland'. In: *Zeitschrift für Slawistik*, 5 (1960), pp. 317–55.

Guerre, Danielle: *Le 'traité des faiz de haultes prouesses de Cyrus' par Vasque de Lucène d'après Xénophon.* Dissertation, Paris, 1957. 246 pp. (typescript) 4°. (Summary in *Positions des Thèses,* 1957, pp. 79–82.)

Habicht, Victor Curt: 'Das Brandenburger Evangelistar und Niedersachsen'. In: *Niedersachsen,* 38 (1933), pp. 424–35.

Haebler, Konrad: *Deutsche Bibliophilen des 16. Jahrhunderts. Die Fürsten von Anhalt...* Leipzig, Hiersemann, 1923. 98 pp., 35 pl. Fol.

Handbuch der Bibliothekswissenschaft. Ed. Fritz Milkau. 3 vols and index. Leipzig, Harrassowitz, 1931–42. 4°.

Hannemann, Kurt: 'Unterweisung zur Vollkommenheit'. In: *Die deutsche Literatur des Mittelalters, Verfasserlexikon* 4 (1952), coll. 639–50.

Hansel, Hans: 'Zur Herkunft des handschriftlichen Missale der Universitätsbibliothek Greifswald'. In: *Pommersche Jahrbücher* 34 (1940), pp. 58–75.

Hartmann, Albert: *Deutsche Buchmalerei des Mittelalters.* (Exhibition at the Bayerische Staatsbibliothek.) Munich, Wolf, 1938. 103 pp., 12 pl.

Haseloff, Arthur: 'Die mittelalterliche Kunst'. In: *Meisterwerke der Kunst aus Sachsen und Thüringen.* Magdeburg, Baensch (1906). pp. 87–110, pl. 101–28.

Haseloff, Arthur: *Eine Thüringisch-Sächsische Malerschule des 13. Jahrhunderts.* Strassburg, Heitz, 1897. 377 pp., 42 pl. (*Studien zur deutschen Kunstgeschichte,* 9.)

Hauser, Arnold: *Sozialgeschichte der Kunst und Literatur.* 2 vols. Munich, Beck, 1953. xi, 536, viii, 586 pp.

Heidrich, Ernst: 'Zur Chronologie des Dürerschen Marienlebens'. In: *Repertorium für Kunstwissenschaft* 29 (1906), pp. 227–41.

Helssig, Rudolf: *Katalog der lateinischen und deutschen Handschriften der Universitätsbibliothek zu Leipzig.* Vol. I, pt. I: *Die theologischen Handschriften.* Leipzig, Hirzel, 1926–35. 815 pp. (*Katalog der Handschriften der Universitätsbibliothek zu Leipzig,* IV, I.)

Hesse, Ludwig Friedrich: 'Über das *Speculum humanae salvationis*'. In: *Serapeum* 16 (1855), pp. 193–203, 209–21, 225–37, 241–55, 257–67.

Hinz, Paulus: *Gegenwärtige Vergangenheit. Dom und Domschatz zu Halberstadt.* Berlin, Evangelische Verlagsanstalt (1962). 239 pp., ill.

Holder-Egger, Oswald: *Monumenta Erphesfurtensia saeculum XII, XIII, XIV.* Ed. ... Hanover and Leipzig, Hahn, 1899. viii, 919 pp. (*Scriptorum rerum Germanicarum in usum scholarum.*)

Homeyer, Gustav: *Die deutschen Rechtsbücher des Mittelalters und ihre Handschriften.* New edn. by Conrad Borchling et al. Pts 1 & 2. Weimar, Böhlau, 1931–4. xiii, 61, 323 pp.

Hosäus, Wilhelm: 'Deutsche mittelalterliche Handschriften der Fürst-Georgs-Bibliothek zu Dessau'. In: *Mitteilungen des Vereins für Anhaltische Geschichte und Altertumskunde* 4 (1886), pp. 203–19.

Jacobs, Friedrich, and F. A. Uckert: *Beiträge zur älteren Literatur oder Merkwürdigkeiten der Herzoglichen öffentlichen Bibliothek zu Gotha.* 3 vols. Leipzig, Dyk, 1835–8.

Jacobus de Voragine: *Legenda aurea.* Transl. from Latin by Richard Benz. Berlin, Union Verlag (1963). xliii, 1116 pp.

Jähns, Max: *Geschichte der Kriegswissenschaften vornehmlich in Deutschland.* 2 pts. Munich and Leipzig, Oldenbourg, 1889–90. xlvi, xxxix, 1766 pp. (*Geschichte der Wissenschaften in Deutschland,* 21.)

Jahn, Johannes: *Wörterbuch der Kunst.* Written in collaboration with Robert Heidenreich and

Wilhelm von Jenny. Stuttgart, Kröner (1940). vi, 617 pp., 189 figs. (*Kröners Taschenausgaben*, 165.)

Jantzen, Hans: 'Ottonische Kunst'. Hamburg, Rowohlt (1959). 175 pp. (*Rowohlts deutsche Enzyklopädie*, 89.)

Johannes von Saaz: *Der Ackermann und der Tod. Ein Streit- und Trostgespräch vom Tode aus dem Jahre 1400.* Leipzig, Insel-Verlag (1918). 55 pp. (*Insel-Bücherei*, 198.)

Johannes von Tepl: *Der ackerman...* Ed. by Willy Krogmann. Wiesbaden, Brockhaus, 1954. 264 pp., 2 figs. (*Deutsche Klassiker des Mittelalters*, n.s. 1.)

Johannsen, Christa: 'In der Stille gehütete Schätze. Die Handschriften- und Inkunabel-abteilung der Deutschen Staatsbibliothek und ihr Direktor Dr Hans Lülfing'. In: *Weltoffen-heit als Lebensprinzip.* Berlin, Union Verlag (1962), pp. 90-8.

Kästner, Erhard: *Bekränzter Jahreslauf. Ein festlicher Kalender für alle Zeit.* (With illustrations from a Flemish Book of Hours of the Dresden Landes-bibliothek.) Leipzig, Bibliographisches Institut (1935). Unpaginated.

Kappner, Hermann: *Die Geschichtswissenschaft an der Universität Jena vom Humanismus bis zur Auf-klärung.* Jena, Fischer, 1931. 136 pp.

Karbe, W.: 'Herzog Heinrich V und die Vor-geschichte'. In: *Mecklenburg*, 34 (1939), pp. 163-6.

Karl der Grosse. Werk und Wirkung. (Exhibition, Aachen, 1965.) (Düsseldorf, Schwann, 1965.) xl, 568 pp., 158 figs.

Katalog der Ausstellung Alt-Lausitzer Kunst im Stadtmuseum Bautzen... (Exhibition arranged by the Kunstverein zu Bautzen.) 2nd ed. Bautzen, Donnerhak, 1935. 111 pp., 32 unno. pl.

Katalog der Handschriften der Kgl. öffentlichen Bibli-othek, (later) Sächsischen Landesbibliothek. 4 vols. Leipzig, Teubner, 1883-1923. Vols 1 & 2 ed. by Franz Schnorr von Carolsfeld; vols 3 & 4 by Ludwig Schmidt.

Kirchner, Joachim: *Beschreibendes Verzeichnis der Miniaturen und des Initialschmuckes in den Phillipps-Handschriften.* Leipzig, Weber, 1926. 140 pp., 131 figs, 6 col. pl. 4°. (*Beschreibendes Verzeichnis der Miniatur-Handschriften der Preussi-schen Staatsbibliothek zu Berlin*, 1.)

Kirchner, Joachim: 'Die Heimat des Egino-codex'. In: *Archiv für Urkundenforschungen* 10 (1928), pp. 111-27, with 7 figs in text.

Kirchner, J.: *Scriptura latina libraria a saeculo primo usque ad finem medii aevi.* Munich, Oldenbourg, 1955. 54 pp., 52 pl. 4°.

Kloss, Ernst: *Die schlesische Buchmalerei des Mittel-alters.* Berlin, Deutscher Verein für Kunst-wissenschaft, 1942. x, 243 pp., 282 figs. 4°.

Köhler, Wilhelm: *Die karolingischen Miniaturen.* Vol. 1: *Die Schule von Tours* (in 2 vols, text and plates); vol. 2: *Die Hofschule Karls des Grossen* (text and plates in one vol.). Berlin, Cassirer and Deutscher Verein für Kunst-wissenschaft, 1930-3; 1958. 8° and 2°. (*Denk-mäler deutscher Kunst.*)

Kunstdenkmäler, Die, von Stadt und Dom Branden-burg. Ed. Paul Eichholz et al. Berlin, Voss, 1912. xviii, 388 pp., 74 pl. (*Die Kunstdenkmäler der Provinz Brandenburg*, vol. 2, pt. 3.)

Laborde, A.: *Les manuscrits à peintures de la cité de Dieu de Saint Augustin.* 3 vols. Paris, Rahir, 1909. 2°.

Lehfeld, P.: *Bau- und Kunstdenkmäler Thüringens.* Jena, Fischer, 1888. x, xvi, 306 pp. (*Bau- und Kunstdenkmäler Grossherzogtum Sachsen-Weimar-Eisenach*, vol. 2, pt. 1.)

Lehmann, Paul: *Mittelalterliche Bibliothekskataloge Deutschlands und der Schweiz.* Vol. 2: *Bistum Mainz, Erfurt.* Munich, Beck, 1928. vi, 812 pp. 4°.

Leidinger, Georg: *Das Perikopenbuch Kaiser Heinrichs II. (cod. lat. 4452).* Munich, Riehn & Tietze, n.d. 62 pp., 67 pl. 4°. *(Miniaturen aus Handschriften der Kgl. Hof- und Staatsbibliothek in München, 5.)*

Lemm, Siegfried: *Kurzes Verzeichnis der romanischen Handschriften.* Berlin, Weidmann, 1918. 141 pp. *(Mitteilungen aus der Kgl. Bibliothek, 4.)*

Lexikon des gesamten Buchwesens. Ed. by Karl Löffler and Joachim Kirchner. 3 vols. Leipzig, Hiersemann, 1935–7. 4°. – 2nd edn., ed. by Joachim Kirchner. 4 vols, Stuttgart, Hiersemann, 1952–6.

Lexikon für Theologie und Kirche. 2nd edn. 10 vols. Freiburg im Breisgau, Herder, 1930–8.

Lindner, F.: 'Ein französisches Breviarium des 15. Jahrhunderts'. In: *Zeitschrift für neufranzösische Sprache und Literatur* 1 (1879), pp. 41–6.

Lindner, F.: 'Ein französisches Calendarium aus dem Anfang des 15. Jahrhunderts'. In: *Zeitschrift für romanische Philologie* 6 (1882), pp. 352–71.

Lindner, F.: *Lobgedicht auf die Zusammenkunft Franz I. mit Karl V. in Aiguesmortes.* (Ed. from the original in the library of Rostock university on the occasion of the 30th congress of German philologists and scholars.) Rostock, Adler, 1875. 29 pp.

Lisch, G. C. F.: 'Ernst von Kirchberg. Mecklenburgische Reim-Chronik'. In: *Jahrbücher des Vereins für mecklenburgische Geschichte* 6 (1841), p. 171 f.

Lisch, G. C. F.: 'Ernst von Kirchberg, Verfasser der mecklenburgischen Reimchronik vom Jahre 1378'. In: *Jahrbücher des Vereins für*
mecklenburgische Geschichte 12 (1847), pp. 36 bis 58.

Löffler, Karl: *Der Landgrafenpsalter. Eine Bilderhandschrift...* Leipzig, Hiersemann, 1925. 62 pp., 28 pl. 4°.

Lowe, E. A.: *Codices latini antiquiores. A paleographical guide to Latin manuscripts prior to the ninth century.* Pts 8, 9: Germany. Oxford, Clarendon Press, 1959. xii, 69 pp. Large fol.

Lülfing, Hans: 'Deutsche Staatsbibliothek. Die Handschriftenabteilung'. In: *Deutsche Staatsbibliothek 1661–1961*, vol. 1 (1961), pp. 319–80.

Lutz, J., and P. Perdrizet: *Speculum humanae salvationis. Texte critique. Traduction... Les sources et l'influence iconographiques...* Vol. 1, pts 1–3. Mulhouse, Meininger, 1907. xix, 343 pp. Fol.

Marx, E.: 'Bericht über ein Dokument mittelalterlicher Technik'. In: *Beiträge zur Geschichte der Technik und Industrie* 16 (1926), pp. 317–21.

Matthaei, Kurt: 'Altdeutsche Handschriften der Fürst-Georg-Bibliothek in Dessau'. In: *Mitteilungen des Vereins für Anhaltische Geschichte und Altertumskunde* 11 (1912), pp. 528–38.

Meder, Joseph: *Dürer-Katalog. Ein Handbuch über Albrecht Dürers Stiche, Radierungen, Holzschnitte...* Vienna, Gilhofer & Ranschburg, 1932. xxiii, 357 pp. 190 figs., 52 pl.

Merton, Adolf: *Die Buchmalerei in St Gallen vom neunten bis elften Jahrhundert.* 2nd ed. Leipzig, Hiersemann, 1923. 111 pp., 96 pl., 8 col. pl. 4°.

Meyer, Erich: *Das Dommuseum Halberstadt. Ein Führer...* Halberstadt, Domgemeindekirchenrat (1936). 31 pp., 38 figs.

Morenz, Siegfried: *Altägyptischer Jenseitsführer. Papyrus Berlin 3127. Mit Bemerkungen zur Totenliteratur der Ägypter.* Leipzig, Edition Leipzig, 1964. 22 pp., 1 facs. roll.

Mrusek, Hans Joachim, and Klaus G. Beyer:

Drei deutsche Dome. Dresden, Verlag der Kunst (1963). 335 pp. 4°.

Müffelmann, L.: *Die Reim-Chronik des Marschalk Thurius und ihre Quellen.* Phil. diss. Rostock, Boldt, 1876. 80 pp.

Müller, H.: 'Verzeichnis der theologischen Handschriften in der Kgl. Universitätsbibliothek zu Greifswald'. In: *Neuer Anzeiger für Bibliographie und Bibliothekswissenschaft Jg 1876*, pp. 13–19.

Mylius, Johann Christoph: *Memorabilia Bibliothecae Academicae Jenensis.* Jena and Weissenfels, Croker, 1746. 640 pp.

Naumann, Robert: *Catalogus librorum manuscriptorum qui in bibliotheca senatoria civitatis Lipsiensis asservantur...* Grimmae, Gebhardt, 1838. xxiv, 562, lvi pp., 15 pl.

Naumann, Robert: *Die Malereien in den Handschriften der Stadtbibliothek zu Leipzig.* Leipzig, Weigel, 1855. 103 pp.

Neumeister, Ingeburg: *Die Miniaturen eines deutschen Prosamartyrologiums in der Hs. Bos. q.3 der Universitätsbibliothek Jena. Ein Beitrag...* Diss., Jena, 1958. Typescript. 4°.

Oechelhaeuser, Adolf von: *Der Bilderkreis zum 'Wälschen Gaste' des Thomasin von Zerclaere. Nach den vorhandenen Handschriften untersucht und beschrieben.* Heidelberg, Koester, 1890. 86 pp., 8 pl. 4°.

Olschki, Leonardo: *Manuscrits français à peintures des bibliothèques d'Allemagne.* Geneva, Olschki, 1932. 725 pp., 80 pl. Fol.

Otto von Freising: *Chronik oder die Geschichte der zwei Staaten,* trans. Adolf Schmidt, ed. Walter Lammers. Berlin, Rütten & Loening (1960). lxx, 760 pp., 14 pl. *(Ausgewählte Quellen zur deutschen Geschichte des Mittelalters, 16.)*

Pahnke, Robert: *Schulpforta. Geschichte des Zisterzienserklosters Pforte.* Leipzig, Koehler & Amelang, 1956. 198 pp.

Pfister, Kurt: *Die mittelalterliche Buchmalerei des Abendlandes.* Munich, Holbein-Verlag (1922). 40 pp., 40 pl. 4°.

Porcher, Jean: *L'enluminure française.* (Paris) Arts et métiers graphiques (1959). 271 pp., 94 col. pl.

Porcher, Jean: *French miniatures from illuminated manuscripts.* Translated (from *L'enluminure française*) by Julian Brown. London, Collins, 1960. 275 pp., col. pl.

Putzger, F. W.: *Historischer Schul-Atlas zur alten, mittleren und neuen Geschichte.* 234 maps. Ed. Alfred Baldamus and Ernst Schwabe. 25th edn. Bielefeld and Leipzig, Velhagen & Klasing, 1901. xvi pp., 40 folding leaves.

Rademacher, Otto: 'Über die Merseburger Kalendarien'. In: *Thüringisch-sächsische Zeitschrift für Geschichte und Kunst 2* (1912), pp. 171–223, 1 pl.

Rathgeber, Georg: *Bibliotheca Gothana. Section der abendländischen mit Gemälden geschmückten Handschriften.* Gotha, Müller, 1839. x, 32 pp. 4°.

Reimann, Georg, and Horst Büttner: *Mittelalterliche Buchmalerei in Sammlungen volksdemokratischer Länder.* (Leipzig) Seemann, 1961. 42 pp., 57 pl. 4°.

Roediger, Karl Erich: *Die geistlichen Musikhandschriften der Universitätsbibliothek Jena.* (Vol. 1: text; vol. 2: catalogue of music.) Jena, Frommann, 1935. xi, 139, 207 pp. 8° and 4°.

Roob, Helmut: 'Unvollendete Miniaturen in einer Ovid-Handschrift der Gothaer Bibliothek'. In: *Forschungen und Fortschritte 38* (1964), pp. 174–7.

Rose, Valentin: *Verzeichnis der lateinischen Hand-*

schriften der Kgl. Bibliothek zu Berlin. Vols 1 & 2, pts i–iii. Berlin, Asher, 1893–1905. *(Die Hand- schriften-Verzeichnisse der Kgl. Bibliothek zu Ber- lin, 12, 13.)*

Rosen, Gert: *Versteigerung 11. Freitag, 28 April 1950.* (Auction catalogue.) (Charlottenburg, Find- eisen, 1950.) 95 pp. 8 pl.

Rosenfeld, Felix: *Urkundenbuch des Hochstifts Naumburg.* Vol. 1 (967–1207). Magdeburg, Historische Kommission, 1925. viii, 450 pp. *(Geschichtsquellen der Provinz Sachsen, n.s. 1.)*

Rothe, Edith: *Das Kirchenjahr. Wort und Bild im Dienst des Glaubens.* Berlin, Union Verlag (1956). 158 pp.

Salmi, Mario: *La miniatura italiana.* Milan, Electa Editrice (1956). 256 pp. 4°.

Saunders, O. Elfrida: *English Illumination:* 2 vols. Florence, Pantheon; Paris, Pegasus (1928). xx, 132 pp., 129 pl. 4°.

Scheidig, Walther: *Der Miniaturzyklus zur Welt- chronik Ottos von Freising im Codex Jenensis Bose q.6.* Strassburg, Heitz, 1928. 125 pp., 11 pl. *(Studien zur deutschen Kunstgeschichte, 257.)*

Schenk zu Schweinsberg, Eberhard: 'Margarete von Rodemachern, eine deutsche Bücherfreun- din in Lothringen'. In: *Aus der Geschichte der Landesbibliothek Weimar... Festschrift zur Feier ihres 250jährigen Bestehens.* Jena 1941. pp. 117–52, with 2 figs & 5 pl. *(Zeitschrift des Vereins für Thüringer Geschichte, Beiheft 23.)*

Schirrmacher, Friedrich: 'Ernst von Kirchberg'. In: *Allgemeine deutsche Biographie* 15 (1882), p. 788 f.

Schirrmacher, Friedrich: 'Ernst von Kirchberg, kein Mecklenburger, sondern ein Thüringer'. In: *Beiträge zur Geschichte Mecklenburgs* 2 (1875), no. 4. 28 pp.

Schlesinger, Walter: *Kirchengeschichte Sachsens im* Mittelalter. 2 vols. Cologne and Graz, Böhlau, 1962. xii, 397, viii, 762 pp. *(Mittelalterliche Forschungen, 27.)*

Schmidt, Adolf: 'Das Reichenauer Evangelistar. Hs. 190 der Stadtbibliothek zu Leipzig'. In: Hofmann, Johannes: *Die Bibliothek und ihre Kleinodien. Festschrift...* Leipzig, Hiersemann, 1927. pp. 22–40.

Schmidt, Eva: *Die Zisterzienserinnenabtei St. Ma- rienstern und die Wallfahrtskirche zu Rosenthal.* Leipzig, St Benno-Verlag, 1959. 101 pp.

Schmidt, Gerhard: *Die Armenbibeln des 14. Jahr- hunderts.* Cologne and Graz, Böhlau, 1959. xii, 163 pp., 44 pl. 4°.

Schmidt, Gustav: 'Die Handschriften der Gym- nasial-Bibliothek', 2 pts. In: *Kgl. Dom-Gym- nasium zu Halberstadt. Oster-Programm 1878,* no. 190. 38 pp.; *1881,* no. 197, pp. 1–132.

Schmidt, Ludwig: 'Beiträge zur Geschichte der wissenschaftlichen Studien in sächsischen Klö- stern. 1: Altzella; 2: Pegau'. In: *Neues Archiv für sächsische Geschichte* 18 (1897), pp. 201–72; & 20 (1899), pp. 13–24.

Schmidt, Wieland: 'Das Berliner Exemplar der Gutenberg-Bibel'. In: *Edwin Redslob zum 70. Geburtstag 1955,* pp. 96–123.

Schöne, Wolfgang: *Über das Licht in der Malerei.* Berlin, Mann, 1954. 303 pp. 4°.

Schöne Handschriften aus dem Besitz der Preussischen Staatsbibliothek. Berlin, Reichsdruckerei, 1931. 135 pp. 4°.

Schott, Max: *Zwei Lütticher Sakramentare.* Strass- burg, Heitz, 1931. 207 pp., 13 pl. *(Studien zur deutschen Kunstgeschichte, 284.)*

Schramm, Albert: *Der Bilderschmuck der Früh- drucke. 1: Die Drucke von Albrecht Pfister in Bam- berg.* Leipzig, Hiersemann, 1922. 7 pp., 38 pl. Fol.

Schröder, Carl: *Mecklenburg und die Mecklenburger*

294

in der schönen Literatur. Berlin, Süsserott, 1909. viii, 488 pp. *(Mecklenburgische Geschichte in Einzeldarstellungen,* 11, 12.)

Schultze, Victor: *Die Quedlinburger Itala-Miniaturen der Kgl. Bibliothek in Berlin. Fragmente der ältesten christlichen Buchmalerei.* Munich, Beck, 1898. 44 pp., 7 pl., 8 figs. 4°.

Schum, Wilhelm: *Beschreibendes Verzeichnis der Amplonianischen Handschriften-Sammlung zu Erfurt...* Berlin, Weidmann, 1887. lviii, 1010 pp., 2 pl. 4°.

Schunke, Ilse: *Das europäische Buch seit der Einführung des Papiers.* (Exhibition mounted by the Sächsische Landesbibliothek at the Dresden Show of 1927.) (Dresden, Liepsch & Reichardt, 1927.) 23 pp., 6 figs. 4°.

Schuster, Julius: 'Secreta Salernitana und Gart der Gesundheit. Eine Studie...' In: *Mittelalterliche Handschriften. Festgabe Hermann Degering 1926,* pp.203–37, with 2 pl. and 6 figs.

Seidlitz, W. von: 'Die illustrierten Handschriften der Hamilton-Sammlung zu Berlin'. In: *Repertorium für Kunstwissenschaft* 6 (1883), pp.256–73; 7 (1884), pp.78–89, 295–301; 8 (1885), pp.94–110.

Sordo, Enrique: *Maurisches Spanien. Córdoba, Sevilla, Granada.* Frankfurt am Main, Umschau-Verlag (1964). 233 pp., 92 photos. 4°.

Springer, Anton: 'Die Psalterillustration im frühen Mittelalter'. In: *Abhandlungen der philologisch-historischen Classe der Kgl. Sächsischen Gesellschaft der Wissenschaften* 8 (1883), pp.189 to 296.

Stange, Alfred: 'Beiträge zur sächsischen Buchmalerei des 13.Jahrhunderts'. In: *Münchener Jahrbuch der bildenden Kunst.* n.s. 6 (1929), pp.302–44.

Stange, Alfred: *Deutsche Malerei der Gotik.* 9 vols. Berlin, Deutscher Kunstverlag, 1934–58.

Stechow, Wolfgang: *Apollo und Daphne.* Leipzig and Berlin, Teubner, 1932. xiii, 76 pp., 34 pl. *(Studien der Bibliothek Warburg,* 23.)

Swarzenski, Hanns: 'The Anhalt Morgan Gospels'. In: *The Art Bulletin* 31 (1949), pp.77–83.

Swarzenski, Hanns: *Vorgotische Miniaturen. Die ersten Jahrhunderte deutscher Malerei.* Königstein im Taunus and Leipzig, Langewiesche, 1927. 96 pp., 87 pp. ill. 4°.

Theele, Joseph: *Die Handschriften des Benediktiner-Klosters S.Petri zu Erfurt...* Leipzig, Harrassowitz, 1920. xi, 220 pp. *(Beihefte zum Zentralblatt für Bibliothekswesen,* 48.)

Thieme, Ulrich, and Felix Becker: *Allgemeines Lexikon der bildenden Künstler.* 37 vols. Leipzig, Engelmann und Seemann, 1907–50.

Thoms, Heinrich: 'Die Mecklenburgische Reimchronik des Ernst von Kirchberg und ihre Quellen'. In: *Beiträge zur Geschichte Mecklenburgs* 2 (1875), no. 2. 54 pp.

Thulin, Oskar: *Cranach-Altäre der Reformationszeit.* Berlin, Evangelische Verlagsanstalt (1955). 167 pp., photos. 4°.

Troschke, Asmus von: 'Miniaturbildnisse von Cranach d.J. in Lutherbibeln'. In: *Zeitschrift des deutschen Vereins für Kunstwissenschaft* 6 (1939), pp.15–28.

Vöge, Wilhelm: 'Die Mindener Bilderhandschriftengruppe'. In: *Repertorium für Kunstwissenschaft* 16 (1893), pp.198–213.

Vöge, Wilhelm: *Eine deutsche Malerschule um die Wende des ersten Jahrtausends.* Trier, Lintz, 1891. ix, 389 pp., 46 figs. *(Westdeutsche Zschr. für Geschichte und Kunst,* Erg. H.7.)

Vom Advent zum Advent. Wegweiser durch das katholische Kirchenjahr. Leipzig, St Benno, 1952–.

Vulpius, Christian August: 'Sogenanntes Scan-

derbegisches Ingenieurkunst- und Wunderbuch...' In: *Curiositäten der physikalisch-lite-
risch-artistisch-historischen Vor- und Mitwelt* 10
(1824), pt. 4, pp.289–308.

Wegele: 'Nicolaus Marschalk, gen. Thurius'. In:
Allgemeine deutsche Biographie 20 (1884), p.431f.

Wegener, P.: 'Verzeichnis der auf der Zeitzer
Stifts-Bibliothek befindlichen Handschriften'.
In: *Programm des Kgl. Stifts-Gymnasium in Zeitz
1876*, no.206, pp.1–22.

Weiske, Karl: *Mitteilungen über die Handschriften-
sammlungen der Hauptbibliothek der Franckeschen
Stiftungen zu Halle an der Saale.* (1903) 24 pp.

Weissenborn, J.C.Hermann: *Acten der Erfurter
Universität.* 2 vols. Halle, Hendel, 1881–4.
xxvii, 442, xix, 560 pp., 8 pl. *(Geschichtsquellen
der Provinz Sachsen 8, 1 & 2.)*

Weitzmann, Kurt: *Aus den Bibliotheken des Athos.
Ill. Handschriften aus mittel- und spätbyzantinischer
Zeit.* Hamburg, Wittig (1963). 114 pp.

Westphalen, Ernst Joachim von: *Monumenta
inedita rerum Germanicarum praecipue Cimbricarum
et Megapolensium.* Vol.1. Leipzig, Martin, 1739.
123 pp., 2106 coll. Fol.

Wetzer & Welte: *Kirchenlexikon oder Enzyklopädie
der katholischen Theologie und ihrer Hilfswissen-
schaften.* 2nd ed. 12 vols, index. Freiburg im
Breisgau, Herder, 1880–1903.

Wiegand, Fritz: 'Die Erfurter Studentenmatrikel.
Ein Beitrag...' In: *Marginalien. Blätter der Pirck-
heimer-Gesellschaft* 17 (1964), pp.42–9.

Wilhelm, Friedrich: 'Das Jenaer Martyrologium
und die Unterweisung zur Vollkommenheit'.

In: *Münchner Museum für Philologie...* 5 (1928),
pp.1–105.

Willkomm, Bernhard: *Die Jenaer Universitätsbibliothek...* Jena, Palles-Verlag, 1930. 8 pp., 8 pl.

Winkler, Friedrich: *Die flämische Buchmalerei des
15. und 16.Jahrhunderts.* Leipzig, Seemann, 1925.
210 pp., 91 pl. 4°.

Winkler, Friedrich: *Der Leipziger Valerius Maximus. Mit einer Einl. über die Anfänge des Sitten-
bildes in den Niederlanden.* Leipzig, Seemann,
1921. 15 pp., 5 pl. Fol.

Wirtgen, Bernhard: *Die Handschriften des Klosters
St Peter und Paul zu Erfurt bis zum Ende des
13.Jahrhunderts.* Berlin phil. diss., 10 Dec. 1936.
Gräfenhainichen, Heine, 1936. 138 pp., 28 figs.

Wit, J. de: *Die Miniaturen des Virgilius Vaticanus.*
Amsterdam, Swets & Zeitlinger, 1959. 216 pp.,
40 pl. 4°.

Worringer, Wilhelm: *Die altdeutsche Buchillustration.*
3rd ed. Munich, Piper, 1921. 152 pp., 103 figs.

Zeidler, J.: 'Der Prosaroman *Ysage le Triste*'. In:
Zeitschrift für romanische Philologie 25 (1901),
pp. 175–214, 472–89, 641–68.

Zimmermann, E.Heinrich: 'Die Fuldaer Buch-
malerei in karolingischer und ottonischer Zeit'.
In: *Kunstgeschichtliches Jahrbuch der K.K. Zentral-
Kommission...* 4 (1910), pp. 1–104.

Zimmermann, E.Heinrich: *Vorkarolingische Miniaturen.* Berlin, Deutscher Verein für Kunst-
wissenschaft, 1916. Text: 329 pp., 25 figs in
1 vol., 8°. 341 pl. in 4 folders, 2°. *(Denkmäler
deutscher Kunst, Section 3, pt 1.)*

GLOSSARY

INDEX

ACKNOWLEDGMENTS

GLOSSARY

Acanthus. Plant whose leaves, in a stylized form, are a common ornamental device.

Antiphonary. Collection of antiphons, the anthems, versicles and responses sung alternately by the two halves of a church choir.

Bible historiale. A free version of bible stories in the vernacular.

Biblia pauperum. Picture bible, in which scenes from Old and New Testaments are juxtaposed.

Body-colour. Paint rendered opaque by having white mixed with the coloured pigment.

Book of Hours. Layman's prayerbook, giving prayers for each part of the day.

Breviary. Contains the daily offices, or prayers, which must be recited by priests and others in holy orders.

Canon major. Central section of the Mass, during which transsubstantiation takes place.

Canones. Collection of church, or other, laws.

Canons. Tables of synoptic passages of the gospels, devised by Eusebius of Caesarea.

Capital. Latin script of large, angular letters.

Clef. In musical notation, a letter indicating the pitch, usually of F or C only.

Codex. Late Roman and mediaeval book composed of manuscript sections.

Concordance. Index of a work, or of works of one author, with references and contexts.

Corpus juris canonici. Collection of primary sources of canon law.

Cruciferous nimbus. A halo, incorporating a cross.

Cursive. A script in which words are written without raising the pen between letters.

Decretals. Collection of papal decrees on individual matters, which were incorporated in canon law.

Decretum Gratiani. The second, and more impor-

tant, part of the *Corpus juris canonici*, written by Gratian in *c.* 1150.

Digests. Summary, made by order of Justinian, of the *corpus juris civilis*, the official record of Roman law. They contain fifty extracts from the writings of Roman jurists.

Epistolary. Contains all the passages from the Epistles appointed to be read at mass throughout the year.

Evangelistary. Contains the passages from the four Gospels appointed to be read at mass throughout the year.

Filigree. Ornamental work of fine gold or silver wire; in illumination, decoration with very fine lines, speckled with dots of gold and silver.

Fleuron. Cruciform, leaf-like ornament set on the tip of Gothic towers and gables.

Gospel-book. Book containing the text of the four Gospels.

Gradual. Originally the antiphon sung between the epistle and gospel in the mass, as the officiating priests mounted the chancel steps *(gradus)*. It came to mean a book containing such antiphons.

Homilies. Sermons of the Fathers of the Church, arranged to be read during the Church year.

Illuminate. To decorate a manuscript with coloured initials, borders and miniatures.

Itala. Name given to the Latin translation of the Bible done in the second century A.D., probably in North Africa.

Labarum. The banner of the late Roman emperors, adopted by Constantine, bearing the initial X (for Christos).

Lectionary. Contains bible passages appointed to be read in services.

Livre d'Heures. See Book of Hours.

Majuscule. A script formed of large or capital letters.

Mandorla (Ital.: 'almond'). A pointed oval halo, surrounding the whole figure of the Risen Christ.

Martyrology. A calendar of martyrs' feast days with biographies.

Matricula. A list or register of members of a university.

Matutinal. Contains the prayers for matins, properly a midnight office, usually said in the early morning.

Meander. Key pattern: continuous ornament which winds in and out with right-angled bends, named after the river Maiandros in Asia Minor.

Mensural note. Symbol indicating the duration of a musical note.

Miniator. One who illuminates a manuscript.

Miniature. A picture or illustration in a manuscript.

Minuscule. A script formed of small letters in a four-line system.

Missal. Contains forms of the Mass, special prayers, etc., for use throughout the year.

Neumes. Symbols used in the notation of music (especially liturgical chants) between the eighth and thirteenth centuries.

Orantes. Praying figures in early Christian art.

Papyrus. Paper made of the paper reed, a sedge.

Parchment. Animal skin specially prepared for writing on.

Responsorial. Contains the responsories, the verses said or sung alternately by the priest and congregation or choir.

Sachsenspiegel. Collection of laws of mediaeval Saxony, written by Eike von Repkow in the early thirteenth century. Earliest book of its kind in Germany.

Sacramentary. Contains the prayers belonging to the various sacraments.

Scriptorium. Writing room of a monastery.

Semi-uncial. A script used between the fifth and ninth centuries, consisting of small uncial letters in a four-line system.

Spandrel. Corner of a square or rectangle when it frames a circular or rounded picture, archway, etc.

Speculum humanae salvationis. Series of illustrated stories of the life of Christ, juxtaposed with Old Testament scenes.

Speculum virginum. 'Maidens' mirror'. A moral tract.

Summa juris canonici. A summary of church law made by Monaldus of Capodistria in the early fourteenth century.

Typology. Interpretation of the Old Testament in the light of the New, by juxtaposing appropriate images; e.g. the lowering of Joseph into the pit by his brothers and the Entombment of Christ.

Uncial. Greek and Latin script formed of large, characteristically rounded letters.

Universal chronicle. A history of the world from the Creation to the time of writing; the early part usually based on the Old Testament, the latter part, dealing with the author's lifetime, often of real historical value.

Vesperal. Contains the canticles, psalms, etc., sung at Vespers.

Vulgate. St Jerome's Latin translation of the Bible, undertaken by order of Pope Damasius and completed c. A.D.405.

Weichbild. Nowadays, the area administered by a municipal authority; in the fourteenth century a book describing the basis of that authority, the law in force in a particular town.

Zoomorph. Animal form used in decorative patterns.

INDEX

Italic figures refer to the plates

ACKNOWLEDGMENTS

Most of the photographic reproductions were made especially for this volume by Klaus G. Beyer of Weimar. *Pls 110 and 142* are by Ballin & Rabe of Halle; *pls 1 and 92* by Deutsche Fotothek of Dresden; *pl. 57* by Christel Gohlke of Berlin.